A WAYFARER IN CHINA

THE LITTLE "FU T'OU" (CARAVAN HEADMAN)

A WAYFARER IN CHINA

IMPRESSIONS OF A TRIP
ACROSS WEST CHINA AND MONGOLIA

By ELIZABETH KENDALL

WITH ILLUSTRATIONS

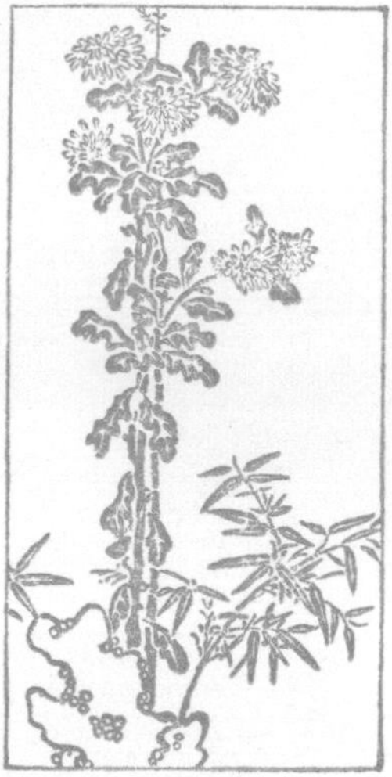

BOSTON AND NEW YORK
HOUGHTON MIFFLIN COMPANY
The Riverside Press Cambridge

Published February 1913

TO
THE HAPPY MEMORY OF MY MOTHER
THE ONE WHO
ALWAYS UNDERSTOOD

PREFACE

A WORD of explanation may help to an understanding of this record of a brief journey in China, in 1911, in the last quiet months before the revolution.

No one who has ever known the joy of hunting impressions of strange peoples and strange lands in the out-of-the-way corners of the world can ever feel quite free again, for he hears always a compelling voice that "calls him night and day" to go forth on the chase once more. Years ago, for a beginning, I pursued impressions and experiences in the Far West on the frontier, — there was a frontier then. And since that time, whenever chance has offered, that has been my holiday pastime, among the Kentucky mountains, in the Taurus, in Montenegro, in India. Everywhere there is interest, for everywhere there is human nature, but whoever has once come under the spell of the Orient knows that henceforth there is no choice; footloose, he must always turn eastwards.

But really to see the East one must shun the half-Europeanized town and the treaty port, must leave behind the comforts of hotel and railway, and be ready to accept the rough and the smooth of unbeaten trails. But the compensations are many: changing scenes, long days out of doors, freedom from the bondage of conventional life, and above all, the fascination of living among peoples of primitive simplicity and yet of a civilization so ancient that it makes all that is oldest in the West seem raw and crude and unfinished. So when two years ago my feet sought again the "open road," it was towards the East that I naturally turned, and this time it was China that called me. I did not go in pursuit of any information in particular, but just to get for myself an impression of the country and the people. My idea of the Chinese had been derived, like that of most Americans, from books and chance observation of the handful of Kwangtung men who are earning their living among us by washing our clothes. Silent, inscrutable, they flit through the American scene, alien to the last. What lies behind the riddle of their impassive faces? Perhaps I could find an answer. Then, too, it was clear, even to the most unintelligent, that a change was coming over the East, though few realized how speedily. I longed to see the old China before I made ready to welcome the new. But not the China of the coast, for there the West had already left its stamp. So I turned to the interior, to the western provinces of Yunnan and Szechuan. Wonderful for scenery, important in commerce and politics, still unspoiled, there I could find what I wanted.

Of course I was told not to do it, it would not be safe, but that is what one is always told. A long, solitary summer spent a few years ago among the Himalayas of Western Tibet, in Ladakh and Baltistan, gave me heart to face such discouragement, and I found, as I had found before, that those who knew the country best were most ready to speed me onward. And as the following pages show, there was nothing to fear. I had no difficulties, no adventures, hardly enough to make the tale interesting.

It is true, I had some special advantages. I was an American and a woman, and no longer young. Chinese respect for grey hair is a very real thing; a woman is not feared as a man may be, and hostility is often nothing more than fear; and even in remote Szechuan I met men who knew that the American Government had returned the Boxer indemnity, and who looked kindly upon me for that reason. If the word of certain foreigners is to be trusted, I gained in not knowing the language; the people would not take advantage of my helplessness. That seems rather incredible; if it is true, the whole Western world has something to learn of China.

But I could not have done what I did without the wise and generous aid of many whom I met along the way, Europeans and Chinese, officials, merchants, and above all missionaries, everywhere the pioneers. To them all I tender here my grateful thanks. And to the representatives of the Hong Kong and Shanghai Bank wherever I met them, and also to those of the Russo-Asiatic Bank I would express my gratitude for many courtesies shown me.

As I look back I know it was worth while, all of it. Half a dozen months count for little toward the real understanding of a strange civilization, but it is something to have seen a great people in its home, to have watched it at work and at play, for you have been forced once again to realize that although "East is East and West is West," the thing that most matters is the nature of the man, and that everywhere human nature is much the same.

THE ORCHARD,
WELLESLEY, MASSACHUSETTS,
November, 1912.

CONTENTS

ILLUSTRATIONS

My thanks are due to Robert J. Davidson, Esq., of Chengtu, Szechuan, for kind permission to use the photograph of the Yangtse Gorges. Also to Messrs. Underwood & Underwood, of New York, for the photographs of the Tartar Wall, Peking. With these exceptions the illustrations are from photographs made by myself on the journey. I should like to express here my appreciation of the care and skill shown by the staff of the Kodak Agency, Regent Street, West, in handling films often used under very unfavourable conditions.

E. K.

SUGGESTIONS FOR PRONOUNCING CHINESE NAMES IN THE TEXT

IN general vowels are pronounced as in Italian.

a preceded by *w* and followed by *ng* is like *a* in *fall*.
ü like the French *u*.
ai like *i* in *mine*.
ao like *ou* in *proud*.
ei like *ey* in *they*.
ie like *e-e* in *re-enter*.
ui with vowels distinct.
ou with vowels distinct and stress on *o*.

Of the consonants, *ch*, *k*, *p*, *t*, *ts* are softer than in English, approaching respectively *j*, *g*, *b*, *d*, *dz*.
hs is approximately *sh* (hsien = she-en).

MONEY, WEIGHTS AND MEASURES

Tael, roughly two-thirds of a dollar gold.
Dollar or dollar Mex., about fifty cents gold.
Cash, about the twentieth part of a cent gold.
Li, a scant third of an English mile.
Catty, about one and one-third pounds avoirdupois.

A WAYFARER IN CHINA

For the wander-thirst is on me
And my soul is in Cathay.

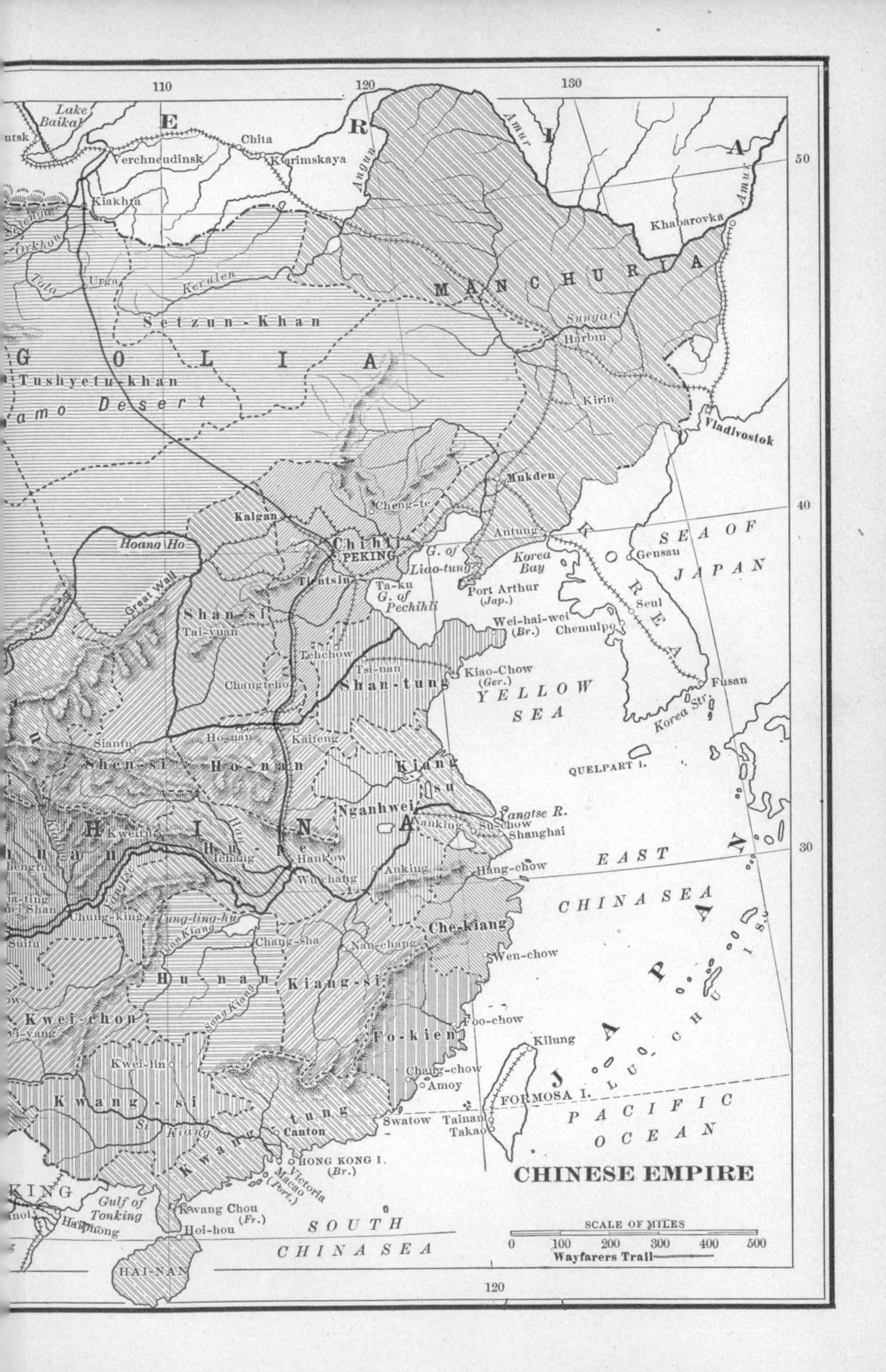
CHINESE EMPIRE
SCALE OF MILES
0 100 200 300 400 500
Wayfarers Trail
110
120
130
50
40
30
Lake Baikal
Chita
Verchneudinsk
Karimskaya
Kiakhta
Urga
Argun
Amur
Khabarovka
MANCHURIA
Sungari
Harbin
Kirin
Vladivostok
Setzun-Khan
Tushyetu-khan
Desert
Kerulen
Tola
Orkhon
Selenga
Mukden
Cheng-te
Kalgan
Hoang Ho
Great Wall
Chihli
PEKING
Tientsin
Ta-ku
G. of Pechihli
G. of Liao-tung
Port Arthur
(Jap.)
Antung
Korea Bay
KOREA
Gensan
Seul
Chemulpo
Fusan
Korea Str.
SEA OF JAPAN
Wei-hai-wei
(Br.)
Kiao-Chow
(Ger.)
YELLOW SEA
QUELPART I.
Shan-si
Tai-yuan
Tehchow
Tsi-nan
Shan-tung
Changteho
Siantu
Ho-nan
Kaifeng
Shen-si
Kiang-su
Nganhwei
Yangtse R.
Nanking
Su-chow
Shanghai
Hu-pe
Ichang
Hankow
Wuchang
Anking
Hang-chow
EAST CHINA SEA
Chung-king
Tung-ling-hu
Chang-sha
Nan-chang
Che-kiang
Wen-chow
Suifu
Hu-nan
Kiang-si
Kwei-chou
Fo-kien
Foo-chow
Kilung
Kwei-lin
Chang-chow
Amoy
FORMOSA I.
Kwang-si
Si Kiang
Canton
Kwang-tung
Swatow
Tainan
Takao
PACIFIC OCEAN
LUO CHU IS.
JAPAN
HONG KONG I.
(Br.)
Victoria
Macao
(Port.)
Gulf of Tonking
Kwang Chou
(Fr.)
Haiphong
Hoi-hou
SOUTH CHINA SEA
HAI-NAN

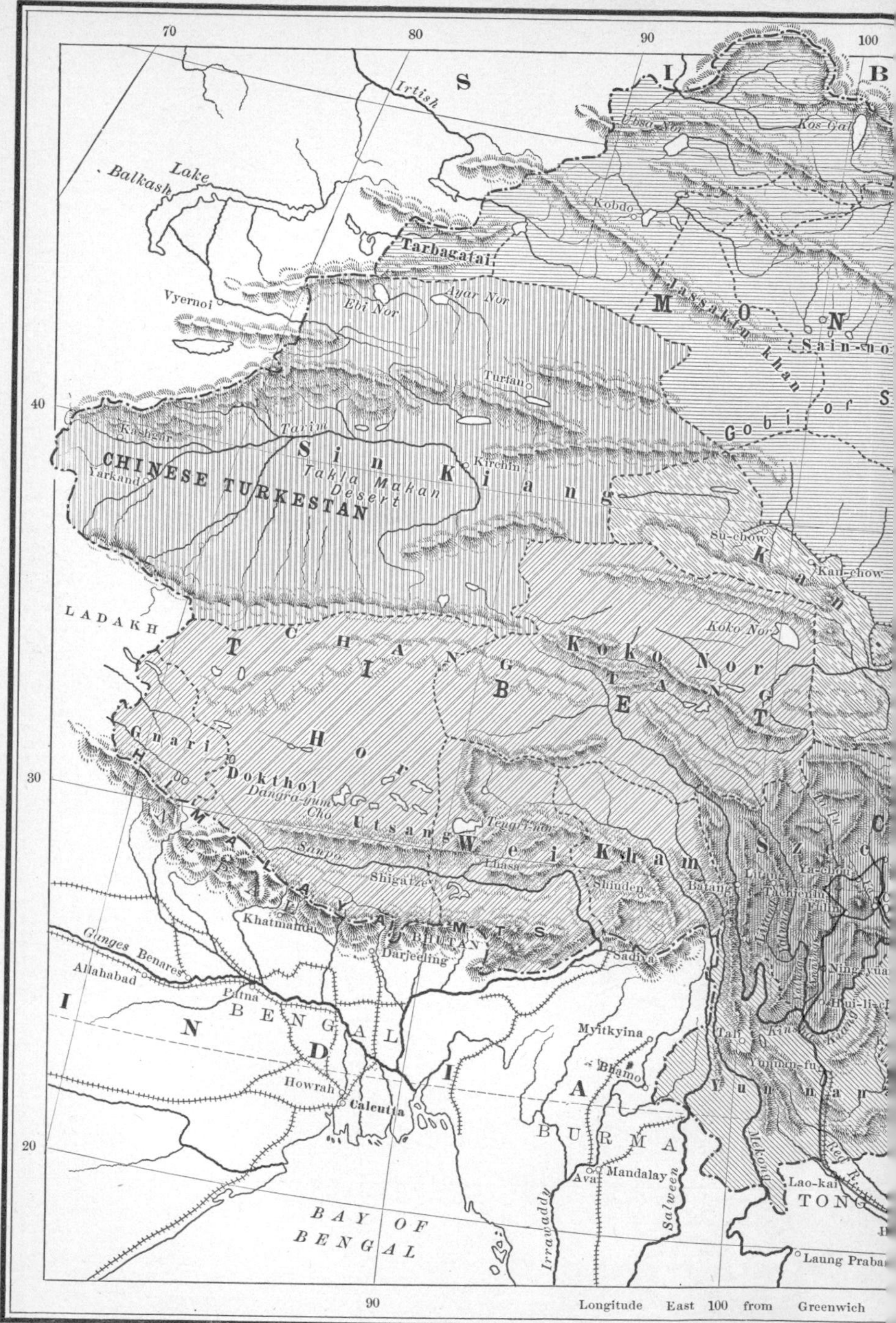

70
80
90
100
Irtish
Lake Balkash
Tarbagatai
Vyernoi
Ebi Nor
Ayar Nor
Ubsa Nor
Kos Gol
Kobdo
Turfan
Tarim
Kashgar
Yarkand
CHINESE TURKESTAN
Sin Kiang
Takla Makan Desert
Kirchin
Su-chow
Kan-chow
Koko Nor
LADAKH
Gnari
Dokthol
Dangra-yum Cho
Utsang
Tengri-nor
Sanpo
Lhasa
Shigatze
Shiuden
Batang
Litang
Khatmandu
BHUTAN
Darjeeling
Sadiya
Ganges
Benares
Allahabad
Patna
BENGAL
INDIA
Howrah
Calcutta
Myitkyina
Bhamo
BURMA
Ava
Mandalay
Irrawaddy
Salween
Mekong
Tali
Yunnan-fu
Ning-yuan
Lao-kai
Laung Praban
BAY OF BENGAL
40
30
20
Longitude East 100 from Greenwich

A WAYFARER IN CHINA

CHAPTER I

ACROSS TONKING

THREE years ago West China seemed at the back of beyond. To make your way in you had either to traverse the length of Upper Burma and then cross the great rivers and ranges of western Yunnan, a weary month-long journey, or else spend tedious weeks ascending the Yangtse, the monotony of the trip tempered by occasional shipwreck. To-day, thanks to French enterprise, you can slip in between mountain and river and find yourself at Yunnan-fu, the provincial capital, after a railway journey of only three days and a half from Haiphong, the port of Tonking.

When first planning a visit to West China, I set my heart on going in from the west, for I had long wished to see the wild, picturesque country that lies between the Burmese frontier and the Yangtse. Years before, I had looked across the border and promised myself that some day I would find out what lay on the other side. But when the time came the difficulty of securing a Chinese interpreter in Burma forced me to go to Hong Kong, and once there, lack of time made it necessary that I should choose the shortest route into West China, and that was by way of Haiphong and the Red River railway. After all, there were compensations. Even a fleeting vision from the windows of a railway carriage gives some idea of what the French are doing in their great Eastern colony. Moreover, there could be no better starting-point for such a trip as I had before me than the free port of Hong Kong, and the comfort of arranging an outfit in a place where East and West meet untrammelled by custom-houses is not to be despised. As a rule it is a mistake to bring an elaborate outfit from home. Generally each place has worked out just the devices that best serve its particular needs, and much of Western travelling equipment does not fit in with the conditions of Eastern life. Shoes and saddles the traveller from the West wisely brings with him, and of course all scientific apparatus is best provided in Europe. But in the main I found all that I needed, whether of Eastern or Western manufacture, in Hong Kong, and at surprisingly low prices. Interpreter and cook I had secured from Shanghai. The former, a Kiangsi man, was the product of mission schools and a year in an American Western college. He spoke English fairly well, and was sufficiently at home in the various forms of Mandarin to get on in

Yunnan and Szechuan. The cook had come down the "Great River" from Chung-king with an English family returning home, and was glad to work his way back, even though by a round-about route. Although he spoke no English, he understood European ways and was quick to comprehend my wishes. And he proved a faithful, hard-working fellow, and a very passable cook.

By the end of March my preparations were complete. The boat for Haiphong was to leave at nine o'clock on the morning of the 29th, and the evening before two sampans took me and my kit, together with the interpreter and the cook, out to where she lay at her moorings. My belongings looked rather formidable as they lay heaped up on the deck of the Sikiang, of the Est Asiatique Français line, but, after all, there was only a moderate supply of stores, such as tea, jam, biscuit, sugar, cereals, tinned meats and tinned milk, together with a few enamelled iron dishes and the cook's stew-pans, all packed in wooden boxes. The bedding-roll and clothing were put in camp-bags of waterproof canvas, while the necessary maps and cameras and films were carried in suit-cases for safe-keeping. An English cross saddle brought from Shanghai proved more satisfactory for the small Yunnan ponies than would have been the Mexican saddle which I had tried in vain to secure. Acting on a timely word of warning I bought in Hong Kong a most comfortable sedan-chair, a well-made bamboo affair fitted with a top and adjustable screens and curtains to keep out either rain or sun. I had been told that I should have no use for a tent, but that a camp-bed was a necessity, and so it proved. The bed I took with me was of American manufacture; compact and light, and fitted with a mosquito frame, it served me throughout all my journeyings and was finally left in Urga in North Mongolia, on the chance that it might serve another traveller a good turn. An important part of my outfit, a small Irish terrier, arrived from Japan the next morning, when I had about given him up. He was dropped into my waiting sampan as his ship, homeward bound to Calcutta from Kobe, came into her moorings, and we climbed up the side of the Sikiang not fifteen minutes before she was off. All's well that ends well. We were safe on board, and I had secured a gay little comrade in my solitary journeying, while before Jack lay a glorious run of two thousand odd miles.

The mail boat to Haiphong, due to make the trip in fifty-three hours, had once been a royal Portuguese yacht, but the only remaining traces of her former glory were the royal monogram, "M.R.P.," conspicuous in glass and woodwork, and her long, graceful lines, charming to look at, but not well fitted to contend with the cross-currents of the China Sea. As the only lady passenger I had very comfortable quarters, and the kindest attention from French officers and Annamese stewards. The second afternoon there came a welcome diversion when the boat put into Kwang-chou-wan, two hundred miles southwest of Hong Kong, to visit the new free port of Fort Bayard, the commercial and military station which the French are creating in the cession they secured from China in 1898, and which, if all goes well, is some day to rival Hong Kong. The Bay of Kwang-chou is very fine, affording a safe harbour to the two or three ships that were riding at anchor, or to two or three navies if need came, but Fort Bayard displays as yet few signs of the prophesied greatness. To while away the hours of waiting I went on shore and wandered about the empty, grass-grown roads of the tiny settlement. To the right as one walked up from the beach stretched a long line of substantial-looking barracks, and many of the houses were of European appearance, attractively set in large gardens. Above the whole towered a rather pretentious two-spired church. The one native and business street running parallel with the beach showed little life; people did not wake up even at the coming of the fortnightly mail from Hong Kong, and the native population seemed no more than sufficient to serve the needs of the foreign element.

We were joined here by two or three French officials attended by an escort of Annamese policemen

These latter had a decidedly ladylike, genteel air with their hair smoothly brushed and twisted in a low knot at the back of the neck, the whole bound round with a black kerchief laid in neat folds. Their uniform was of dark blue woollen set off by putties of a lighter blue, and their appearance was decidedly shipshape. I talked with one of the Frenchmen returning from an official visit to Fort Bayard. He seemed to have little faith in the new settlement, declaring the Government had poured in money like water, and with no adequate return.

It is more than a century since France began to interest herself in this part of the world, dreaming dreams of an Eastern empire to offset the one she had just lost in America. Then came the French Revolution, and the dream went the way of many more substantial things, and it was not until the days of the Second Empire that Napoleon III, looking east and west, again took up the question. Little by little the French strengthened their hold upon the Indo-China peninsula, and the final contest came in the eighties, a part of the universal game of grab then going on in Africa and Asia. Although China gave up her claim to the territory a quarter of a century ago, it took many years longer to pacify the country, and there is still something to be done. The cost in men and money has been very great, and at one time the whole policy of colonial expansion became so unpopular that it spelled political ruin to the man most identified with it, Jules Ferry, "l'homme de Tonking."

The real history of Tonking dates from the administration of M. Doumer, Governor-General of Indo-China from 1897 to 1902. During these five years the Parisian printer, turned Radical politician and administrator, showed what one able and determined man could do. When he arrived in the East, piracy and brigandage were rife, there was an annual deficit of some three million francs, and the feeble administration had done nothing to develop the possibilities of the country. When he left, the colony was upon its feet, lawlessness had been suppressed, the administration reformed, and the deficit turned into a substantial surplus. He had built towns and telegraphs, encouraged the native industries of rice planting and silk culture, and by offering special inducements to French enterprise had developed tea, coffee, and rubber growing.

Nor did the energetic imperialist stop here. Believing that "a nation to be great should be always striving to be greater," he began to develop a vigorous forward policy which seemed to have as its goal nothing less than the control of Yunnan and Southeast China. Colonial expansion was necessary to the continued existence of France, he declared. In his last report, looking back to the achievements of a past generation, he concluded, "We are the same men, but we no longer believe in ourselves. We act as if we were a vanquished people, and in any case we appear so to the world. This is the result of our policy of effacement for which must be substituted at all costs a policy of action which will permit us to hold our rank."

It is true the forward policy did not originate with M. Doumer, for the value of Tonking as the key to China had been recognized by French statesmen before ever he put foot in the colony, but it was his task to make that policy something more than a pious aspiration. Not only did he set about making the French possessions the needed commercial and industrial base for such an undertaking, but he also initiated the next move in the game, the development of railway systems which would bring French traders, and if need be French soldiers, into the heart of the coveted territory. He worked out all the plans, urged them upon the Government, and did more than any other man to secure the necessary support of the French financiers; to-day railways linked up with Hanoi and Haiphong have crossed the Chinese frontier at two points, Dong Dang and Ho-k'ou.

The colony, to call it by its correct name, of Kwangchou held an important place in M. Doumer's scheme, and he predicted for it a "brilliant future as a port of commerce." Like the rest of his party he regretted the mistaken moderation of the Government in not acquiring at the same time a lease of the island of Hainan. Something is being done now to repair this unfortunate error by industriously developing French hold upon that territory, and the big consulate and the French post-office and hospital at Hoi-hou, the chief port, are significant of future hopes, even if not justified by present conditions.

The following noon, after we left Kwang-chou, we were approaching Haiphong through muddy red channels between the low-lying meadow lands which here border the river Cua-Cam, on the right bank of which lies the chief commercial centre of Tonking. But its days as a shipping port are said to be numbered, because of the difficult approach. Much money has been spent in efforts to improve the waterway, but with no satisfactory results, and now it is proposed to create a new port in the beautiful Baie d'Along, a little farther east. There was some doubt in my mind as to the reception awaiting us. We had been told that the customs inspection was severe, and we had many packages; no Chinese would be admitted without passports, and I had neglected to provide any for my men; there was a strict muzzling law on, and Jack had not even a collar. But the graceful courtesy of the French officials smoothed away every difficulty. We were bowed out of the custom-house with our packages unopened. At the police headquarters, where I at once reported myself with my Chinese men, we were met by one of my fellow passengers from Kwang-chou who had hurried ahead to explain the situation, and thanks to his efforts the lack of passports was kindly overlooked. As for Jack, he was quickly furnished with all the equipment of the civilized dog — muzzle, collar, chain — at one of the large outfitting-shops, of which there seemed quite enough for the needs of the place.

Haiphong is an attractive town of some twenty thousand inhabitants, of whom perhaps one thousand are Europeans. It is planned with an eye to the future, like all French colonial centres, with broad streets and imposing public buildings. But a deep calm brooded over everything; there was no bustle in the thoroughfares, and the shops seemed unvisited, nor did their proprietors show interest in attracting custom. In one of the largest I offered a piastre, fifty cents gold, in payment for a few picture post-cards, but they could not change the coin, and seemed disinclined to make the effort to do it, so I went without my cards. The Annamese, who form the bulk of the population, are attractive in appearance, finer in feature and gentler in manner than the Chinese. Save for a serious cast of face, they are much like the Burmese. Their dress is quieter in tone than that of either their Burmese cousins or their Chinese neighbours, and is severely utilitarian in cut, differing little for men or women. The working dress of Haiphong was full, long, square-cut trousers over which fell a sort of prolonged shirt slashed to the waist. When at work the front panel was tucked up out of the way. All alike wore huge straw hats tied under the chin.

But I saw little of Haiphong, as I left the same evening, and even less of Hanoi, the capital, where we arrived at half-past ten, starting off again before eight o'clock the next morning. I was sorry not to see more of the latter place, for it is one of the finest cities in the Far East. But I carried away a vision of a good hotel, an imposing capitol, and a pretentious station, all set on wide streets lined with European-looking houses surrounded by real green grass lawns. A twenty-minute run in a rickshaw soon after dawn showed fine chaussées leading out into the country and filled, even at this early hour, with crowds of country-folk bringing their produce to market. I believe there are over one hundred miles of metalled roads in the capital and the suburbs, all due to untiring M. Doumer. But his most enduring monument in Hanoi is the fine exposition buildings. When he went home to raise a second loan of two hundred million francs for the development of the colony, the men to whom he appealed naturally asked what were the resources of the country. His convincing reply was the famous exposition of 1902.

There is one through train daily each way between

Haiphong and Yunnan-fu. The distance is about six hundred miles, and it took three days and an evening to make the trip. There is no traffic by night, and this seems to be the rule on these adventurous railways, for I met the same thing on the Anatolian and Bagdad lines between Constantinople and Eregli. The corridor trains are equipped with four classes. The first was inferior to the same class on Continental lines, but that seemed to matter little, for it was usually empty. As a gay young Englishman in Yunnan-fu remarked, no one went first-class unless he was travelling at some one's else expense. The second and third class were very good of their kind, and the fourth was far and away the most comfortable arrangement of the sort I had ever seen, with benches along the sides and large unglazed window openings. Most of the passengers and all the jollity went in this class. Everywhere there were other than human travellers; birds, dogs, goats, and pigs were given room, always on condition of having a ticket. I paid four dollars gold for my dog's ticket from Haiphong to Yunnan-fu, but having paid, Jack's right in the carriage was as unquestioned as mine, and I found this true in all my railway travel in China.

The Tonking-Yunnan railway is a remarkable undertaking, and shows the seriousness with which the French are attacking the problems of Far Eastern colonization. The lower half of the line, which here follows up the Red River valley, presented few serious engineering difficulties, although calling for at least one hundred and seventy-five bridges on the section south of Lao-kai, but it was almost impossible to secure labourers for the construction work. Annamese refused to lend a hand, and the Chinese died like flies from the malarial conditions. For a time work was at a standstill, and in the end it had to be suspended during the summer months. The upper part, on the other hand, especially that section which runs through the Namti valley, tested to the utmost the skill of the French engineers. And the cost was correspondingly great. Even as it is, much of the embanking seems to be of a rather slight character, and quite unfit to stand the tremendous tropical downpours of the early summer months. After leaving China I learned that I had passed over the line just in time, for the rains set in very early in the summer of 1911, and for weeks traffic was fearfully interrupted by landslips and broken bridges.

Whether the line will prove a financial success depends on some things not wholly under control. The present customs regulations certainly tend to check the development of trade in Tonking, and the transportation rates are perhaps more than traffic can bear. The French, however, can change their policy in these respects if they think best. But the proposed construction by the Chinese Government of a railway connecting Yunnan-fu and the West River valley would cut the ground out from under their feet. For the moment, the Revolution has stopped the enterprise, but it is certain to be taken up again, as there are no insuperable engineering obstacles in the way, and every economic and political reason for giving Yunnan an outlet to the sea through Chinese territory.

On leaving Hanoi in the early morning light we struck across a wide fertile plain, beautifully cultivated; fields of rice alternating with maize stretched away to a wall of feathery bamboo broken by stately palms and glossy mangoes. After a little the country became more broken, rolling near by, mountainous in the distance. The vegetation, dense and tropical, hemmed in the line on both sides, but here and there charming trails led away through the jungle to villages on higher land; a delightful region to pass through, perhaps to live in if one were a duck, but for human beings the steamy heat must be very depressing. At Yun Bay the valley narrowed, and we drew nearer the mountains, but there was no change in the atmosphere, and had not the sky been cloudy, we should have suffered greatly from the heat.

My fellow travellers were chiefly officials of the civil administration or connected with the railway, who chatted or slept or quietly drank away the weary hours; for them there was no novelty in the trip to dull the feeling of discomfort. At one small station a man who might have been a planter got in, followed by an attractive-looking Annamese woman carrying a little child. She cried bitterly as she waved good-bye to a group of natives on the station platform. The man seemed well known on the line, and was soon the centre of a group of his fellows who paid no attention to the woman. After a while the trio went to sleep, the man on the carriage bench, the woman and child on the floor. She was what is euphemistically called a "cook" in Tonking; just another name for an arrangement so often resulting from the lonely life of Europeans among a slack-fibred dependent alien population. It is the same thing that confronts the stray visitor to the isolated tea plantations of the Assam hills, where young English lads are set down by themselves, perhaps a day's journey from the next European. What wonder that they find it difficult to hold fast to the standards and principles of the home that seems so far away, or that if they once ignore their inherited traditions, no matter in how slight a thing, there seems to be no natural stopping-place short of the abyss. As once said to me an aged American missionary, who perhaps had never worn an evening coat a dozen times in his life, "A nice young fellow, clean in body and soul, comes out from England, and finds himself shut up for the year on one of these plantations, no one of his kind within reach. He means well, but the test is too great. First he stops dressing for dinner. What's the use? Then he gets careless about his manners. And the end of it all is black-and-tan babies in the compound." Here in Tonking the woman is perhaps as well off as in her native hut until the planter goes home or brings out a European wife, but in some way or another there is usually an untoward ending. As for the children, they go to swell the class that is neither here nor there, and their lot is probably happier than that of the unfortunate Eurasians of India, since race prejudice is far less strong among the French than with the Anglo-Saxon.

At Lao-kai on the Tonking frontier I stopped over for a day's rest, having learned that it boasted a comfortable European inn. The little town is built on the opposite high banks of the Red River near its junction with the Namti. Just across the latter stream lie China and the Chinese town of Ho-k'ou. There is a distinct European aspect to Lao-kai, and as a frontier post it has a good-sized garrison of the Annamese Tirailleurs and the French Foreign Legion. The latter did not look as black as they are painted, and it was hard to realize that behind their friendly, courteous bearing were ruined careers; but the contrast of their sturdy forms and weather-beaten faces with the slender figures and delicate features of the Tirailleurs was very striking. I did not wonder that the French soldiers have dubbed their Annamese companions-in-arms the "Young Ladies." The inn, which was most efficiently managed by two Frenchwomen, served as a sort of club for the Europeans of both Lao-kai and Ho-k'ou, and incidentally also for innumerable dogs and cats. At dinner each person was the centre of an expectant group of the four-footed habitués of the inn, and no one seemed to object. Just another instance of the liking of the most civilized peoples of the West and the East, English, French, and Chinese, for pet animals.

A small church on the right bank of the river showed white among the bamboos, and in the early evening the bells rang with a homelike sound. Crossing by the ferry I found the place empty save for two Annamese soldiers kneeling quietly and reverently. In going back and forth on the ferry-boat as I did several times, I had a chance to observe the people. As in the case of the Burmans the difference between men and women is not marked; indeed, among the younger ones it is often difficult to tell them apart. The great palm-leaf hat generally worn took me back to hot Sunday afternoons in an old church in the Berkshire hills of Massachusetts, when my restless little mind busied itself with wondering what palm leaves looked like when they were not fans. I now had a chance to see, for I was in the land of palms, and the church-going fans of my childhood seemed to have transformed themselves into a universal headgear. In shape the Annamese hat resembles a tea-tray with edges three inches deep, and of the size of a bicycle wheel. In addition to the band passing under the chin a small crown fits the head snugly, and helps to keep the huge thing in place. Primarily it is a head-covering, a protection against sun or rain, but incidentally it serves as a windbreak, a basket-cover, a tray, or a cradle. Often French soldiers crossed with me, and I noticed that they usually spoke Annamese fluently, unlike Tommy Atkins in India, who rarely knows a word of the vernacular; also they seemed to be on a friendly, not to say familiar footing with the natives.

After a comfortable week-end's rest, I left Lao-kai in the early morning, helped on my journey by those courtesies that so often in strange lands convince one that "less than kin more than kind" quite understates the truth. An Italian on his way down the river wired the landlord of the best inn in Yunnan-fu of my coming, that I might be properly met. That I had already done so myself did not at all take from his kind thoughtfulness. Still another Italian of the Chinese customs service joined me as we left Lao-kai, having come over from Ho-k'ou to escort me across the frontier, that I might have no bother with my luggage. Yet another of these kind strangers wired ahead to warn the solitary American on the line of my coming, thus giving the two compatriots a chance to exchange a few words at the station as the train went through.

On leaving Lao-kai our way led up the valley of the Namti, a small mountain river coming in from the east. The scenery was now much wilder, and as we rose to higher levels the vegetation changed, the pathless jungle which comes up to the very doors of Lao-kai gave way to sparsely covered grass slopes, and they in turn to barren, rocky walls. It was here that the French engineers encountered their most difficult problems. We wound up the narrow valley in splendid loops and curves, turning upon our tracks, running through numerous tunnels, and at one time crossing a chasm so narrow and with sides so steep and precipitous that it was found necessary to build the bridge in two parts, each against the face of the cliff, and then gradually lower them until they met above the river, three hundred and fifty feet below. Finally by an almost intolerable gradient we topped the divide and found ourselves overlooking a wonderful, well-watered plain five thousand feet above the sea, and cultivated as far as the vision could carry with the care and precision of a market-garden.

That night I spent at A-Mi-chou in a semi-Chinese inn. The cooking was good, and, thanks to the thoughtfulness of a railway official who wired ahead, I had one of the two good rooms of the house, the others being given over to rats. This was truly China, and the European railway with its Frenchified trains and stations seemed indeed an invasion, a world apart. The French officials apparently shared this feeling, and had a nice way of regarding themselves as your hosts and protectors.

All the next day we were crossing the great plateau of Yunnan, now climbing a pass in the mountain-ranges that tower above the level, now making our way up a narrow rocky valley, the gray limestone cliffs gay with bright blue flowers and pink blossoming shrubs. Just what they were I could not tell as the train rolled by. Mostly the road led through long stretches of tiny garden-like fields, broken here and there by prosperous looking villages half concealed in bamboo groves. The scenery was very fine and varied; above, the rocky hills, below, the green valleys. The mingling, too, of tropical and temperate vegetation was striking. We were in latitude 24° and 25°, about the same as Calcutta, but at an elevation of nearly seven thousand feet, and the combination seemed to work confusion among the growing things, for rice and wheat were found not far apart, and here at last Heine's palm and pine had come together.

Late on the second afternoon after leaving Lao-kai we were approaching Yunnan-fu. Seen across the plain, the capital of the province looked very imposing as it lay stretched along a low ridge running east and west. Rice-fields interspersed with ruins, sad re-

A YUNNAN VALLEY

OUTSIDE THE WALLS OF YUNNAN-FU

minders of the terrible Mohammedan rebellion of a generation ago, crowd up to the very walls on the near side of the town. Outside the South Gate is the station, and not far distant the Chinese house which an enterprising French couple had turned into a very comfortable inn, where I stayed the three days needed for arranging my caravan and seeing the sights of the place.

CHAPTER II

DAYS IN YUNNAN-FU

THE situation of Yunnan's capital is extraordinarily picturesque. It stands in a wide plain, its northern wall running along a low rocky ridge from which there is a charming view over city and lake to the great mountains that skirt the plain on all sides. Lying at an elevation of nearly seven thousand feet, it is blessed with a white man's climate. Eighty-five degrees in the shade marks the highest summer temperature, and the winters are just pleasantly bracing. Europeans who have experienced the biting winds of Peking, the damp heat of Canton, or the gray skies of Chengtu find in the bright days and cool breezes of Yunnan some mitigation of their exile to this remote corner of the empire. The city itself is not very attractive in spite of its many trees, for it seems a network of narrow lanes, only broken here and there by a temple enclosure or a stretch of waste land, the whole shut in by sound thirty-foot high walls; nor are there any sights of special interest, with the exception of a rather fine Confucian temple. But the country roundabout affords many charming excursions. The waters of the lake, some twenty-three miles in length, once perhaps washed the west wall, but it is gradually silting up, and to-day it is five miles away and is reached by heavy sampans which ply the narrow canals that intersect the rice-fields. Farm buildings, tea-houses, and temples buried in groves of bamboo are dotted over the plain, which is crossed at intervals by high, stone-paved dykes lined with trees. The rich cultivation of the lowland is in sharp contrast with the surrounding hills, bare and barren save where the presence of a temple has preserved the forest.

Yunnan-fu, with a population of some eighty thousand, seems a fairly prosperous town. Copper is found on the neighbouring hills, and the metal-work of the place is famous, although by law all copper mined must be sent to Peking. But the importance of the city depends mainly upon its trade. It is the centre of a large though rather scantily populated district abounding in the great staples, rice, beans, and millet, as well as in fruit and vegetables. Formerly Yunnan stood in the forefront of opium-producing provinces, but when I was there not a poppy-field was to be seen. The last viceroy, the much respected Hsi Liang, the one Mongol in the Chinese service, himself not an opium smoker, had shown great determination in carrying out the imperial edicts against its use or production, and rather unwillingly Yunnan was brought into line with the new order.

Under his successor, Li Ching Hsi, a man known to be given over to the use of the drug, unwilling converts hoped for better days, only to be disappointed. After a more or less serious effort to reform, he announced that he was too old to change, but the province had a long life before it, and must obey the law. So he made amends for his own short-comings by enforcing the restrictions almost as vigorously as his predecessor had done. What was true at that time in Yunnan was also the case in Szechuan. Although always on the watch for the poppy, nowhere did I see it cultivated. Probably in remote valleys off the regular trails a stray field might now and then have been found, innocently or intentionally overlooked by the inspector, but in the main poppy-growing had really been stamped out; and this where a generation ago that careful observer, Baber, estimated that poppy-fields constituted a third of the whole cultivation. Credit where credit is due. Manchu rule may have been weak and corrupt, but at least in respect of one great popular vice it achieved more than any Western power ever thought of attempting. Certainly not last among the causes for its overthrow was the discontent aroused by its anti-opium policy. And now it is reported that individualism run mad among the revolutionary leaders has led to a slackening in the enforcement of the rules, and the revival of poppy cultivation.

For half a century Yunnan has known little peace. Twenty years long the terrible Mohammedan rebellion raged, and the unhappy province was swept from end to end with fire and sword. Marks of the devastation of that time are everywhere visible. Hardly had it been put down when the war with the French in the eighties again involved Yunnan. Later came the outbreak of the tribesmen, while the Boxer movement of the north found a vigorous response here. Bloodshed and disorder have given the country a set-back from which it is only beginning to recover.

But the coming of the railway has brought fresh life to Yunnan, and the prospects for the future economic development are very promising. In the capital there were many signs of a new day. The Reform movement had taken good hold in this remote corner of the empire. A hospital with eight wards and under Chinese control was doing fine work. Schools were flourishing, and there was even a university of sorts. The newly organized police force pervaded the whole place and was reputed quite efficient. But it was the new military spirit that most forced itself upon you; you simply could not get away from it. Bugle practice made hideous night and day. Everywhere you met marching soldiers, and the great drill ground was the most active place in the town. Dread of the foreigner underlies much of the present activity and openmindedness towards Western ideas. The willingness to adopt our ways does not necessarily mean that the Chinese prefer them to their own, but simply that they realize if they would meet us on equal terms they must meet us with our own weapons. Writing of the Boxer rising, Sir Charles Eliot summed up the Chinese position in a sentence, "Let us learn their tricks before we make an end of them." Now it might read, "Let us learn their tricks before they make an end of us." The drilling soldiers, the modern barracks, the elaborately equipped arsenals, as well as the military schools found all over China to-day, show which one of the Western "tricks" seems to the man of the Middle Kingdom of most immediate value. At the military school of Yunnan-fu they have a graphic way of enforcing the lesson to be learned. A short time ago the students gave a public dramatic performance, a sort of thing for which the Chinese have decided talent. One of the scenes showed an Englishman kicking his Hindu servant, while another represented an Annamese undergoing a beating at the hands of a Frenchman. The teaching was plain. "This will be your fate unless you are strong to resist." The English and French consuls protested formally, and the proper apologies were made, but no one believes that the lesson was forgotten.

It is not to be wondered at that the people of Yunnan are alive to the danger of foreign interference, for they see the British on the west and much more the French on the south, peering with greedy eyes and clutching hands over the border. In the last fifteen years commissions of the one and the other have scoured the province with scarcely so much as "by your leave," investigating the mineral resources and planning out practicable railway routes. Within the capital city the French seem entrenched. A French post-office, a French hospital, French shops, hotels, missions, and above all the huge consulate, are there like advance posts of a greater invasion. There is an ominous look to these pretentious establishments holding strategic points in this or that debatable territory. Take the French consulates, here in Yunnan-fu and in Hoi-hou, or the Russian in Urga, the North Mongolian capital, they have more the aspect of a fortified outpost in a hostile country than the residence of the peaceful representative of a friendly power.

And Yunnan is beginning to move. For some time past the Government has been considering seriously the project of a railway across the province on the east to the Si Kiang and Canton, and just before I arrived in Yunnan-fu two engineers (significantly enough Americans) started northwards to make the preliminary surveys for a line connecting the capital with the Yangtse. If these two schemes can be carried through under Chinese control, good-by to the hopes of the French. Just at the time that I was in Yunnan there was much excitement over the Pien-ma matter, a boundary question between the province and Burma. A boycott of British goods had been started which would have been more effective if there had been more goods to boycott, but it indicated the feeling of the people, and the viceroy, Li Ching Hsi, was winning golden opinions for the stand he took in the matter, which, however, did not save him from ignominious deportation by the Revolutionary party only a few months later.

But whatever the feeling towards foreigners in the mass, the individual foreigner seemed to meet with no unfriendliness on the part of the people in Yunnan-fu, and apparently official relations were on a cordial footing. I found the Bureau of Foreign Affairs ready to do all it could to smooth my way across Yunnan, but perhaps that was due in part to the fact that the chief of the bureau had been for several years consul in New York. By arrangement I called one afternoon, in company with a missionary lady, upon his wife. Threading our way through narrow, winding streets, our chairs turned in at an inconspicuous doorway and we found ourselves in a large compound, containing not so much one house as a number of houses set down among gay gardens. The building in which we were received consisted apparently of two rooms, an anteroom and a reception room. The latter was furnished in the usual style (invariable, it seems to me, from country inn to prince's palace), heavy high chairs, heavy high tables ranged against walls decorated with kakemonos and gay mottoes; only in the centre of the room was a large table covered with a cloth of European manufacture on which were set out dishes of English biscuits and sweets. Our hostess, dressed in a modified Chinese costume, received us with graceful dignity. Her fine-featured face bore a marked likeness to many that one meets on the street or in the church of an old New England town, and its rather anxious expression somewhat emphasized the resemblance. She spoke with much pleasure of the years she had spent in America, and her daughter, who had been educated in a well-known private school in New York, looked back longingly to those days, complaining that there was no society in Yunnan-fu; but she brightened up at a reference to the arrival of a new and young English vice-consul, hoping that it might mean some tennis. It was an unexpected touch of New China in this out-of-the-way corner. Before we left, two younger children were brought in, both born in America, and one bearing the name "Daisy," the other "Lincoln," but already they were forgetting their English.

During my three days in Yunnan-fu,[1] through the

[1] The words "fu" and "chou" and "hsien," attached to so many Chinese place-names, are terms denoting administrative divisions. "Fu" may be translated prefecture, "chou," department, and "hsien," a district. The towns having these terminations are the headquarters of the respective divisions.

kindness of the British Consul-General I was given a chance to make one or two excursions into the surrounding country. An especially charming trip that we took one afternoon was to Chin Tien, or "Golden Temple," a celebrated copper temple about five miles out. Near the town our chairs were borne along the narrow earth balk between the bean- and rice-fields, but farther on our way led over the top of a high dyke lined with trees. We mounted by a charming winding road to the temple, set high on the hillside among its own groves of conifers, the courts of the temple, which rose one behind the other, being connected by long, steep flights of steps. In the upper court we were met by the friendly priests, the quiet dignity of their reception being somewhat disturbed by the din of the temple dogs, goaded almost to madness at Jack's imperturbable bearing. Chinese temples rarely offer much of interest; the construction is usually simple and their treasures are few, but everything is freely shown, there are no dark corners, and the spacious courts gay with flowers are full of charm. The sacred images which they contain are generally grotesque or hideous. Not often does one show a trace of the gracious serenity that marks the traditional representations of Buddha; on the other hand, they are never indecent.

While I was seeing a little of Yunnan-fu and its people, the preparations for my overland trip were

MY SEDAN CHAIR AND BEARERS

A MEMORIAL ARCH NEAR YUNNAN-FU

moving forward, thanks chiefly to the kind helpfulness of Mr. Stevenson, of the China Inland Mission. For many years a resident of the province, and wise in the ways of the country and of the country-folk, his advice served me at every turn. Engaging the coolies was of course the matter of chief importance. On them would depend the success of the first stage of my journey, the two and a half or three weeks' trip to Ning-yüan-fu in the Chien-ch'ang valley. A representative of the coolie "hong," or guild, a dignified, substantial-looking man, was brought to the inn by Mr. Stevenson. After looking over my kit carefully (even the dog was "hefted" on the chance he might have to ride at times), he decided the number of coolies necessary. As I wished to travel fast if need came, I threw in another man that the loads might be light. The average load is seventy or eighty catties, a catty equalling about one pound and a quarter. In Yunnan the coolies generally carry on the shoulder, the burden, fairly divided, being suspended from the two ends of a bamboo pole. For myself I had four men, as I had a four-bearer chair, the grandest of all things on the road save the mandarin's chair with its curved poles raising the occupant high above the common herd. At first I did not realize the significance of the number, although I marked the interest with which my interpreter inquired how many bearers I should have. What I did appreciate was the extreme comfort of my travelling arrangements. Seated in my chair, which was open above and enclosed below, and furnished with a water-proof top and with curtains that could be lowered to protect me against sun or rain, wind or importunate curiosity, I felt as though on a throne. Under the seat was a compartment just large enough for dressing-bag, camera, and thermos bottle, while at my feet there was ample room for Jack. For my interpreter there was a two-bearer chair, with which he was vastly discontented, and I, too, had my doubts about it, although our reasons were not the same. He felt it beneath his dignity to travel with two bearers only; I feared that it was too great a burden for two men, even though the chair was light and the Chinese literatus, small-boned and lacking in muscle, is no heavy burden. Anyway, the arrangement did not work well, and at Ning-yüan-fu the interpreter was provided with a closed chair and three bearers, to his own satisfaction and to mine also, again for different reasons.

A sedan-chair is too luxurious to be long endurable, so I added a pony to our caravan, purchased, from a home-going Dane of the customs service, for forty-four dollars Mexican. The Yunnanese ponies are small and sturdy, and as active as cats. They are all warranted to kick, and mine was no exception. Although he was described as a gentleman's steed, he had the manners of a pack-horse. I doubt if any one of our party escaped the touch of his hoofs, and it was a joy to see him exchange salutations with the ponies we met on the trail. However, he was sure-footed and willing, and although hardly up to so long a trip as mine, yet with care he came out very well at the end. But it required constant watchfulness to make sure that he was properly watered and fed, even though most of the time I took along a coolie for no other purpose save to look after the horse, and lead him when I was not riding. And to the very last it meant an order each time to insure that the girths were loosened and the stirrups tied up when I was out of the saddle. When we started from Yunnan-fu our caravan was made up of thirteen coolies, — six chair-men, six baggage-carriers, and a "fu t'ou," or head coolie, whose duty it was to keep the others up to their work, to settle disputes, or to meet any difficulty that arose. In short, he was responsible both to me and to the hong for the carrying-out of the contract which had been duly agreed upon. In my limited experience, the fu t'ou is a great blessing. I found mine capable, reliable men, adroit in smoothing away difficulties and very ready to meet my wishes. As for the contract, that was a serious matter. Each detail was carefully entered in a formidable document, the route, the stages, the number of men, the amount to be paid, and the how and where of payment. The hong had one copy and I another which was handed over to the fu t'ou at the end of the trip, that he might show it to the chief of the hong as proof that he had carried out the contract. Each coolie was to receive $7.00 Mexican, or about $3.50 gold, for his journey from Yunnan-fu to Ning-yüan-fu, reckoned usually as sixteen stages. About one third the amount was to be paid before starting, the remainder in specified sums at stated intervals en route. I had no concern with the men's daily food, but from time to time I was expected to give them "pork money" if they behaved well. It would have been cheaper, I believe, to have hired coolies off the street, but far less satisfactory, for the hong holds itself responsible to you for the behavior of its men. And in their turn the coolies pay a definite percentage of their earnings to the hong.

My stores and bedding and other things were packed in large covered baskets insecurely fastened with padlocks. As time went on, covers became loose and padlocks were knocked off by projecting rocks, but nothing was ever lost or stolen. To keep out wet or vermin I had the baskets lined with Chinese oiled cotton, perishable but cheap, and effective as long as it lasts. Other sheets of the same material were provided for use in the inn. One was laid on the floor and my camp-bed set up in the middle of it, while others were spread over the wooden Chinese beds with which the room was generally well supplied, and on them my clothes, saddle, etc., were placed. When new the oiled cotton has a strong, pungent odour, not pleasant but very effective against vermin.

A most important item was the money to be used on the journey. I had an account with the Hong Kong and Shanghai Bank at Shanghai, and wherever there were Europeans it was possible to get checks cashed, but from Yunnan-fu to Ning-yüan, a journey of two and a half weeks or more, I should be quite off the track of foreigners. Fortunately Yunnan is waking up in money matters as well as in other ways, and has a silver coinage of its own; moreover, one that the inhabitants are willing to accept, which is not always the case, as I found later to my cost. With the help of native bankers I was duly furnished with a supply of Yunnan dollars, akin to Mexican dollars in value, and I obtained also some Szechuan coins to use when I entered that province. In addition I became the proud possessor of some seventy dollars in Hupeh money. This I was told would pass anywhere after crossing the Yangtse. When I reached Ning-yüan-fu, however, I found that no one would take it save at a heavy discount. Unwilling to burden myself with it longer, I decided to let the Chinese bankers have it, even though at a loss, but when they discovered that the money was in twenty-cent pieces they would have nothing to do with it at any price. So I carried it some two thousand miles farther, to Hupeh itself. But even there it was not willingly accepted. In the railway offices at Hankow not more than forty cents would be received in small coins. If your ticket cost $10.50, you paid for it in unbroken dollars, giving the railway a chance to unload some of the undesirable change upon you. In the end I found myself reduced to peddling twenty-cent pieces among friends and friends of friends. For small change on my journey I carried rolls of copper cents, while the cook festooned himself with long ropes of copper "cash," about twenty to the American cent.

By the arrangement of the Foreign Office two soldiers were detailed to escort me across Yunnan. It is by the wish of the officials rather than at the traveller's request that this escort is given. The Chinese have learned through an experience not wholly to our credit that injury or even annoyance to the European may bring a punishment quite out of proportion to the harm done; so to avoid difficulties the official is inclined to insist upon sending soldiers with the foreigners passing through his district, and the traveller as a rule perforce accepts the arrangement. If he refuses, he will find it more difficult to secure redress for any loss or injury suffered. For my part I did not feel inclined to object. The expense is borne by the Government, save for the customary tip, and in more ways than one I found my escort useful. At irregular intervals they were changed. When we reached the end of the last stage for which they were detailed, I gave them my card to carry to the proper local official. This was replied to by sending a new pair bearing the official's card.

Some of the men were old-time soldiers, hardly to be distinguished from yamen runners in their untidy black and scarlet jackets decorated with bold lettering on the back; and their weapons consisted simply of something that might be described as a small sword or a huge carving-knife in a leather sheath. After entering Szechuan I was usually accompanied by quite real soldiers, men of the new service, fairly shipshape in khaki and putties and carrying up-to-date guns. But whether of the old order or of the new, I found the men at all times very courteous and friendly, and ready to do any little service that came their way. It was the duty of one man to stay with me, while the other looked after the baggage coolies. As more at home in the particular district through which we were passing, they were often very helpful to my coolies in pointing out a short cut or in finding our intricate way across the fields. Sometimes one was sent in advance to make sure of the best quarters the village where we were to pass the night could afford, and they often showed great zeal in tidying up the room for my coming. The preparations consisted usually in stirring up the dust of ages on the floor, a proceeding I did not like, and in ruthlessly tearing out the paper that covered the lattice opening, of which I much approved. Glass is rarely seen in West China, and the paper excluded both light and air, but never the gaze of the curious, as a peephole was very easily punched. On the march my escort, quick to notice my interest in the flowers, were active in bringing me huge nosegays gathered along the trail, so that my chair was often turned into a gay flowery bower; and they sometimes showed their love for dogs, or perhaps sought to prove their zeal in my service, by picking up Jack and carrying him for the half-hour, to his great disgust, as his sturdy legs were untiring, and equally so was his desire to investigate every nook and corner. "Little fu t'ou," the coolies called him, because of the careful watch he kept for any stragglers of the caravan.

CHAPTER III

ACROSS YUNNAN

MY departure was set for the 8th of April, and by half-past four of that morning the coolies, marshalled by the hong man, were at the door; but it was after nine before we were really under way. It is always a triumphant moment when one's caravan actually starts; there have been so many times when starting at all seemed doubtful. Mine looked quite imposing as it moved off, headed by Mr. Stevenson on his sturdy pony, I following in my chair, while servants and coolies straggled on behind, but, as usual, something was missing. This time it was one of the two soldiers detailed by the Foreign Office to accompany me the first stages of my journey. We were told he would join us farther on. Fortunately Mr. Stevenson was up to the wiles of the native, and he at once scented the favourite device for two to take the travelling allowance, and then, by some amicable arrangement, for only one to go. So messengers were sent in haste to look up the recreant, who finally joined us with cheerful face at the West Gate, which we reached by a rough path outside the north wall.

Here I bade Mr. Stevenson good-bye, and turned

my face away from the city. Once more I was on the "open road." Above me shone the bright sun of Yunnan, before me lay the long trail leading into the unknown. Seven hundred miles of wild mountainous country, six weeks of steady travelling lay between me and Chengtu, the great western capital. The road I planned to follow would lead nearly due north at first, traversing the famous Chien-ch'ang valley after crossing the Yangtse. But at Fulin on the Ta Tu I intended to make a détour to the west as far as Tachienlu, that I might see a little of the Tibetans even though I could not enter Tibet. I did not fear trouble of any sort in spite of a last letter of warning received at Hong Kong from our Peking Legation, but there was just enough of a touch of adventure to the trip to make the roughnesses of the way endurable. Days would pass before I could again talk with my own kind, but I was not afraid of being lonely. "The scene was savage, but the scene was new," and the hours would be filled full with the constantly changing interests of the road, and as I looked at my men I felt already the comradeship that would come with long days of effort and hardship passed together. These men of the East — Turk, Indian, Chinese, Mongol — are much of a muchness, it seems to me; pay them fairly, treat them considerately, laugh instead of storm at the inevitable mishaps of the way, and generally they will give you faithful, willing service.

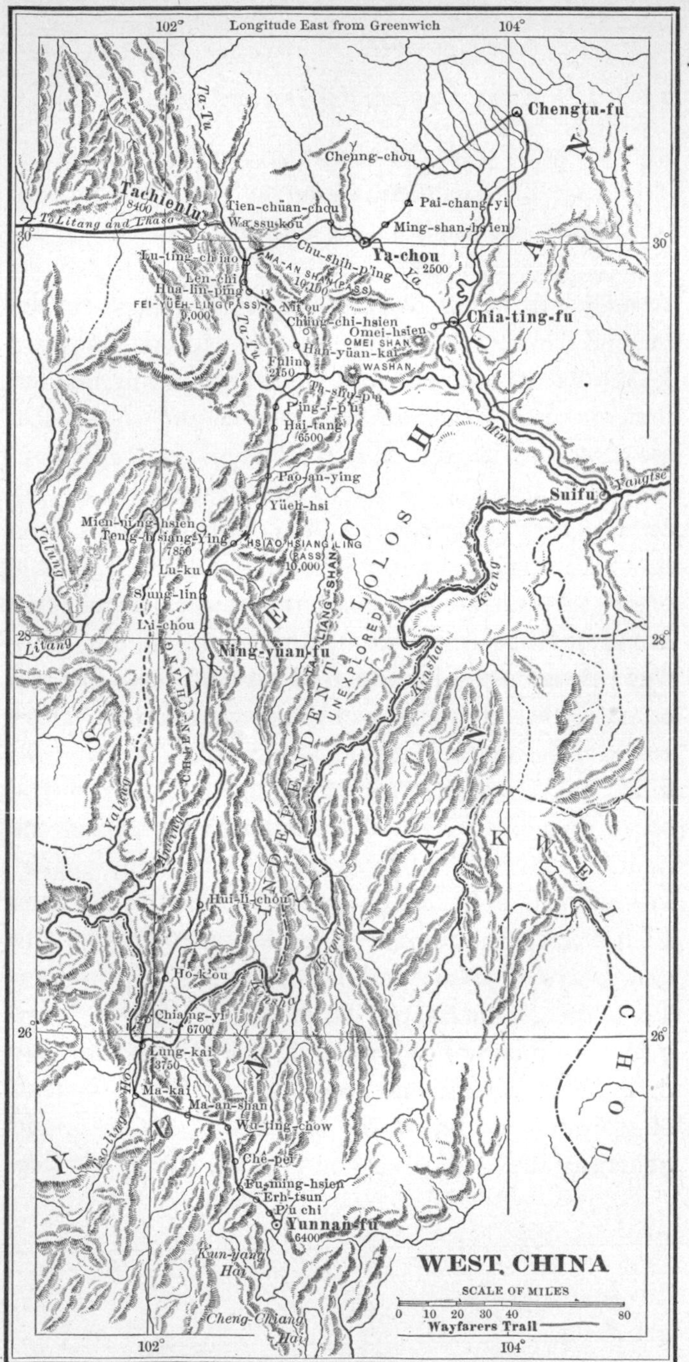

WEST CHINA
Longitude East from Greenwich
102°
104°
30°
28°
26°
Chengtu-fu
Cheung-chou
Pai-chang-yi
Ming-shan-hsien
Tachienlu
8400
To Litang and Lhasa
Tien-chüan-chou
Wa ssu-kou
Ya-chou
2500
Ya
Chu-shih-p'ing
MA-AN SHAN (PASS)
10,100
Lu-ting-ch'iao
Len-chi
Hua-lin-ping
FEI-YÜEH-LING (PASS)
9,000
Ni-tou
Ch'ing-chi-hsien
Omei-hsien
OMEI SHAN
Chia-ting-fu
Han-yüan-kai
Fulin
2150
WASHAN
Ta-shu-pu
Ping-i-pu
Hai-tang
6500
Min
Pao-an-ying
Yüeh-hsi
Suifu
Yangtse
Ta-Tu
Mien-ning-hsien
Teng-h'siang-Ying
7850
HSIAO HSIANG LING (PASS)
10,000
Lu-ku
Sung-lin
Li-chou
Yalung
Litang
Ning-yüan-fu
TA LIANG SHAN
INDEPENDENT LOLOS
UNEXPLORED
Kiang
Kinsha
Kinsha Kiang
SZ CH'UAN
YUNNAN
KWEICHOU
Yalung
CHIEN CH'ANG
Anning
Hui-li-chou
Ho-k'ou
Chiang-yi
6700
Lung-kai
3750
Ho
Ma-kai
Ma-an-shan
Wu-ting-chow
Chê-pei
Tso-ling
Fu-ming-hsien
Erh-tsun
P'u chi
Yunnan-fu
6400
Kun-yang Hai
Cheng-Chiang Hai
SCALE OF MILES
0 10 20 30 40 80
Wayfarers Trail

It is only when they have been spoiled by overpayment, or by bullying of a sort they do not understand, that the foreigner finds them exacting and untrustworthy. And the Chinese is an eminently reasonable man. He does not expect reward without work, and he works easily and cheerfully. But as yet he was to me an unknown quantity, and I looked over my group of coolies with some interest and a little uncertainty. They were mostly strong, sound-looking men; two or three were middle-aged, the rest young. No one looked unequal to the work, and no one proved so. All wore the inevitable blue cotton of the Chinese, varying with wear and patching from blue-black to bluish-white, and the fashion of the dress was always the same; short, full trousers, square-cut, topped by a belted shirt with long sleeves falling over the hands or rolled up to the elbow according to the weather. About their heads they generally twisted a strip of cotton, save when blazing sun or pouring rain called for the protection of their wide straw hats covered with oiled cotton. Generally they wore the queue tucked into the girdle to keep it out of the way, but occasionally it was put to use, as, for example, if a man's hat was not at hand to ward off the glare of the sun, he would deftly arrange a thatch of leaves over his eyes, binding it firm with his long braid of black hair. On their feet they wore the inevitable straw sandal of these parts. Comfortable for those who know how to wear them, cheap even though not durable (they cost only four cents Mexican the pair), and a great safeguard against slipping, they seemed as satisfactory footwear as the ordinary shoes of the better-class Chinese seemed unsatisfactory. Throughout the East it is only the barefooted peasant or the sandalled mountaineer who does not seem encumbered by his feet. The felt shoe of the Chinese gentleman and the flapping, heelless slipper of the Indian are alike uncomfortable and hampering. Nor have Asiatics learned as yet to wear proper European shoes, or to wear them properly, for they stub along in badly cut, ill-fitting things too short for their feet. Why does not the shoemaker of the West, if he wishes to secure an Eastern market, study the foot of the native, and make him shoes suited to his need?

Our order of march through Yunnan varied little from day to day. We all had breakfast before starting at about seven, and we all had much the same thing, tea and rice, but mine came from the coast; the coolies bought theirs by the way. At intervals during the forenoon we stopped at one of the many tea-houses along the road to give the men a chance to rest and smoke and drink tea. Sometimes I stayed in my chair by the roadside; more often I escaped from the noise and dirt of the village to some spot outside, among the rice- and bean-fields, where the pony could gather a few scant mouthfuls of grass while I sat hard-by on

MY CARAVAN

THE MILITARY ESCORT

ON A YUNNAN ROAD

a turf balk and enjoyed the quiet and clean air. Of course I was often found out and followed by the village-folk, but their curiosity was not very offensive. Generally they squatted down in a semi-circle about me, settling themselves deliberately to gaze their fill. If they came too near I laughed and waved them back, and they always complied good-naturedly. The little children were often really quite charming under the dirt, but until they had learned to wash their faces and wipe their noses I must confess I liked them best at a distance.

At noon we stopped at a handy inn or tea-house for tiffin and a long rest. I was ordinarily served at the back of the big eating-room open to the street in as dignified seclusion as my cook could achieve. Rice again, with perhaps stewed fowl or tinned beef, and a dessert of jam and biscuit, usually formed my luncheon, and dinner was like unto it, save that occasionally we succeeded in securing some onions or potatoes. The setting-forth of my table with clean cloth and changes of plates was of never-failing interest to the crowds that darkened the front of the eating-house, and excitement reached a climax when the coolie, whom my cook had installed as helper, — there is no Chinese too poor to lack some one to do his bidding, — served Jack his midday meal of rice in his own dish. Then men stood on tiptoe and children climbed on each other's shoulders to see a dog fed like — the Chinese equivalent of Christian. They never seemed to begrudge him his food; on the contrary, they often smiled approvingly. We were thousands of miles away from the famine-stricken regions of eastern China, and through much of the country where I journeyed I saw almost no beggars or hungry-looking folk. In the afternoon we stopped as before at short intervals at some roadside tea-house, for the coolies generally expect to rest every hour.

Our day's stage usually ended in a good-sized town. I should have preferred it otherwise, for there is more quiet and freedom in the villages. But my coolies would have it so; they liked the stir and better fare of the towns, and the regular stages are arranged accordingly. Our entrance was noisy and imposing. My coming seemed always expected, for as by magic the narrow streets filled with staring crowds. Through them the soldiers fought a way for my chair, borne at smart pace by the coolies all shouting at the top of their voices. I tried to cultivate the superior impassiveness of the Chinese official, but generally the delighted shrieks of the children at the sight of Jack at my feet, and his gay yelps in response, "upset the apple cart." There was a rush to see the "foreign dog." I gripped him tighter and only breathed freely when with a sharp turn to right or left my chair was lifted high over a threshold and borne through the inn door into the courtyard, the crowd in no wise baffled swarming at our heels, sometimes not even stopping at the entrance to the inner court, sacred (more or less) to the so-called mandarin rooms, the best rooms of the place. I could not but sympathize with the inn-keeper, the order of his establishment thus upset, but he took it in good part; perhaps the turmoil had its value in making known to the whole world that the wandering foreigner had bestowed her patronage upon his house. I am sure he had some reward in the many cups of tea drunk while the crowd lingered on the chance of another sight of the unusual visitor. Anyway we were always made welcome, and no objections were offered when my men took possession of the place in very unceremonious fashion, as it seemed to me, filling the court with their din, blocking the ways with the chairs and baskets, seeking the best room for me, and then testing the door and putting things to rights after a fashion, while the owner looked on in helpless wonder.

In the villages one stepped directly from the road into a large living-room, kitchen, and dining-room in one, and out of this opened the places for sleeping. The inns in the towns are built more or less after one and the same pattern. Entrance is through a large restaurant open to the street, and filled with tables occupied at all hours save early dawn with men sipping and smoking. From the restaurant one passes into a stone-paved court surrounded usually by low, one-story buildings, although occasionally there is a second story opening into a gallery. Here are kitchens and sleeping-rooms, while store-rooms and stables are tucked in anywhere. In the largest inns there is often an inner court into which open the better rooms.

While the cook bustled about to get hot water, and the head coolie saw to the setting-up of my bed, I generally went with the "ma-fu," or horse boy, to see that the pony was properly cared for. Usually he was handy, sometimes tethered by my door, often just under my room, once overhead. Meanwhile the coolies were freshening themselves up a bit after the day's work. Sitting about the court they rinsed chest and head and legs with the unfailing supply of hot water which is the one luxury of a Chinese inn. I can speak authoritatively on the cleanliness of the Chinese coolie, for I had the chance daily to see my men scrub themselves. Their cotton clothing loosely cut was well ventilated, even though infrequently cleansed, and there hung about them nothing of the odour of the great unwashed of the Western world. I wish one could say as much for the inns, but alas, they were foul-smelling, one and all, and occasionally the room offered me was so filthy that I refused to occupy it, and went on the war-path for myself, followed by a crowd of perplexed servants and coolies. Almost always I found a loft or a stable-yard that had at least the advantage of plenty of fresh air, and without demur my innkeeper made me free of it, although I expect it cut him to the heart to have his best room so flouted.

Generally I went to bed soon after dinner; there was nothing else to do, for the dim lantern light made reading difficult, and anyway my books were few. But while the nights were none too long for me, the Chinese, like most Asiatics, make little distinction between day and night. They sleep if there is nothing else to do, they wake when work or pleasure calls, and it was long after midnight when the inn settled itself to rest, and by four o'clock it was again awake, and before seven we were once more on the road.

In Yunnan, or "South of the Clouds," as the word signifies, you are in a land of sunshine, of wild grandeur and beauty, of unfailing interest. Its one hundred and fifty-five thousand square miles are pretty much on end; no matter which way you cross the country you are always going up or going down, and the contrasts of vegetation and lack of it are just as emphatic; barren snow-topped mountains overhang tiny valleys, veritable gems of tropical beauty; you pass with one step from a waste of rock and sand to a garden-like oasis of soft green and rippling waters. Yunnan's chequered history is revealed in the varied peoples that inhabit the deep valleys and narrow river banks. Nominally annexed to the empire by Kublai Khan, the Mongol, in the thirteenth century, ever since the Chinese people have been at work peacefully and irresistibly making the conquest real, and now they are found all over the province, as a matter of course occupying the best places. But they have not exterminated the aborigines, nor have they assimilated them to any degree. To-day the tribes constitute more than one half the population, and an ethnological map of Yunnan is a wonderful patchwork, for side by side and yet quite distinct, you find scattered about settlements of Chinese, Shans, Lolos, Miaos, Losus, and just what some of these are is still an unsolved riddle. To add to the confusion there is a division of religions hardly known elsewhere, for out of the population of twelve millions it is estimated that three or four millions are Mohammedans. To be sure, they seem much like the others, and generally all get on together very well, for Moslem pride of religion does not find much response with the practical Chinese, and the Buddhist is as tolerant here as elsewhere. But the Mohammedan rebellion of half a century ago has left terrible memories ; then add to that the ill-feeling between the Chinese and the tribesmen, and the general discontent at the prohibition of poppy-growing, and it is plain that Yunnan offers a fine field for long-continued civil disorder with all the possibility of foreign interference.

The early hours of our first day's march led us

along the great western trade route, and we met scores of people hurrying towards the capital, mostly coolies carrying on their backs, or slung from a bamboo pole across their shoulders, great loads of wood, charcoal, fowls, rice, vegetables. Every one was afoot or astride a pony, for there was nothing on wheels, not even a barrow. The crowd lacked the variety in colour and cut of dress of a Hindu gathering; all had black hair and all wore blue clothes, and one realized at once how much China loses in not having a picturesque and significant head covering like the Indian turban. But the faces showed more diversity both in hue and in feature than I had looked for. In America we come in contact chiefly with Chinese of one class, and usually from the one province of Kwangtung. But the men of Yunnan and Szechuan are of a different type, larger, sturdier, of better carriage. It takes experience commonly to mark differences in face and expression among men of an alien race, and to the Asiatic all Europeans look much alike, but already I was discerning variety in the faces I met along the trail, and they did not seem as unfamiliar to me as I had expected. I was constantly surprised by resemblances to types and individuals at home. One of my chair coolies, for example, a young, smooth-faced fellow, bore a disconcerting likeness to one of my former students. But fair or dark, fine-featured or foul, all greeted me in a friendly way, generally stopping after I had passed to ask my coolies more about me. My four-bearer chair testified to my standing, and my men, Eastern fashion, glorified themselves in glorifying me. I was a "scholar," a "learned lady," but what I had come for was not so clear. A missionary I certainly was not. Anyway, as a mere woman I was not likely to do harm.

The road after crossing the plain entered the hills, winding up and down, but always paved with cobbles and flags laid with infinite pains generations ago, and now illustrating the Chinese saying of "good for ten years, bad for ten thousand." It was so hopelessly out of repair that men and ponies alike had to pick their way with caution. Long flights of irregular and broken stone stairs led up and down the hillsides over which my freshly shod pony slipped and floundered awkwardly, and I always breathed a sigh of relief when a stretch of hard red earth gave a little respite. It was neither courage nor pride that kept me in the saddle, but the knowledge that much of the way would be worse rather than better, and I would wisely face it at the outset. If it got too nerve-racking I could always betake myself to my chair and, trusting in the eight sturdy legs of my bearers, abandon myself to enjoying the sights along the way.

Our first day's halt for tiffin was at the small hamlet of P'u chi. The eating-house was small and crowded, and my cook set my table perforce in the midst of the peering, pointing throng. I was the target of scores of black eyes, and I felt that every movement was discussed, every mouthful counted. As a first experience it was a little embarrassing, but the people seemed good-humoured and very ready to fall into place or move out of the way in obedience to my gestures when I tried to take some pictures, not too successfully. Here for a moment I was again in touch with my own world, as a runner, most thoughtfully sent by Mr. Stevenson with the morning's letters, overtook me. According to arrangement he had been paid beforehand, but not knowing that I knew that, he clamoured for more. The crowd pressed closer to listen to the discussion, and grinned with a rather malicious satisfaction when the man was forced to confess that he had already received what they knew was a generous tip. Chinese business instinct kept them impartial, even between one of their own people and a foreigner.

That night we stopped, after a stage of some sixty li, about nineteen miles, at Erh-tsun, a small, uninteresting village. The inn was very poor, and I would have consoled myself by thinking that it was well to get used to the worst at once, only I was not sure that it was the worst. My room, off the public gathering place, had but one window looking directly on the street. From the moment of my arrival the opening was filled with the faces of a staring, curious crowd, pushing each other, stretching their necks to get a better view. My servants put up an oiled cotton sheet, but it was promptly drawn aside, so there was nothing for me to do but wash, eat, and go to bed in public, like a royal personage of former times.

It was a beautiful spring morning when we started the next day. We were now among the mountains, and much of our way led along barren hillsides, but the air was intoxicating, and the views across the ridges were charming. At times we dropped into a small valley, each having its little group of houses nestling among feathery bamboos and surrounded by tiny green fields. Dogs barked, children ran after us, men and women stopped for a moment to smile a greeting and exchange a word with our coolies. As a rule, the people looked comfortable and well fed, but here and there we passed a group of ruined, abandoned hovels. The explanation varied. Sometimes the ruin dated back more than a generation to the terrible days of the Mohammedan rebellion. In other cases the trouble was more recent. The irrigating system had broken down, or water was scant, or more frequently the cutting-off of the opium crop had driven the people from their homes. But in general there was little tillable land that was unoccupied. In fact, the painstaking effort to utilize every bit of soil was tragic to American eyes, accustomed to long stretches of countryside awaiting the plough. At the close of the troubles that devastated the province during the third quarter of the nineteenth century it is said that the population of Yunnan had fallen to about a million, but now, owing in part to the great natural increase of the Chinese, and in part to immigration chiefly from overpopulated Szechuan and Kwei-chou, it is estimated at twelve million. At any rate, those who know the country well declare there is little vacant land fit for agriculture, that the province has about as many inhabitants as it can support, and can afford no relief to the overcrowded eastern districts. This is a thing to keep in mind when Japan urges her need of Manchuria for her teeming millions.

We stopped for tiffin at Fu-ming-hsien, a prosperous-looking town of some eight hundred families. As usual, I lunched in public, the crowd pressing close about my table in spite of the efforts of a real, khaki-clad policeman; but it was a jolly, friendly crowd, its interest easily diverted from me to the dog. Here we changed soldiers, for this was a hsien town, or district centre. Those who had come with me from Yunnan-fu were dismissed with a tip amounting to about three cents gold a day each. They seemed perfectly satisfied. It was the regulation amount; had I given more they would have clamoured for something additional. That afternoon we stopped for a long rest at a tiny, lonely inn, perched most picturesquely on a spur of the mountain. I sat in my chair while the coolies drank tea inside, and a number of children gathered about me, ready to run if I seemed dangerous. Finally one, taking his courage in both hands, presented me with the local substitute for candy, — raw peas in the pod, which I nibbled and found refreshing. In turn I doled out some biscuits, to the children's great delight, while fathers and mothers looked on approvingly. The way to the heart of the Chinese is not far to seek. They dote on children, and children the world over are much alike. More than once I have solved an awkward situation by ignoring the inhospitable or unwilling elders and devoting myself to the little ones, always at hand. Please the children and you have won the parents.

We stopped that night at Chê-pei, a small town lying at an elevation of about six thousand feet. My room, the best the inn afforded, was dirty, but large and airy. On one side a table was arranged for the ancestral family worship, and I delayed turning in at night to give the people a chance to burn a few joss sticks, which they did in a very matter-of-fact fashion, nowise disturbed at my washing-things, which Liu, the cook, had set out among the gods.

Our path the next day led high on the mountain-side and along a beautiful ridge. We stopped for an early rest at a little walled village, Jee-ka ("Cock's street"), perched picturesquely on the top of the hill.

Later we saw a storm advancing across the mountains, and before we could reach cover the clouds broke over our heads, drenching the poor coolies to the skin, but they took it in good part, laughing as they scuttled along the trail. The rain kept on for some hours, and the road was alternately a brook or a sea of slippery red mud; the pony, with the cook on his back, rolled over, but fortunately neither was hurt; coolies slid and floundered, and the chair-men went down, greatly to their confusion, for it is deemed inexcusable for a chair-carrier to fall. Toward the end of the day it cleared and the bright sun soon dried the ways, and we raced into Wu-ting-chou in fine shape, the coolies picking their way deftly along the narrow earth balks that form the highway to this rather important town. Our entrance was of the usual character, a cross between a triumphal procession and a circus show, — people rushing to see the sight, children calling, dogs barking, my men shouting as they pushed their way through the throng, while I sat the observed of all, trying to carry off my embarrassment with a benevolent smile. I am told that the interest of a Chinese crowd usually centres on the foreigners' shoes, but in my case, when the gaze got down to my feet, Jack was mostly there to divert attention.

Rain came on again in the night and kept us in Wu-ting-chou over the next day. The Chinese, with their extraordinary adaptability, can stand extremes of heat and cold remarkably well. Hence they are good colonizers, able to work in Manchuria and Singapore, Canada and Panama. But rain they dislike, and a smart shower is a good excuse for stopping. Fortunately for all, the inn was unusually decent. Steps led from the street into an outer court, behind which was a much larger second court, surrounded on all sides by two-story buildings. My room on the upper floor had beautiful views over the town, more attractive at close range than most Chinese towns. The temples and yamen buildings were exceptionally fine, while the houses, of sun-dried brick of the colour of the red soil of Yunnan, had a comfortable look, their tip-tilted tiled roofs showing picturesquely among the trees.

I spent the rainy forenoon in writing and in leaning over the gallery to watch the life going on below. After the first excitement people went about their business undisturbed by my presence. At one side cooking was carried on at a long, crescent-shaped range of some sort of cement, and containing half a dozen openings for fires. Above each fire was a bowl-shaped depression in the range, and into this was fitted a big iron pot. The food of the country is generally boiled, and is often seasoned with a good deal of care. Barring the lack of cleanliness, the chief objection to the cooking of the peasant-folk is the failure to cook thoroughly. The Chinese are content if the rice and vegetables are cooked through; they do not insist, as we do, that they be cooked soft. In the smaller inns my men prepared their food themselves, and some showed considerable skill. One soldier in particular was past-master in making savoury stews much appreciated by the others.

Wu-ting-chou being a place designated for the payment of an instalment of wages, and also the time having come for pork money, my coolies had a grand feast, after which they devoted themselves to gambling away their hard-earned money in games of "fan t'an." As they played entirely among themselves the result was that some staggered the following day under heavy ropes of cash, while others were forced to sell their hats to pay for their food. I could only hope that the next pay-day would mean a readjustment of spoils.

In the afternoon it cleared, and I went out in my chair, escorted by two policemen, to a charming grove outside the walls, where I rested for a time in a quiet nook, enjoying the views over the valley and thankful to get away from the din of the inn. Curling up, I went fast asleep, to wake with an uncomfortable sense of being watched; and sure enough, peering over the top of the bank where I was lying were two pairs of startled black eyes. I laughed, and thereupon the owners of the eyes, who had stumbled upon me as they came up the hill, seated themselves in front of me and began to ply me with questions, to which I could only answer with another laugh; so they relapsed into friendly silence, gingerly stroking Jack while they kept a watchful eye on me. What does it matter if words are lacking, a laugh is understood, and will often smooth a way where speech would bring confusion. Once, years ago in Western Tibet, I crossed a high pass with just one coolie, in advance of my caravan. Without warning we dropped down into a little village above the Shyok. Most of the people had never before seen a European. I could not talk with them nor they with my coolie, — for he came from the other side of the range, — nor he with me. But I laughed, and every one else laughed, and in five minutes I was sitting on the grass under the walnut trees, offerings of flowers and mulberries on my lap, and while the whole population sat around on stone walls and house roofs, the village head man took off my shoes and rubbed my weary feet.

When I emerged from my retreat I found that a priest from the neighbouring temple had come to beg a visit from me. It turned out to be a Buddhist temple on the usual plan, noteworthy only for a rather good figure of Buddha made of sun-dried clay and painted. The priest was inclined to refuse a fee, saying he had done nothing, but he was keen to have me take some pictures.

TEMPLE GATEWAY

TEMPLE CORNER

WU-TING-CHOU

The next three days our path led us across the mountains separating the Yangtse and Red River basins. We were now off the main roads; villages and travellers were few. To my delight we had left for a time the paved trails over which the pony scraped and slipped; the hard dirt made a surer footing, and it was possible to let him out for a trot now and then. The start and finish of the day were usually by winding narrow paths carried along the strips of turf dividing the fields or over the top of a stone wall. I learned to respect both the sure-footedness of the Yunnan pony and the thrift of the Yunnan peasant who wasted no bit of tillable land on roads. From time to time we crossed a stone bridge, rarely of more than one arch, and that so pointed that the ponies on the road, which followed closely the line of the arch, clambered up with difficulty only to slide headlong on the other side. The bridges of these parts are very picturesque, giving an added charm to the landscape, in glaring contrast to the hideous, shed-like structures that disfigure many a beautiful stream of New England.

Our way led alternately over barren or pine-clad hills, showing everywhere signs of charcoal burners, or through deep gorges, or dipped down into tiny emerald valleys. At one point we descended an interminable rock staircase guarded by soldiers top and bottom. Formerly this was a haunt of robbers, but now the Government was making a vigorous effort to insure the safety of traffic along this way. Our stay that night was in a tiny hamlet, and a special guard was stationed at the door of the inn to defend us against real or fancied danger from marauders.

It was still early in April, but even on these high levels the flowers were in their glory, and each day revealed a new wonder. Roses were abundant, white and scentless, or small, pink, and spicy, and the ground was carpeted with yellow and blue flowers. From time to time we passed a group of comfortable farm buildings, but much of the country had a desolate look and the villages were nothing more than forlorn hamlets, and once we stopped for the night in a solitary house far from any settlement. A week after leaving Yunnan-fu we entered the valley of the Tso-ling Ho, a tributary of the Great River, and a more fertile region. As I had been warned, the weather changed here, and for the next twenty-four hours we sweltered in the steamy heat of the Yangtse basin. From now on, there was no lack of water. On all sides brooks large and small dashed down, swelling the Tso-ling almost to the size of the main river itself. At one spot, sending the men on to the village, I stopped on the river bank to bathe my tired feet, and was startled by the passing of a stray fisherman, but he seemed in no wise surprised, and greeting me courteously went on with his work. China shares with us the bad fame of being unpleasantly inquisitive.

Would the rural American, happening upon a Chinese woman, — an alien apparition from her smoothly plastered hair to her tiny bound feet, — by the brookside in one of his home fields, have shown the same restraint?

At five o'clock that same day we reached the ferry across the Yangtse, too late to cross that night. I was hot and weary after a long march, and the only place available in the village of Lung-kai was a cramped, windowless hole opening into a small, filthy court, the best room of the inn being occupied by a sick man. Through an open doorway I caught a glimpse into a stable-yard well filled with pigs. On one side was a small, open, shrine-like structure reached by a short flight of steps. In spite of the shocked remonstrances of my men I insisted on taking possession of this; the yard, though dirty, was dry, and at least I was sure of plenty of air. Fresh straw was spread in the shrine and my bed set up on it; the pigs were given my pony's stable, as I preferred his company to theirs; and I had an unusually pleasant evening, spite of the fact that the roofs of the adjoining buildings were crowded with onlookers, mostly children, until it grew too dark for them to see anything.

We crossed the Yangtse the next day on a large flat-bottomed boat into which we all crowded higgledy-piggledy, the men and their loads, pony and chairs. The current was so swift that we were carried some distance downstream before making a landing. At this point, and indeed from Tibet to Suifu, the Yangtse is, I believe, generally known as the Kinsha Kiang, or "River of Golden Sand." The Chinese have no idea of the continuing identity of a river, and most of theirs have different names at different parts of their course, but in this case there is some reason for the failure to regard the upper and the lower Yangtse as one and the same stream, for at Suifu, where the Min joins the Yangtse, it is much the larger body of water throughout most of the year, and is generally held by the natives to be the true source of the Great River. Moreover, above the junction the Yangtse is not navigable, owing to the swift current and obstructing rocks, while the Min serves as one of China's great waterways, bearing the products of the famous Chengtu plain to the eastern markets.

After leaving the ferry we followed for some miles the dry bed of a river whose name I could not learn. The scene was desolate and barren in the extreme, nothing but rock and sand; and had it not been cloudy the heat would have been very trying. But we were now among the Cloud Mountains, where the bright days are so few that it is said the Szechuan dogs bark when the sun comes out. After a short stop at a lonely inn near a trickle of a brook we turned abruptly up the mountain-side, by a zigzag trail so steep that even the interpreter was forced to walk.

As I toiled wearily upward, I looked back to find my dog riding comfortably in my chair. Tired and hot, he had barked to be taken up. The coolies thought it a fine joke, and when I whistled him down they at once put him back again, explaining that it was hard work for short legs. At one of the worst bits of the trail we met some finely dressed men on horseback, who stared in a superior way at me on foot. The Chinese sees no reason for walking if he has a chair or pony. What are the chair and the pony for? They must lack imagination, or how can they ride down the awful staircases of a West China road, the pony plunging from step to step under his heavy load? I doubt if they realize either the pony's suffering or the rider's danger. I did both, and so I often walked. After a climb of three thousand feet we came out on a wide open plateau, beautifully cultivated, which we crossed to our night stopping-place, Chiang-yi, nearly seven thousand feet above sea level.

We started the next morning in the rain, which kept up pretty much all day. The country through which we now passed was rather bare of cultivation and of inhabitants, but the wealth and variety of flowers and shrubs more than made amends. Nowhere have I seen such numbers of flowering shrubs as all through this region, a few known to me, but most of them quite new. It was with much gratification that I learned at a later time of the remarkable work done in connection with the Arnold Arboretum near Boston in seeking out and bringing to America specimens of many of China's beautiful trees and plants. At the head of one small valley we passed a charming temple half buried in oleanders and surrounded by its own shimmering green rice-fields, and a little farther on we came to a farmhouse enclosed in a rose hedge some twelve feet high and in full bloom. There was no sign of life about, and it might have served as the refuge of the Sleeping Princess, but a nearer inspection would probably have been disillusioning.

We stopped that night at Ho-k'ou, a small place of which I saw little, for the heavy rain that kept us there over a day held me a prisoner in the inn. I had a small room over the pony's stable, and I spent the forenoon writing to the tune of comfortable crunching of corn and beans. The rest of the day I amused myself in entertaining the women of the inn with the contents of my dressing-case, and when it grew cold in my open loft I joined the circle round the good coal fire burning in a brazier in the public room. Every one was friendly, and persistent, men and women alike, in urging me to take whiffs from their long-stemmed tobacco pipes. All smoke, using sometimes this long-stemmed, small-bowled pipe, and sometimes the water pipe, akin in principle to the Indian hubble-bubble. In this part of Szechuan I saw few smoking cigarettes, but thanks to the untiring efforts of the British American Tobacco Company, they are fast becoming known, and my men were vastly pleased when I doled some out at the end of a hard day.

From Ho-k'ou it was a two days' journey to Hui-li-chou, the first large town on my trip. The scenery was charmingly varied. At times the trail led along high ridges with beautiful glimpses down into the valleys, or affording splendid views to right and left, to the mysterious, forbidden Lololand to the east, and to the unsurveyed country beyond the Yalung, west of us, or again it dropped to the banks of the streams, leading us through attractive hamlets buried in palms and bamboo, pines and cactus, while the surrounding hillsides were white or red with masses of rhododendron just coming into flower. Entering one village I heard a sound as of swarming bees raised to the one hundredth power. On inquiry it turned out to be a school kept in a small temple. While the coolies were resting I sent my card to the schoolmaster, and was promptly invited to pay a visit of inspection. It proved to be a private school of some thirty boys and one girl, the master's daughter. They were of all ages from six years upwards, and, I was told, generally stayed from one to five years at school. Instruction was limited to reading and writing, and two boys were called up to show what they could do. To ignorant me they seemed to do very well, reading glibly down their pages of hieroglyphics.

At another stop I had a talk with the village headman. He was elected for one year, he told me, by the people of the hamlet, comprising about forty families. He confessed his inability to read or write, but his face was intelligent and his bearing showed dignity and self-respect. Petty disputes and breaches of the peace were settled by him according to unwritten custom and his native shrewdness; and he was also responsible for the collection of the land tax due from the village.

The people in this part of Szechuan seemed fairly prosperous, but the prevalence of goitre was very unpleasant. The natives account for it in various ways, — the use of white salt or the drinking of water made from melting snow.

On the 20th of April we reached Hui-li-chou. The approach to the town or group of towns which make up this, the largest place in southern Szechuan, was charming, through high hedges gay with pink and white flowers. In the suburbs weaving or dyeing seemed to be going on in every house. Sometimes whole streets were given over to the dyers, naked men at work above huge vats filled with the inevitable blue of China. After crossing the half-dry bed of a small river we found ourselves under the great wall of Hui-li proper. Turning in at the South Gate we rapidly traversed the town to our night's lodging-place near the North Gate, the crowds becoming ever denser, people swarming out from the restaurants and side streets, as the news spread of the arrival of a "yang-potsz" (foreign woman). The interest was not surprising, as I was only the third or fourth European woman to come this way, but it was my first experience alone in a large town, and the pressing, staring crowd was rather dismaying; however, I found comfortable companionship in the smiling face of a little lad running beside my chair, his swift feet keeping pace with the carriers. I smiled back, and when the heavy doors of our night's lodging-house closed behind us, I found the small gamin was inside, too, — self-installed errand boy. He proved quick and alert beyond the common run of boys, East or West, and made himself very useful, but save when out on errands he was always at my side, watching me with dog-like interest, and kowtowing to the ground when I gave him a small reward. The next morning he was on duty at dawn, and trotted beside my chair until we were well on our way, when I sent him back. I should have been glad to have borrowed or bought or stolen him.

Hui-li-chou, with a population of some forty thousand, is in the middle of an important mining region, both zinc and copper ore being found in the neighbouring hills in good quantity; but the bad roads and government restrictions combine to keep down industry. In spite of its being a trading centre the inns are notoriously bad, and we were fortunate in finding rooms in a small mission chapel maintained by a handful of native Christians. In the course of the evening some of them paid me a call. They seemed intelligent and alert, and although in the past the town has had an unpleasant reputation for hostility to missions, conditions at the present time were declared to be satisfactory.

CHAPTER IV

THE CHIEN-CH'ANG

THE second day after leaving Hui-li-chou we entered the valley of the Anning Ho, a grey, fast-flowing stream whose course runs parallel with the meridian like all the others of that interesting group of rivers between Assam and eastern Szechuan, the Irrawaddy, the Salween, the Mekong, the Yangtse, the Yalung. The Anning, the smallest of these, lies enclosed in a wilderness of tangled ranges, and its valley forms the shortest trade route between Szechuan and the Indo-Chinese peninsula. For about eight marches, north and south, it runs through a district known as Chien-ch'ang, celebrated throughout China for its fertility and the variety of its products. At the lower end the valley is very narrow, and level ground is limited, but the gentle slopes on either side are beautifully cultivated in tiny terraced fields. Farther north, however, in the neighbourhood of Ning-yüan-fu, the valley widens out into a broad, open plain. Apparently in this favoured region tropics and temperate zone meet, for I never saw before such motley vegetation. Rice and cotton alternate with wheat and maize and beans, while saffron and indigo fit in anywhere. Fruits, too, of many kinds are abundant. A short time ago the poppy made every turn brilliant, but to-day imperial edicts, ruthlessly enforced, are saving the Chinese unwillingly from themselves, and the poppy has disappeared from sight. In spite of complaints it would seem as though the Chien-ch'ang farmers, better than many in West China, could support the loss of that remunerative crop, for their resources, properly exploited, seem almost exhaustless. Mulberry trees are grown about every village and farmhouse, and the silk export is of considerable value to the community.

But one of the most interesting products of this region has lost much of its importance in late years. All over China, but especially in this part of Szechuan, there grows a tree of the large-leaved privet species. On the bark of the branches and twigs are discovered attached little brown scales of the size and shape of a small pea. When opened in the spring they are found to contain a swarming mass of minute insects. Toward the end of April, the time when I passed through this region, these scales were being carefully gathered and packed in small parcels, and already the journey northward was beginning. Porters bearing loads of about sixty pounds were hurrying up the valley, often travelling only by night to save their precious burden from the burning sun's rays which would cause too rapid development.

Their destination was Chia-ting, which lies on the Min River at the eastern edge of a great plain, the home of the so-called "pai-la shu," or "white wax tree," a species of ash. The whole countryside is dotted over with this tree, so cut as to resemble the pollard willow. On arrival the scales are carefully made up into small packets of twenty or thirty scales each, wrapped in leaves and attached to the branches of the white wax tree. After a short interval the insects emerge from the scales and secrete a waxlike substance, covering the boughs and twigs with a white deposit about a quarter of an inch thick. This is carefully gathered, and after purification by boiling is made up into the small cakes of commerce to be put to various uses. It forms an important ingredient in sizing and polish, and also in giving a gloss to silk; but especially it is valued as imparting a greater consistency to tallow for candles, as it melts only at a temperature of 160° Fahrenheit. But the Standard Oil activities have dealt a serious blow to the white wax industry. Kerosene is now in general use where there is any lighting at all, and whereas formerly ten thousand coolies annually hurried up the valley carrying scales to Chia-ting, we now saw only a few hundred.

A generation ago Chien-ch'ang was perhaps the least known part of all China to the outside world. About the middle of the thirteenth century the Mongol, Kublai Khan, acting as general of the forces of his brother, Genghis Khan, went through here to the conquest of Tali, then an independent kingdom in the southwest, and the untiring Venetian following in his train noted a few of the characteristics of Caindu, the name he gave both to the valley and the capital city. Six centuries elapsed before the next traveller from the West came this way. In the late seventies Colborne Baber, Chinese Secretary of the British Legation, traversed the valley from north to south, being the first European since the time of Marco Polo to enter Ning-yüan-fu, save for an unfortunate French priest who arrived a few months earlier, only to be driven out with stones. At that time, according to Baber, "two or three sentences in the book of Ser Marco to the effect that after crossing high mountains he reached a fertile country containing many villages and towns, and inhabited by a very immoral population," constituted the only existing description of the district.

In spite of the importance of this route it remained until a few years ago very insecure. Overhung almost its entire length by the inaccessible fastnesses of Lololand, the passing caravans dared journey only with convoy, and even then were frequently overwhelmed by raiders from the hills, who carried off both trader and goods into the mountains, the former to lifelong servitude. The Ta Liang Shan, or "Great

Cold Mountains," the country of the independent Lolos, is a mountainous region extending north and south some three hundred miles, which constitutes to this day an almost impenetrable barrier between east and west, crossed voluntarily by no Chinese, unless in force, and from which but one European party has returned to tell the tale. On the outskirts of this territory a little mission work has been undertaken with some success, but as yet no real impression has been made upon the people. Chinese hold upon the country is limited to an occasional more or less ineffective punitive expedition organized after some unusual outrage, such as the murder, a few years back, of Lieutenant Brooke, the English explorer. Naturally the Government does not care to assume any responsibility for the foolhardy foreigner bent on risking his life. Lieutenant Brooke went without permission, and during my stay in Ning-yüan I learned that two French travellers had just sought in vain for leave to attempt the crossing of the mountains to Suifu.

Within Lololand, of course, no Chinese writ runs, no Chinese magistrate holds sway, and the people, more or less divided among themselves, are under the government of their tribal chiefs. The little that is known of this interesting race has been learned from the so-called tame Lolos who have accepted Chinese rule, and are found scattered in small villages in the western part of Szechuan and Yunnan, being perhaps most numerous in the neighbourhood of the Anning and Yalung rivers, where an appreciable proportion of the population is of aboriginal or mixed aboriginal and Chinese stock. Accepting Chinese rule does not generally mean accepting Chinese customs. They hold to their own language and religion, one a dialect akin to Tibetan, and the other a form of animism. It is very easy to distinguish conquerors and conquered, for the Lolos are darker as well as taller and better formed than the Chinese. Their features are good and they have a frank, direct expression which is very attractive. In dress also they have not conformed to the ways of their masters. Instead of a queue the men wear the hair in a horn above the forehead, while the women hold firmly to the feminine petticoats, surrounded though they are by the trousered Chinese women. Nor do they bind their feet, but stride bravely along on the feet nature gave them.

What these people really are is one of the unsettled ethnological problems of the East, but probably they are of the same stock as the Shans and Burmese. Even their proper appellation is in doubt. The Chinese call them Lolos, which means simply "barbarians" or "wild men." By the people themselves the term is regarded as insulting, and one should avoid using it before them; but they are not agreed among themselves on a common name, and use ordinarily local tribal names.

Half a dozen years ago travellers were warned against the dangers of the road, but since then matters have been taken vigorously in hand by the Chinese authorities. Guard-houses have been erected at short intervals, the passes are strongly fortified, and a large force of well-trained men is stationed permanently in the valley. The journey can now be made in entire safety, but there are numerous signs of past dangers, and the precautions taken are very evident. Perhaps I was made especially conscious of possible danger because, as my interpreter said, though the officials were careful to secure the safety of every one of us, they were particularly anxious that nothing should happen to me; not, of course, from any personal concern for the foreigner, but because the foreigner's Government has such a way of making things unpleasant if anything happens to him.

From Hui-li-chou northwards I was escorted by real soldiers, quite of the new service. They looked rather shipshape in khaki suits and puttees, and their guns were of a good model, but they handled them in careless fashion at first, belabouring laden ponies and even coolies who were slow in getting out of the way of my chair. I am told that they are very ready to lord it over their countrymen when escorting Europeans, taking advantage of the fearful respect in which the foreigner is held. I checked them vigorously at the time, and before the next morning's start I called them up, and with the aid of the interpreter harangued them to the effect that I was pleased to see that they knew how to use their guns, and if need came I hoped they would give a good account of themselves in China's defence, but in the mean time they should be very slow to use their weapons on men or beasts, and if I saw them do it while they were with me they would get no "wine money." The soldiers took my orders very meekly, and the bystanders (there are always bystanders in China) grinned approvingly.

The first two marches out from Hui-li led over the range into the Anning valley, a high, rocky trail without much vegetation for the most part, but after we struck the river, cultivation was almost continuous, one hamlet following fast on another. This part of the valley is available for irrigation, and the skill and ingenuity shown in making use of the water supply is nothing short of marvellous. At one point we ascended a long, wide, gentle slope all laid out in tiny fields, and well watered from two large, fast-flowing streams. But where did they come from, for the slope ended abruptly in a sharp, high precipice overlooking a gorge through which flowed the Chin Ch'uan, a tributary of the Anning. But on turning a corner at the head of the slope we saw that from high up on the mountain-side an artificial channel had been constructed with infinite labour, bringing water from the upper course of the stream to the thirsty fields below.

Late on this same day the trail crossed a bare, rocky hillside, at one point passing between masses of stone ruins; something like a tower to the right, and on the left a sort of walled enclosure. I had lingered behind to gather a nosegay of the small blue flowers that marked the day's march. As I approached I saw some twenty or thirty men clad in long white or black cloaks hanging about the ruins, and my big chair coolie, who had constituted himself my special protector, coming to meet me, hurried me by without stopping. When I joined the interpreter, who was waiting for me at a discreet distance, I learned that the men were Lolos, "half-tame wild men," employed by merchants and others to guard this rather dangerous place where the trail approached somewhat closely the territory of the independent Lolos. In spite of protests I went back, accompanied by the big coolie and a soldier, to take some pictures. A few of the men ran away, but most made no objection and good-humouredly grouped themselves at my direction while I photographed them as best I could in the waning light. Their independent bearing and bold, free look interested me, and I should have been glad to talk with them, but the interpreter was disinclined to come near, and it was doubtful, too, if they could have spoken Chinese well enough to have been understood.

The 25th of April was our last day into Ning-yüan-fu, and I was glad; it was getting very hot, and the coolies were tired from their long journey. Several were hiring substitutes from the village-folk, paying less than half what they received from me. To avoid the heat we were off before sunrise. Often on that part of the trip we started in the half-light of the early dawn, and there was something very delightful in our unnoticed departure through the empty, echoing streets of the sleeping town where, the evening before, the whole population had been at our heels. And outside the stifling walls the joy of another day's ride through a new world was awaiting me.

For a time we followed up the narrow, winding valley, gradually opening out until we turned off to cross the low hills that barred the southern end of the Ning-yüan plain. Every inch of ground was under cultivation, but as yet few crops were up. Mulberries, however, were ripening fast, forerunners of the abundant fruit of this region. Shortly before tiffin we crossed a stream over which the bridge of stone was actually being repaired. In China, as elsewhere in Asia, it is a work of merit to construct a new building or road, but waste of time to repair the old. I wondered if by any chance some high official was expected, for the East fulfils quite literally the

LOLO GIRLS

"TAME, WILD" LOLOS

Scriptural injunction, "Prepare ye the way of the Lord, make straight his path before him"; more than once I realized the advantage of following in the footsteps of the great.

Toward the end of the day we crossed a spur of the hills, and descended abruptly into the Ning-yüan plain; half concealed among the trees lay the town, while off to the southeast sparkled the water of the lake noted by Marco Polo. As we sat resting for a few moments at a tea-house, I saw galloping towards us two horsemen, Europeans, the first I had seen for nearly three weeks. They turned out to be Mr. Wellwood and Dr. Humphreys, of the American Baptist Mission, who had ridden out to make me welcome. An hour later we crossed the parade ground outside the city gate, and shortly, turning in by a building of unmistakable European architecture, found ourselves in the mission compound. It was most delightful to be again among my own kind, and the three days spent in Ning-yüan while I was reorganizing my little caravan for the next stage were very enjoyable, barring the excessive heat.

Ning-yüan-fu is the largest town in this part of Szechuan, having a population of perhaps fifty thousand. It is surrounded by a well-built wall, high and broad and nearly three miles in length. Within are few buildings of interest, due perhaps to the fact that about fifty years ago it was almost demolished by an earthquake. According to tradition, the same thing happened in the early part of the Ming period, when the town, which, so it is said, then stood in the hollow where the lake now lies, was first shaken by an earthquake and then overwhelmed by a rush of water from underground. Later a new city was built on the present site. If the natives are to be believed, the ruins of the drowned city may still be seen on calm days lying at the bottom of the lake, while after a storm beds and chairs of strange patterns are sometimes found floating about on the water.

Even this remote corner of China shows the influence of the new movement, and Western ideas are making their way. Something had been done to improve the city schools, and I can testify to the desire of the military force stationed at Ning-yüan to form itself on European models, for the morning's sleep was broken by the vigorous bugle practice of the band, and at every turn one met soldiers, marching along with a good deal of vim. The large parade ground was given over in the afternoon to the testing and speeding of ponies. We rode out there one day, and I was pleased to see that the interest and wise ways of the missionaries in horseflesh were much appreciated by the owners of the ponies, men of a class not easily reached by the ordinary channels of mission work.

As my contract with the Yunnan hong was only to

Ning-yüan-fu, it was necessary to make new arrangements here. My old men had expressed a wish to go on with me, but in the end only one did so, the others disliking the détour to Tachienlu which they knew I had in mind. Moreover, it would have been necessary for them to register in the Ning-yüan hong, which they were not anxious to do, nor was the hong anxious to have them. So I let them go, well contented with their "wine money," which was, indeed, outrageously large. Soon after starting from Yunnan-fu I had realized that the men were inclined to ask for a day's halt more frequently than I liked, as I was anxious to push ahead, knowing that the spring rains were shortly due. I did not know then the custom of the road, which decrees no payment at all if it is the coolies who insist on stopping, although a small payment, usually five cents gold, is the rule for each day of halt for your convenience. So I felt that my only check upon the men was to hold out a reward. Accordingly I offered them a definite tip and a good one, if they would get me to Ning-yüan-fu at a certain day, which they did, making the journey, as I learned later, simply in the ordinary time. I was advised not to pay them the sum promised, as they were profiting by my ignorance, and it might make me trouble afterwards. But I reasoned that my ignorance was my own fault; they had not asked, I had offered the reward, and I was sure the evil of a broken promise was greater than any bad precedent. So the men got their tip, and I am certain I gained by the reputation I thus acquired of keeping my word. I never again gave such rewards, but I always had good service.

I was sorry to see the Yunnan men go; they were sturdy, willing fellows, quick to learn my ways. In particular, one of my chair coolies, the big fellow called Liu, I should have been glad to keep on, in spite of unexpected revelations at Ning-yüan. He had made the trip from Yunnan with Mr. Wellwood a few weeks earlier, behaving well, but after receiving his pay he got gloriously drunk and was expelled from the inn, whereupon he turned up at the mission, still drunk. As he was not taken in, he proceeded to tear up the chapel palings and make himself a nuisance. So after repeated warnings he was turned over to the police, who shut him up for a night and then gave him a whipping. Probably he had learned a lesson, for he made me no bother. This was the only case within my own knowledge of a coolie's giving trouble through drinking. Out-of-the-way travel in the East is much simpler for being among non-drinking people. Years ago I made a canoeing trip in northern Maine with two friends. Almost we were forced to rob the traditional cradle and grave to secure guides warranted sober — the only sort safe for a party of women; but in the East that question is scarcely considered, and personally I have never had any difficulty.

The men that I took on at Ning-yüan were on the whole younger and smaller than the Yunnan men, but they too did their work well. The new fu t'ou was a Chengtu man of a type quite unlike the others, tall, slender, well made, and with decidedly good features. He seemed young for his post, but soon showed himself quite equal to the task of keeping the men up to the mark, and of meeting any difficulty that arose.

To my surprise I was able to buy oil for our lanterns on the street here. One does not think of the Standard Oil Company as a missionary agency, but it has certainly done a great deal to light up the dark corners of China, morally as well as physically, by providing the people with a cheap way of lighting their houses. Formerly when darkness fell, there was nothing to do but gamble and smoke. Now the industrious Chinese can ply his trade as late as he chooses.

I was sorry to say farewell to my kind hosts, but it was good to get away from the trying heat of Ning-yüan plain, all the more oppressive because of the confined limits of the mission quarters set in the heart of the city. The only escape for the missionaries during the hot months was to a temple on one of the surrounding hills. I was glad to learn that land had been secured at a little distance from the present compound for more spacious accommodations. People at home do not realize the difficulty of getting fresh air and exercise in a Chinese town. Walking inside the walls is almost impossible because of the dirt and crowds, while near the city all unoccupied land is usually given over to graves. In Ning-yüan really the only chance for exercise short of a half-day's excursion, perhaps, was on the city wall, where I had a delightful ride one afternoon.

It was the morning of April 29, when we finally started, my caravan being now increased to seventeen men, as I had advanced the interpreter to a three-bearer chair and given his old one to the cook, who as a Szechuan man should have been able to walk. But he seemed hardly up to it, — in fact he gave me the impression of an elderly man, although he owned to forty-one years only. It needs a trained eye, I imagine, to judge of the age of men of an alien race.

On passing out from the suburbs of the town, charmingly embowered in fruit orchards, we struck across the open, treeless plain. There was little land that could be cultivated that was not under cultivation, but as yet the fields lay bare and baked in the burning sun, waiting the belated rain, as this part of the valley cannot be irrigated, owing to the lie of the land. Rain fell the first night, and after that neither the soil nor I could complain of dryness. Our first stop was at Li-chou, a small, comfortable town at the head of the valley, with a bad inn. It, not Ning-yüan, which lies a little off the main trail, is the centre of the carrying business between Yunnan and the north, and from this time on, we found the village population everywhere chiefly occupied as carrier coolies.

Our first day from Li-chou was a short stage, and we had a long, leisurely tiffin at Sung-lin, where there was an exceptionally good inn. The proprietor was away, but his wife, who was in charge, seemed very competent and friendly, and took me into their private rooms, fairly clean and airy, and quite spacious. In one was a large, grave-shaped mound of cement-like substance. On inquiry I learned that it enclosed the coffin and body of the mother of the proprietor. She had been dead a year, but the body could not receive final burial until his return. The Chinese custom of keeping unburied their dead awaiting a propitious moment strikes one as most unpleasant and unwholesome, but the worst consequences are usually avoided by hermetically sealing the ponderous coffin. In Canton the House of the Dead is visited by all travellers. It is a great stretch of small buildings set in flower gardens, each room commanding a definite rent, and usually occupied by the waiting dead, whose fancied wants are meantime carefully supplied. The dead hand rests heavy on China. Not merely is much valuable land given over to graves, and the hills denuded of forest to make the five-inch coffin boards, but the daily order of life is often unduly sacrificed to the departed.

On my way from Calcutta to Hong Kong there joined us at Singapore the Chinese Consul-General at that place. He was returning with his family to Canton to attend the funeral of his mother. In talk with him I learned that he had been one of that famous group of students who came to America in the seventies, only to be suddenly recalled by the Chinese Government. He had since acted as Secretary to the Chinese Legation in Washington, and was quite at home in Western ways. In his dress he combined very effectively both Chinese and occidental symbols of mourning, his white coat-sleeve being adorned with a band of black crape, while in the long black queue he wore braided the white mourning thread of China. He expected to be at home for some months, and during that time, so he told me, it would be unsuitable for him to engage in any sort of worldly business.

We were now leaving behind the close cultivation of the Chien-ch'ang; the valley grew narrower, hemmed in by higher and more barren mountains, but the wild roses made beautiful every turn. One village that we passed was quite surrounded by a hedge of roses several feet high, and all in full bloom. My second night from Ning-yüan-fu was not much better than the first, for the inn at Lu-ku, a rather important little town, was most uncomfortable; but a delightful hour's rest and quiet on the river bank before entering the town freshened me up so much that the night did not matter. One march to the north of Lu-ku, up the valley of the Anning, lay the district town of Mien-ning, reached by a rough trail that finally wandered off into the inextricable gorges of the Ta Tu Ho. It was in these wild defiles that the last contests of the Taiping rebellion were fought. I looked longingly up the valley, but my way turned off to the right, following the pack-road to the ferry at Fulin. At once on starting the next morning we passed out of the main valley into a narrow gorge with precipitous sides opening from the east. The trail wound upwards along the mountain-face, often hewn out of the rock and scarcely more than five feet wide, and at one point it was barred effectually by heavy gates. They opened to us, but not on that day half a century ago when the Taiping leader, Shih Ta-k'ai, failing to force his way through, turned back to meet defeat in the wilds above Mien-ning-hsien.

All along the road we met signs of our nearness to the country of the Lolos. There was much uncultivated land, and the population seemed scanty, but officials and soldiers were numerous, while guard-houses dominated the trail at short intervals. The village type was not always pure Chinese, and occasionally we met people unmistakably of another race. At Teng-hsiang-ying, or "Strong-walled Camp," where we stopped for the night, both soldiers and

Lolos were much in evidence. We were here about two thousand one hundred feet below the summit of the great pass through which the raiders in times not far past made their way into fertile Chien-ch'ang. After getting settled in the inn, I went for a walk, carefully guarded by two soldiers especially detailed for the purpose by the Yamen. In one alley I noticed Lolo women spinning in the doorways, and with the aid of the soldiers, who seemed to be on very friendly terms with them, I succeeded in getting a picture of two. In feature and colour they might have passed for Italians, and their dress was more European than Chinese in cut. On their heads they wore the Tam o' Shanter-like cap of black stuff, common among these people, bound on with their long braids, and their coats were of the usual felt. Their skirts, homespun, were made with what we used to call a Spanish flounce. According to Baber, the Lolo petticoat is of great significance. No one may go among the independent Lolos safely save in the guardianship of a member of the tribe, and a woman is as good a guardian as a man. Before setting out she puts on an extra petticoat, and the traveller thus escorted is sacred. But if the guarantee is not respected she takes off the garment, spreading it on the ground, and there it remains, telling to all the outrage that has been committed, and appealing to Heaven for redress. Altogether the women that I saw had a rather attractive, feminine look, and their manner, though timid, was not cringing. People who know them best have a good word for the Lolos, but few Europeans have come much in contact with them. Those I saw looked miserably poor. Missionaries declare that the hand of the official is heavy upon them, and of course the persistent, hard-working Chinese are certain to have acquired the best land.

The next day we crossed the Hsiao Hsiang Ling, or "Little Elephant Pass," fortunately in fine weather. The approach from the south was very beautiful. For a number of li our road led through a deep, narrow gorge, following up a fine rocky stream. The flowers and blossoming shrubs were wonderful; masses of white and of pink azaleas clothed the lower slopes, and there appeared now for the first time a bush bearing long, feather-like sprays of fragrant white blooms. From time to time we passed a guard-house, and soldiers were everywhere, some on guard, others practising exercises, others lounging. At one place a group had gathered about a fellow who was playing rather nicely an instrument resembling a mandolin. He seemed gratified at my interest, and readily repeated his music for me. As seen in passing, the guard-houses looked clean and substantial, vastly superior to the ordinary Chinese abode. But the country had a rather forbidding aspect as we marched farther up the valley, fit setting for deeds of outrage and bloodshed; its character seemed symbolized in the head of a Lolo robber set up by the wayside.

The final climb to the pass was over gentle, grassy slopes. At the top, nearly ten thousand feet above sea level, the way led through a strongly fortified post where I stopped for a few moments to enjoy the wide view, northwest to the nearer mountains of the Tibetan range, and east to the dark peaks of the Ta Liang Shan. On the northern side of the pass the descent is long and tiring, a succession of steep zigzags and rocky staircases. At the time of day when I crossed, the lines of carriers and baggage ponies were almost continuous. There were guard-houses at intervals of three li, and at each a special detail of two soldiers came out, and, saluting me properly, fell into position, one in front and one behind, to be replaced at the next post by two others. As we descended to lower levels the valley widened out slightly, giving room for a few hard-wrung fields surrounded by broad stone walls reminding one of New England, and now and then we passed a lonely farmhouse built of stones and enclosed in a rather ineffective defence of wattles. But villages were few, hardly more than hamlets that had grown up about the military posts. All were walled, and where the highway passed through the village, dividing it in two, each half was enclosed in its own high wall of mud and stones. Moreover, many of the houses were of fortress-like

A MEMORIAL ARCH. SZECHUAN

FORTIFIED VILLAGE IN THE CHIEN-CH'ANG VALLEY

construction, three stories high, and with only a few slits for windows. Once or twice we passed through an open bazaar strongly walled and with a fortified gate at either end, serving as a brief resting-place for the caravans hurrying over this dangerous stretch of road.

As we travelled northward we saw fewer of the fine stone bridges of the south ; the construction was now generally of wood, not unlike in outline the disfiguring structures of New England, but improved by open sides and a picturesque curly roof of tiles. Usually they were approached by a flight of steps, showing conclusively, if proof were needed, that there were no wheeled vehicles to consider. And, indeed, traffic generally was of limited character after we left the pass. Occasionally we overtook coolies hurrying along with their precious loads of white wax insects, or bending under long, thick pine or cypress boards, sometimes towering high above their heads or else strapped across their shoulders, forcing them to move crab-fashion along the narrow trails. On inquiry I learned that deeply embedded in the soil of the hills are found huge trees, rows of sprouts marking their location. These are dug up with much effort and sawn into boards which are in great request for the ponderous Chinese coffins. It would seem as though the supply must be inexhaustible, for when Sir Alexander Hosie came this way, a generation ago, he noted the same traffic and received the same explanation. With the prohibition of the poppy, the region has for the moment little export trade, while the imports seem to consist mainly of military supplies for the Chien-ch'ang garrisons. However, the road is in unusually good condition, for the whole way from Teng-hsiang-ying to Yüeh-hsi, our next stop, a distance of perhaps thirty-five miles, is well paved with broad flags. As we drew near to the town the valley opened a little, affording a glimpse of a snow peak to the north, while toward the southeast we look up a narrow gorge into Lololand, the border being but some fifteen miles away. This is almost the only break in the flanking hills that wall in the Forbidden Land. Yüeh-hsi itself lies in the centre of a rock-strewn plain broken by a few rice- and maize-fields, and is important as a military post guarding the trade route against this easy way of attack. The best room of the inn smelt to heaven, but on investigation I found an open loft which proved very possible after ejecting a few fowls.

The following day our march led us through a narrow valley bare of people and cultivation. Following this was a welcome change to steep climbs over grass-covered slopes broken by picturesque ravines. I tried to get a picture of a coolie, bearing a huge nine-foot-long coffin plank, whom we overtook on the trail. A handful of cash and cigarettes won his consent, but in spite of my men's efforts to calm his fears, the poor fellow cringed and trembled so, as I got my camera into position, that I gave it up. I felt as I might feel if I kicked a dumb animal.

Our night's stop was at Pao-an-ying, — like so many other hamlets of this region, little more than a camp-village, and showing its origin in the termination "ying" or "jin," meaning regiment. My room at the inn looked out directly on the street, and there was neither quiet nor privacy to be had, so I went out for a walk, escorted by a soldier and a coolie. Discovering a secluded screened place in a graveyard, I fell asleep on the top of a tomb, and my men near by did the same; but presently I was awakened by Jack's barking, to find myself the centre of a crowd of some fifty men silently watching me, and down the hillside I saw others coming, so I gave it up and took a stroll through the town, inspecting the provision shops.

We were off the next morning in the dark. At first the road was wild and picturesque. The track was unusually good, and steep, well-constructed zigzags carried us up and down the hills. Later the valley opened, and we ascended gradually over beautiful slopes gay with rhododendron and iris. The clouds above the mountains were very fine, but presently rain came on, continuing off and on all day.

Late in the afternoon we came in sight of Haitang, a walled town perched picturesquely on the side of a hill. A temple outside the wall looked attractive, and I should have visited it had it not been for the rain which now set in in good earnest. So, instead, I inspected the inn, which seemed unusually interesting. There was the ordinary entrance court roofed over, and behind that an inner court open to the sky and surrounded by galleried buildings. Off from this led a long, high passage into which opened a number of superior rooms. Mine was quite elaborately furnished with carved bedstead and chairs and tables, and best of all, it had a door opening directly on to the city wall, where I could step out and get a breath of fresh air free from observation.

Here I had my first experience of the "squeeze." On directing the interpreter to give the fu t'ou the coolies' pork money, I learned that on the previous occasion the man had kept an undue proportion of it. Apparently a certain squeeze was regarded as legitimate, but he had transgressed the accepted bounds. I hardly knew how to meet the difficulty. Of course I could have paid the coolies directly, but it was most desirable to maintain the fu t'ou's authority over them. Finally, in true Chinese fashion, the interpreter worked out a scheme by which the fu t'ou's "face" might be saved, and yet the coolies not be defrauded. Going out into the court where the men were lounging, he called loudly to the fu t'ou to come for the coolies' money, naming the sum I intended to give, about one hundred cash to a man. In the face of this there was nothing for the fu t'ou to do but give to each his rightful share, which he did with a very sulky air. Afterwards I had a talk with the man, telling him that my idea of a good fu t'ou was one who kept the men up to their work, and at the same time did not bully or mulct them of their hard-earned money. Such a man would get a good reward at the end. My reputation for lavishness stood me here in great stead, for henceforth there was no difficulty on this score. I might be "squeezed," but at least my coolies were not. The fu t'ou, however, tried to get even with the man who told, by discharging him. Fortunately I learned of this, again through the interpreter, and put a stop to it. The idea of the squeeze seems to be ingrained in the Chinese. How difficult it is to eradicate was shown by the delight of a missionary at Chung-king over the low price for which his trusty Christian clerk had secured a boat for me. For once he felt sure no commission could have been taken.

During all this part of my trip I carried no coined silver, only rough lumps of bullion of varying size, converting them into cash as I needed. The rate of exchange varied from place to place, and I was sometimes warned to put off visiting the money-changers until the next town. Of course the visitor stands to lose anyway, and I am sure that in the course of a long journey through China you would see your money vanish in the mere process of change, quite aside from the money you spent.

Rain fell all the next day, but it could not take from the charm of the road, which led much of the time along the bottom of a deep, narrow gorge, the steep sides clothed to the very top with tropical green flecked with splendid splashes of pink and white azaleas, while by the side of the path were masses of blue iris, and of small yellow and red flowers. We reached our night's resting-place, P'ing-i-p'u, early in the afternoon, and in spite of the rain I went for a walk. By dint of peremptory commands, reënforced by the rain, I shook off my military escort, who for the last few marches had dogged my steps at every turn, moving when I moved, stopping when I stopped. To be sure, they had been very thoughtful of my comfort, helping me in and out of my chair, gathering the new flowers which appeared each day, keeping up a brazier fire in my room when it was damp, but I was tired of being treated as either a suspect or a royal personage, and as we were now well beyond the limit of Lolo raids I demanded the freedom of being alone. I found quiet in an overgrown graveyard, with charming views down stream and up the near hillsides cultivated in tiny scallops to the very top, although the slopes were so steep that each plot was shored up with a strong stone wall to keep the crop of maize and buckwheat from slipping down into the river.

As we passed out of the village the next morning at six o'clock we heard the hum of the boys in the government school already at work. Apparently Young China was wasting no time. For perhaps twenty li we followed down a fine stream, the way rather dangerous from the rocks which now and then detached themselves from the steep overhanging hill-sides. After a time an ascent of one thousand feet brought us in sight of the Ta Tu, which we reached some time after noon by a gradual descent of two thousand feet, through a narrow valley to Ta-shu-p'u. Fine clumps of bamboo and groups of palm now cheered our sight, and fruit of several sorts — cherries, pears, loquats — was becoming abundant. It was very refreshing, although scarcely of a fine quality, and usually gathered before it was ripe. The place looked quiet and attractive, but half a century ago the last scenes of the Taiping rebellion were enacted here, when the remnants of Shih Ta-k'ai's force were surrounded and slaughtered.

Later in the day I went for a stroll to inspect the shops, accompanied by my interpreter, and it was on this occasion that I met with the only instance of unfriendliness (that I recognized) in all my journeying in West China. At one shop I noticed an interesting bronze dragon. The interpreter, who had a rather objectionable habit of fingering the wares, began examining it. Thereupon the merchant came forward and snatched it from his hands, and when we passed that way again on our return, he came out before his shop and waved us off vigorously with his flapping sleeves. The interpreter said that the man disliked foreigners, but admitted that he did not wish to have his things handled.

CHAPTER V

ON THE MANDARIN ROAD

FOR once the sun was shining gloriously as we descended the one long street of Ta-Shu-p'u, lined with food-shops, to the ferry across the Ta Tu Ho, here about six hundred feet wide. Unlike the crossing of the Yangtse at Lung-kai, where we were the only ones to be ferried over, we found ourselves here in a crowd of coolies and ponies impatiently waiting their turn, for we were now on a main travelled road. The two great flat-bottomed boats were loaded to the brim, and the crossing was safely accomplished to the tune of much shouting and kicking (by the ponies). Sitting at ease in my chair I enjoyed the grand views up and down the river, which here swings out from the cliffs in a splendid curve. Above and below the ferry the Ta Tu runs through a wild, little-known region. Few trails cross the precipitous mountains that hem in its turbulent waters, which are navigable for short distances only by timber rafts, and even on these the dangers of the journey are so great that the owners of the timber are expected to bind themselves to provide coffins in case of a fatal accident.

On the farther side we landed on a stretch of shingle, across which we picked our way for a mile to the prosperous trading centre of Fulin, lying on the right bank of the Liu Sha, or "River of Flowing Sand," a small stream flowing into the Ta Tu from the north. Our path led outside the town on the top of a narrow earth embankment, which bordered an irrigating ditch carried along the side of the hill. I should gladly have got off, but there was no chance to dismount save into the water on the one hand or into the valley thirty feet down on the other. But I think you can trust the Yunnan pony anywhere he is willing to go, and mine did not hesitate. In fact, he never balked at anything asked of him save once at a shaky "parao," or footway, constructed along the face of the cliff on timbers thrust into holes bored in the solid rock, and another time when he refused a jump from a boggy rice-field to the top of a crumbling wall hardly a foot wide with another bog on the other side.

Fulin was crowded with coming and going coolies and I could hardly force my way through, but one gets used to staring crowds, and I had long since abandoned the practice of taking refuge in my chair on entering a town, save at the largest ones. Then it was certainly pleasanter and perhaps safer to make my way through the throng enthroned high on the shoulders of my coolies, but in the villages I walked or rode my pony as chance served. Even in the smallest places our entrance was the signal for an uproar. The scores of dogs — big, gaunt pariahs — that infested every village, greeted us as we passed through the gate with a chorus of barks, sending the word down the line. To his credit be it said, Jack paid little attention to them, tittupping along, head up, tail up, only when they came too close turning on them with a flash of white teeth that sent the cowardly brutes flying and brought cries of delight from the village folk who crowded nearer to inspect the strange dog, so small, so brave, and so friendly.

Seen from within, Fulin was not attractive and I escaped outside leaving my men to get their breakfast, which they generally had at about nine o'clock, for the Szechuan order of day is not like that of Yunnan. We were on the road often before six o'clock, and my cook always succeeded in getting me some tea before starting, but the coolies fasted until eight or after, when they stopped for a hearty breakfast. At noon there was usually a second long halt, this time for me and the pony, but the coolies took nothing more save the hourly cups of tea until we reached our night's stopping-place about the middle of the afternoon. The start at dawn was delightful; less so getting into the town with half an afternoon before me, and I made it the rule to stop a mile or so outside the town for a nap in peace and quiet, but the quiet was hard to find. Generally there was a retired nook not too far from the trail, most times a graveyard, but then came the difficulty of getting there unobserved, for if seen we were sure to be tracked. Oh, the races I have run, playing hide-and-seek with the crowd, stealing under a village wall like a thief, hiding behind a little shrine, and the end was always the same, — to be wakened from my first nap by Jack barking at a large blue spot a little distance off, which slowly resolved itself into a stolid line of villagers.

For a few miles we followed up the left bank of the Liu Sha, whose waters were turbid with the red soil of Szechuan. The fertile bottom lands were carefully cultivated with rice, and on the higher ground maize and sugar-cane were growing. Dotted about the fields were clumps of mulberry and orange trees, and the flanks of the enclosing mountains were covered with a sparse growth of oak and pine.

After a time we climbed by a long, steep rock staircase to another valley some fifteen hundred feet above the level of Fulin and into cooler weather and clearer air. Just before entering Han Yüan Kai, where we spent the night, we passed under a very beautiful "pailou," or memorial arch, built of stone and elaborately carved with spirited figures representing historic scenes. The workmanship and variety of these arches are very remarkable. They abound all over Szechuan, especially in the Chengtu plain, and usually commemorate the good deeds of an official (his best act, perhaps, was setting up this memorial to himself), or the virtues of some woman whose merit lay almost invariably in many years, or many children, or above all in remaining a widow. I have heard of a pailou in Kwangtung province in honour of a woman marked out among women for her years, her goodness, and above all for her many descendants, who numbered six sons, forty grandsons, one hundred and twenty-one great-grandsons and two great-great-grandsons.

Han Yüan Kai is on the mandarin road that connects Chengtu and Ya-chou with the frontier. Here we entered a new magistracy, and it was necessary to send to Ch'ing Ch'i, the district headquarters, for a fresh relay of soldiers. One of those who had come with me from Ta-shu-p'u started at once on our arrival at Han Yüan Kai about the middle of the afternoon, and made the journey, twenty-five li each way, to Ch'ing Ch'i-hsien and back before night, bringing with him the two men who were to go on with me. Truly the West China man is no weakling.

During the next day we were following the great tea-road, the road by which most of the twelve million pounds of brick tea consumed by the guzzling Tibetans is carried to the frontier market at Tachienlu. At all hours of the day straggling lines of men or ponies or mules were in sight, toiling along under their precious burdens. Between Ya-chou, the starting-point of this traffic, and Tachienlu there are two high passes to cross, seven thousand feet above the level where the journey begins, and the whole length of the road is a wearisome succession of ups and downs. And the loads carried are extraordinary. Baron von Richthofen says, "There is probably no road in the world where such heavy loads are carried by man across high mountains." The oblong package, called "pao," in which the tea is made up, weighs perhaps eighteen pounds, and, according to the German traveller, ten or eleven form an average load. But Baber declares that he had often seen a coolie carrying eighteen pao, and on one occasion a man with a load of twenty-two, certainly equivalent to four hundred pounds. I saw nothing like that, but I passed many a poor wretch sweating under a burden of two hundred and twenty-five or two hundred and fifty pounds. Day after day they creep along, rarely covering more than six or seven miles a day. Every four hundred yards they rest, but the loads are taken off only at noon and night. At other times they relieve themselves for a moment from the intolerable strain by placing an iron-shod crutch under the load. On the march they carry this in the hand, tapping the ground as they go, and all along the road the granite pavement is worn into holes from the taps of centuries. The load, which is fastened to a framework

"MERCURY," MY FLEET COOLIE

CARRIER COOLIES

attached to the carrier's back, towers high over his head, and is usually surmounted by his wide-brimmed hat fastened at such an angle as to give him protection against rain and sun. Even Chinese ingenuity has failed to devise a way by which he can wear it properly on his head. Some of them fanned themselves vigorously as they walked, with respectable black, old-lady fans, and the contrast with their hard, begrimed faces and sturdy frames was very comical. The men looked worn and exhausted, and their work is killing, although I believe they outlast the chair-bearers; but they were patient and cheerful like the rest, ready to laugh and share their cold lunch of corn-cake with the little foreign dog who begged so prettily.

I wondered how many of them were opium smokers. To the untrained eye the signs were not very plain. Among my coolies was one whom I dubbed "Mercury," so untiring and fleet of foot was he, carrying his load of eighty pounds or so with apparent ease, and showing much pride in keeping near my chair, while usually the carrier coolies lagged far behind. I was told he was the worst smoker of the whole lot. In my caravan of seventeen men, seven, including the fu t'ou, used opium. As a rule they limited themselves to one pipe at night, while five years ago travellers complained that a long halt at noon was demanded by the smokers. The fu t'ou was making a valiant effort, with the aid of anti-opium pills, to break off the habit; it was getting too expensive, he said, especially for a married man. In a number of towns places were pointed out where these pills were sold by the Government. Those who know, say they are often as pernicious as the drug itself.

The majority of my men, eleven to be precise, were married, and eight had children. I was interested to note the discreet and indirect way in which this information was procured for me by the interpreter. Such matters are not mentioned in public in China, any more than in India.

My own chair-men, so it happened, were all gay young bachelors, ready to squander their earnings on anything that took their fancy, — beads or tobacco, hats or cakes, especially cakes. There was a particular sort, very sweet with pink frosting, that was a great delicacy, costing two cents Mexican apiece. I had to speak pretty emphatically to one of the men who was trying to win Jack's favour by feeding him with the costly cookies. "But the little dog likes them," he said.

The Chinese generally, unlike the Hindu, is very ready to spend on his food if he has the money. He will live on less than nothing if put to it, but given the chance he does not stint himself. At short intervals on the road were tea-houses and restaurants of the simpler sort especially planned to cater to the coolie class, but they were often not unattractive. Sometimes they were substantial buildings open to the street, and set out with tables on which were ranged dishes of vegetables and curries and cakes, while in the background was a big cauldron of rice cooking over the fire. Occasionally the tea-house was nothing more than a section of the highway roofed over with mats or leafy boughs. On a handy bench was placed a basin of steaming water for the visitor to bathe hands and face before drawing up to the table. It gave me a pleasant surprise to see the Chinese making of the daily repast a jolly social function, instead of each squatting on the ground in a corner, devouring his solitary bowl of rice as is the fashion of most Eastern peoples.

I found much interest in noting the food of my men, the variety and cost of it, and I whiled away many an hour of waiting, in questioning innkeepers and provision dealers. A good bowl of rice, called "cat's head" and costing twenty cash, or one cent gold, was usually the *pièce de résistance*. This in hand, a man fished out with his chopsticks tidbits from various dishes set out on the table, — beans, cabbage, lettuce, peppers, etc., all cooked. Good hot boiled potatoes in their jackets were sometimes to be had at four cash each, or a bowl of stewed turnips at the same price. Beans in some shape were an important part of every menu. You could get a basin of fresh beans for ten cash, dried bean-cake for five, beans cooked and strained to a stiff batter for making soup for seven cash the ounce, while a large square of white bean-cake was sold for one copper cent. A saucer of spun rice or millet, looking much like vermicelli, with a seasoning of vinegar, cost five cash. Bowls of powdered grain mixed with sugar were much in demand. So, too, for those who could afford them, large round cakes at thirty cash for two. Ground pepper (the Chinese are very fond of pepper in any form) was sold at one cash the tiny package, and sugar for three cash the square inch. Almost every coolie had tucked in about his load a large flat cake of coarse corn-meal or maize mixed with water, which he munched as he went along. In Tachienlu, my supply of biscuits having given out, I had my cook buy some of these; split open and toasted, they were not at all bad. Tea, of course, was to be had everywhere; a pinch of tea-leaves in a covered cup and unstinted boiling water cost from five to twenty cash a cup, and most refreshing I found it. On the whole, the food looked attractive, and the fact that whether liquid or solid it was almost invariably boiled must have much to do with saving the people from the legitimate consequences of their sins against sanitary laws. The Chinese have no principles against eating between meals if they can find anything to eat, and there was temptation all along the road. Beside a wayside well, under a spreading tree, would be placed a small table tended perhaps only by a tiny maiden, and set out with pieces of sugar-cane or twigs of loquats or carefully counted clusters of peanuts or seeds, five pieces for a cash,

Our second night from the ferry was spent at Ni T'ou, a rather important frontier village, and attractive with picturesque red temples and pailous. A good sleep in an unusually comfortable inn prepared us for the stiff climb to come. The morning broke grey and the clouds rested low on the mountains, but at least we were spared a start in the rain. The road was so steep and rough that I preferred to walk, and soon getting ahead of my men I did not see them again until midday, and I had a good morning all to myself among the hills. Occasionally I passed through a little hamlet, people and dogs all turning out to greet my dog and me. Once a whole village emptied itself into the fields to show me the way up the hillside. My cold lunch I ate at the head of a wild gorge by a solitary shrine half buried in clumps of bushes, and beautiful with masses of iris. The last part of the climb to Fei Yüeh Ling, or "Fly Beyond Pass," led through an uninhabited glen down which rushed a fine stream turning the horizontally placed wheels of a ruined mill. Hurrying up the rocky zigzag I stood alone at the top of the pass, nine thousand feet above the sea. Before me I knew towered range upon range, peak above peak, one of the finest views the earth affords, but alas, everything was blotted out by thick white clouds, and I could scarcely see ten feet away.

It was maddening to think of the wonders that lay behind that impenetrable wall, but there was nothing to do but to descend by a trail as steep and slippery as the one by which I had just climbed, for the cold, drenching mist showed no signs of lifting. It was on this slope that Rockhill, the American explorer, met a pilgrim on his way to Lhasa. Starting in the Chusan archipelago near Ning-po, he had already spent seven years on the way, and it would be two more before he could attain his goal, which was not to be wondered at, as with every two steps he prostrated himself full length on the ground before the little altar he carried with him. With this primitive mountain world his act was in weird harmony, but there was an incongruity almost stunning in the sight of a Hindu carrying out a similar vow in one of the crowded business streets of Europeanized Calcutta. I nearly stepped on him as I came out one day from the Hong Kong and Shanghai Bank.

Just before reaching Hua-lin-ping, or "Phœnix" Flat, where we were to spend the night, I espied across the narrow valley to our right a picturesque temple perched at the top of a high wooded cliff. As it was still early in the afternoon, I turned off from the trail, and, accompanied by the interpreter, scrambled down the slope, gay with pink azaleas, to a charming wooden bridge spanning the torrent. After a sharp pull through a fine forest, we came out in front of the temple, which was dedicated to Kuan Yin: by the way, it is rather significant that China's favourite deity is the Goddess of Mercy. The place seemed deserted, and we wandered about at will. Apparently extensive repairs were going on, and roofs and gods alike were being refurbished. After a time an old priest turned up, who took us through the timber-built monastery behind the temple. Here, he told us, well-to-do people of the neighbourhood often spent a few weeks in summer, to escape the damp heat of the valley. The practical Chinese do not hesitate to put their sacred places to use, and they serve in turn for schools, political gatherings, summer resorts.

I was half a mind to cry a halt, the place looked so attractive, and all the more when on stepping out of a door there opened before me a wonderful vision of heaven-kissing mountains. While we were inside the clouds had lifted, revealing the whole line of the great peaks that stand as sentinels at the eastern end of the vast Tibetan plateau. Westward from that snow-topped line there is no low land until you reach the plains of India. For a few minutes we stood spell-bound, and then the clouds shut down again, leaving only a glorious memory to cheer the descent through a grey, dripping world.

A generation ago Hua-lin-ping was an important frontier post, but to-day its broad, barrack-lined street is deserted and grass-grown, for the vanguard of effective Chinese occupation is steadily pushing westward into the tribes country. We started the next morning under clouds of more than one sort; rain was falling, the ma-fu, whom I had been dosing for a day or two, had given out, and had to be left behind as well as one of the coolies, and the fu t'ou was cross at having to shoulder the latter's load. Early on this day we again came to the Ta Tu, having descended five thousand feet from the top of the pass; and for the rest of this stage and all the next one we followed up the wild valley of this beautiful river, which may be said to form the real geographical and ethnographical boundary between China and Tibet. Wherever the valley opened out a little, there was the invariable garden-like cultivation of the Chinese; fruit and nut trees abounded, mulberry, peach, apricot, and walnut, and the fields showed good crops of maize, beans, and sugar-cane. But up from the narrow fertile strip of river bank towered on either hand barren mountains, their precipitous granite sides gashed here and there by deep gorges in and out of which the trail wound with sharp turns and steep descents. The grey, forbidding mountains, showing hardly a foothold for man or beast, tree or house, matched the grey, swirling river, here unnav-

A GROUP OF SZECHUAN FARMHOUSES

igable even for rafts. Thrust back by the land, offered only a watery grave by the river, it seemed no country for man to seek a home, and yet the scattered Chinese hamlets were gay and full of life, and the tea-houses at every turn were doing a good business.

At Leng Chi, where we stopped for breakfast, I fled from the noisy restaurant to a small temple across the road, its outer court filled full of coffins, whether occupied or not, I could not say. A nice old priest promptly found me out, and taking me into an inner room made me comfortable with cups of tea. The buzz of voices told that a school was in session near by, and at the request of the teacher, a good-looking young man, I paid it a visit. Some twenty boys were hard at work on the classics and mathematics, undisturbed by the weird-looking gods around them. They seemed wide awake, and showed real disappointment that I could not stop to see a display of their skill in gymnastics. Every good-sized village seems to boast a school of sorts, and not a few do something for the girls.

The rain was falling as we approached Lu Ting Ch'iao, and that meant a long evening cooped up in a noisy, ill-smelling inn, so in desperation I took refuge under a large tree just outside the town where bushes screened me from the passers on the road. My men had long since made up their minds that I was rather mad, so they left me in peace, only posting one of the soldiers in a temple near by to keep watch and ward; but there was no need, for most of the people hereabouts are Tibetan, and they have little of the pertinacious curiosity of the Chinese, whether because of better manners or because less alert I do not know. And it was well I cut short my stay in the inn, for it was about the worst I had come across, as I took pains to inform the landlord the next morning. But there was no choice. Lu Ting Ch'iao, or the "Town of the Iron Bridge," derives its importance as well as its name from its location, and it was crowded to overflowing with east- and west-bound travellers, officials, merchants, soldiers, coolies, for all traffic must cross the Ta Tu here, the one point spanned by a bridge. Indeed, according to Mr. Archibald Little, this is the only bridge across any one of the many large rivers that unite to form the Great River. It is of the suspension sort, built in 1701, in the reign of that energetic ruler, Kang Hi, and is three hundred and eleven feet long. The nine cables of charcoal-smelted iron that compose it are anchored at the ends in the usual Chinese fashion. On these are laid loose planks to serve as a footway, while the only guard is a shaky chain on either hand. When the wind swoops down the gorge, as it does most afternoons, the whole structure swings uncomfortably, and I wondered at the nonchalance with which heavily laden coolies and ponies crossed. But such as it is, this is the one connecting link between China and Tibet, for ferrying across the upper reaches of the Ta Tu is impracticable most of the year.

After passing the bridge we kept up a narrow trail that clung to the face of the cliff, often cut out of the granite rock. There were no villages, but we passed through one or two hamlets set in a small alluvial fan such as is often seen in Western Tibet, only there the fan ended with a steep precipice two or three hundred feet above the river, while here it sloped gently down to the water's edge.

Occasionally we saw across the Ta Tu on the left bank a village unmistakably Tibetan: no trees; grey, flat-roofed, fortress-like houses, often reached only by a ladder; with few signs of life to be seen even with a glass, there was a forbidding aspect to these places in marked contrast to the bustle of a Chinese village.

We were now skirting the lower slopes of the Ta Shueh Shan, or "Great Snow Mountains," the outposts of the Tibetan plateau, but we were too hemmed in to catch a glimpse of the higher ranges, save once, when a break in the mountain wall afforded a brief, magnificent view of the snowy peaks towering more than fifteen thousand feet above our heads. Then another turn in the road shut us in again between grey cliff and grey river and grey sky. Toward the end of the day a sharp bend to the left took us away from the Ta Tu into the wild gorge through which flows the Tarchendo, and with a rough scramble we dropped down into the pretty little village of Wa Ssu Kou, the "Ravine of the Tile Roof Monastery." At the extreme western end of the one long street we found comfortable quarters in a new, clean inn. Like so many of these villages of wood with shingled roofs, Wa Ssu Kou seems to burn down once in so often, which has at least the advantage that there is less chance for dirt to accumulate.

Strolling out from the inn after a wash, I found myself in the fine gardens that border the river, separated from the water, here level with the bank, only by a narrow strip of shingle. Men and women were hard at work even after nightfall. Each plant is brought up by hand, as it were, and there is no waste of fertilizer; by spoonfuls the precious stuff is applied to each root instead of being scattered over the ground. Just across the river towered a precipitous cliff two thousand feet high, quite overshadowing the village, which looked very small and helpless by contrast. Up the face of the cliff zigzagged a steep trail, finally disappearing over the top, and I looked longingly after it, for on this side the river direct Chinese government ends. The other bank is the country of the tribesmen, people of Mantzu stock living under the rule of their tribal chiefs. Northwards from Wa Ssu Kou the Ta Tu changes its name to Chin Ch'uan, or "Golden Stream," and the whole region is known as the Chin Ch'uan country, and is famous in Chinese history as the scene of one of the most hardly fought campaigns against the tribes.

On my return to Wa Ssu Kou a week later a free half-day gave me a chance for a little run over the border. Guided by a respectable villager I crossed the rickety bridge over the Tarchendo and after a breathless climb came out on the top of the cliff, where I overlooked a wide rolling plateau sloping steeply to the Ta Tu on the east, and enclosed north and west by high mountains. The country seemed barren and almost uninhabited, as though removed by hundreds of miles from the hard-won prosperity and swarming life of the line of Chinese advance to Tachienlu. Only occasionally did we meet any one, Chinese or Mantzu, and there was no stir about the few dwellings that we passed, all high, fortress-like buildings of stone. This whole region is almost unknown to Europeans, and the few Chinese who go there are generally passing traders. According to Hosie, they are allowed to take temporary wives from the women of the country on payment of a sum of money to the tribal head, but they must leave them behind when they depart.

The next day we ascended the valley of the Tarchendo to Tachienlu, a distance of about twenty miles. There is a rise of thirty-five hundred feet on this stage, but so gradual is the ascent that one realizes it only in watching the stream, which is almost continuous rapid and cataract. For miles there was scarcely a square yard of smooth water. The only means of crossing from one bank to the other is by the rope bridges, of which I saw three. Several times I had a chance to watch some one making the trip. From a bamboo rope securely anchored on either bank with heavy rocks, a sling-seat is suspended by means of a section of bamboo which travels along the rope. Seated in the sling the weight of the voyager carries him more than halfway across, but after that he must haul himself up by sheer force. A slip would mean certain death, and it is said that often on reaching the middle of the stream the impulse to let go is uncontrollable. Hardy Western explorers have frequently confessed their dread of these bridges, which are found throughout the mountains of eastern Asia, but I saw men and women crossing as though it were all in the day's work. But then the Chinese have no nerves, you know.

Fortunately the need of crossing here did not seem very imperative, for there was little sign of life on the north bank of the Tarchendo. Indeed, on our side there were no villages for the whole distance, only a few hamlets and now and then a solitary rest-house. The river is so closely shut in by the mighty rock walls on either hand that there is scarcely room for more than the narrow trail. There were a good many walnut trees and willows, and I occasionally saw a meagre patch of barley or Indian corn, but even the Chinese would be hard put to wring a living here were it not for the coolie trade. In fact, every other house seemed to be a restaurant or tea-house. At one the soldier who had escorted me from Ni T'ou covered himself with disgrace by getting into a quarrel. Rain was falling, so I stayed in my chair while the coolies were drinking their everlasting cups of tea. Suddenly there was a great outcry, every one pitching in, and I saw the soldier seize the innkeeper by the queue, belabouring him vigorously with the flat of his short broad sword. I called to the interpreter to interfere, but either he did not hear me or would not obey; so I scrambled out of my chair as best I could (a woman, as an inferior being, must always step over the side pole; to touch the pole that rests on the coolie's shoulder would cause him to have sores), and, throwing myself into the fray, hauled the soldier off. I knew, for I had tested it, that the edge of his sword was sharp. When the excitement had died down, I learned that the whole trouble rose from the innkeeper's demanding payment for four cakes, while the soldier insisted that he had eaten only three. Who had the right of it I do not know, but I read the man a lesson at so misbehaving himself when escorting a lady, a truly Western point of view which was probably Greek to him, but anyway he seemed greatly downcast at my rebuke, and for the rest of the day hung about in an apologetic way, occasionally mutely laying a bunch of flowers on the arm of my chair as a peace offering.

CHAPTER VI

TACHIENLU

TACHIENLU is surely *sui generis;* there can be no other town quite like it. Situated eight thousand four hundred feet above the sea, it seems to lie at the bottom of a well, the surrounding snow-capped mountains towering perhaps fifteen thousand feet in the air above the little town which, small as it is, has hardly room to stand, while outside the wall there is scarcely a foot of level ground. It is wedged into the angle where three valleys come together, the Tar and the Chen rivers meeting just below the town to form the Tarchendo, and our first view of the place as we turned the cliff corner that here bars the gorge, was very striking, grey walls and curly roofs standing out sharply from the flanking hillsides.

Within the walls of Tachienlu, China and Tibet meet. As we made our way through the long, dirty main street, here running parallel with the Tar which comes tumbling down from the snow-fields of the Tibetan range, I was struck at once by the varied aspect of the people. The dense crowd that surged through the streets, some on horseback and some on foot, was more Tibetan than Chinese, but the faces that peered out from the shops were unmistakably of the Middle Kingdom. Groups of fierce-looking fellows, clad in skins and felt, strode boldly along, their dark faces bearing indelible marks of the hard, wild life of the Great Plateau. Many of them carried weapons of some sort, for the Chinese have scorned to disarm them. Among them walked impassively the blue-gowned men of the ruling race, fairer, smaller, feebler, and yet undoubtedly master. It was the triumph of the organizing mind over the brute force of the lower animal. Almost one man in five was a red-robed lama, no cleaner in dress nor more intelligent in face than the rest, and above the din of the crowd and the rush of the river rose incessantly weird chanting and the long-drawn wail of horns from the temples scattered about the town. Lamaism has Tachienlu in its grip, and I could have fancied myself back in Himis lamassery, thousands of miles away on the western frontier of Tibet. It was an extraordinarily picturesque scene, full of life and sound and colour.

Marco Polo described the territory lying west of Ya-chou as "Thibeth," and a century ago the Chinese frontier stopped at Tachienlu, but to-day Batang, a hundred and twenty-five miles to the west as the crow flies, is the western limit of Szechuan. In actual fact, however, direct administration by the Chinese stops at the Ta Tu, on the right bank of the river the people being governed by their tribal chiefs. Ta-

A VIEW OF TACHIENLU

TIBETANS

chienlu is in the principality of the King of Chala, whose palace is one of the two or three noteworthy buildings in the place, and the Tibetan population of some seven hundred families, not counting the lamas, is directly under his authority. But there is a power behind the throne, and the town is really governed by the Chinese officials, for it is the key to the country to the west, and the Imperial Government has long been awake to the importance of controlling the great trade and military road to Lhasa. What the effect of the Revolution will be upon the relations of China and Tibet remains to be seen. Already Chao Erh Feng, the man who as Warden of the Marches had made Chinese rule more of a reality in Lhasa than ever before, has fallen a victim to Manchu weakness; hated by Chinese and Tibetan alike, he met his death at the hands of a rebellious soldiery in January, 1912.

Between Tachienlu and Lhasa lie many hundred miles of barren, windswept plateaus and perilous mountain passes. There are, I believe, at least ten of these passes higher than Mont Blanc. Connection between the two places is over one of the most difficult mountain roads in the world, yet it was by this route that the Chinese finally conquered Tibet in the eighteenth century, and to-day most of the trade goes the same way. Those who deny the Chinese all soldierly qualities must have forgotten their achievements against the Tibetans, let alone the still more extraordinary military feat of their victory over the Gurkhas of Nepal, when a force of seventy thousand men of the Middle Kingdom crossed the whole width of the most inaccessible country in the world, and, fighting at a distance of two thousand miles from their base, defeated the crack warriors of the East.

The China Inland Mission has a station at Tachienlu, but to my disappointment the two missionaries were away at the time of my visit, and although their Chinese helpers made me welcome, providing a place for me in one of the buildings of the mission compound, I felt it a real loss not to talk with men who would have had so much of interest to tell. Moreover, I had been looking forward to meeting my own kind once more after two weeks of Chinese society. Fortunately another traveller turned up in Tachienlu about the time I did, an English officer of the Indian army, returning to duty by a roundabout route after two years' leave at home. As he too was installed in the mission compound we soon discovered each other, and I had the pleasure of some interesting talk, and of really dining again. Eating alone in a smelly Chinese inn cannot by any stretch be called dining. I found that Captain Bailey had gone with the Younghusband expedition to Lhasa, and was now on his way to Batang with the hope of being able to cross Tibet from the Chinese side. We had an enjoyable evening comparing experiences. I was impressed, as often before, by the comfort a man manages to secure for himself when travelling. If absolutely necessary, he will get down to the bare bones of living, but ordinarily the woman, if she has made up her mind to rough it, is far more indifferent to soft lying and high living, especially the latter, than the man. One thing I had, however, that Captain Bailey lacked, — a dog, — and I think he rather envied me my four-footed companion. I know I begrudged him his further adventure into the wilds beyond Tachienlu. Months later I learned that although he did not reach Lhasa as he had hoped to do, his explorations in the little-known region between Assam and Tibet and China had won him much fame and the Gill Medal awarded by the Royal Geographical Society.

Thanks to Captain Bailey I suffered no inconvenience from the absence of the missionaries on whom I had relied for help in getting a cheque cashed, as he kindly introduced me to the postmaster, to whom he had brought a letter from the English post-commissioner at Chengtu, and this official most courteously gave me all the money I needed for the next stage of my journey. The Imperial Post-Office was in 1911 still under the same management as the customs service, and was marked by the same efficiency. All over China it had spread a network of post-routes, and by this time, unless the Revolution has upset things, as it probably has, there should be a regular mail service between Tachienlu and Batang and Lhasa. To be sure, the arrangements at Tachienlu were rather primitive, but the surprising thing was that there should be any post-office at all. When I went for my letters the morning after I arrived, I was shown a large heap of stuff on the floor of the little office, and the interpreter and I spent a good half-hour disentangling my things from the dusty pile, most of which was apparently for members of the large French mission in Tachienlu. I was sorry not to have a chance to meet representatives of the mission, which has been established for a long time, and works, I believe, among both Tibetans and Chinese, the Protestants confining themselves to the Chinese community. Nor was I more successful in learning about the Protestant work, owing to the absence of the missionaries on a journey to Batang. But I was greatly impressed by the truly beautiful face and dignified bearing of a native pastor who called upon me at my lodgings. Fine, serene, pure of countenance, he might have posed for a Buddha or a Chinese St. John. In my limited experience of the Chinese, the men who stand out from their fellows for beauty of expression and attractiveness of manner are two or three Christians of the better class. Naturally fine-featured and of dignified presence, the touch of the Christian faith seems to have transformed the supercilious impassiveness of their class into a serenity full of charm. It is a pity that it is not more often so, but the zeal of the West mars as well as mends, and in imparting Western beliefs and Western learning carelessly and needlessly destroys Eastern ideals of conduct and manner, often more reasonable and more attractive than our own. The complacent cocksureness of the Occidental attitude toward Oriental ways and standards has little to rest on. We have reviled the people of the East in the past for their unwillingness to admit that there was anything we could teach them, and they are amending their ways, but we have shown and show still a stupidity quite equal to theirs in our refusal to learn of them. Take, for example, the small matter of manners, — if it be a small matter. More than one teacher in America has confessed the value of the object lesson in good breeding given by the chance student from the East, but how few Westerners in China show any desire to pattern after the dignified, courteous bearing of the Chinese gentleman. I have met bad manners in the Flowery Kingdom, but not among the natives.

It had been a long, hard pull from Ning-yüan-fu; two weeks' continuous travelling is a tax upon every one, but at no place had we found comfortable quarters for the whole of the party, and as the men preferred to push on, I was not inclined to object. But usually a seventh-day rest is very acceptable to them; so we were all glad for a little breathing-space in Tachienlu. The servants and coolies spent the first day in a general tidying-up, getting a shave, face and head, and having their queues washed and combed and replaited. Some also made themselves fine in new clothes, but others were content to wash the old. As none of them, with the exception of the fu t'ou, had ever been in Tachienlu before, they were as keen to see the sights as I was, and in my rambles about the town the next two or three days, I was greeted at every turn by my coolies, enjoying to the full their hard-earned holiday.

There was less to see of interest in Tachienlu than I had expected. The shops are filled mainly with ordinary Chinese wares, and my efforts to find some Tibetan curios were fruitless, those shown to me being of little value. I imagine it is a matter of chance if one secures anything really worth while. At any rate, neither the quaint teapots nor the hand praying-wheels that I was seeking were forthcoming. Nor could I find any decent leopard skins, which a short time ago formed an important article of commerce, so plentiful were they. But at least I had the fun of bartering with the people, whom I found much the most interesting thing in Tachienlu, and thanks to the indifference or the politeness of the Tibetan I was able to wander about freely without being dogged by a throng of men and boys. Chinese soldiers were much in evidence, for this is naturally an important military post as well as the forwarding depot for the troops stationed along the great western trade route to Batang and Lhasa. The Chinese population under their protection, numbering some four hundred families, mostly traders, looked sleek and prosperous. Evidently they made a good living off the country, unlike the Tibetans who were generally dirty and ragged and poor in appearance. I must confess that I was disappointed at the latter. In spite of their hardy, muscular aspect and bold bearing, I did not find them attractive as do most travellers. They lacked the grotesque jollity of the Ladakhis of Western Tibet, their cousins in creed and race, and I met nothing of the manly friendliness which marked the people of Mongolia whom I had to do with later. Never have I seen men of more vicious expression than some I met in my strolls about Tachienlu, and I could well believe the stories told of the ferocity shown by the lamas along the frontier. Very likely the people are better than their priests, but if so, their looks belie them. There is rarely a man — or a people — so low as to lack a defender, and it is a pleasing side to the white man's rule in the East, that if he be half a man he is likely to stand up for the weak folk he governs. It may be due to pride of ownership, or it may be the result of a knowledge born of intimate acquaintance, but whatever the cause, no race is quite without champions in the white man's congress. Captain Bailey who had had long experience of the Tibetans in administrative work on the northeastern borderland of India, was no exception, and he defended them vigorously. I had no knowledge to set against his, but when he declared that they were a clean people it seemed to me he was stretching a point, for I should have thought their dirt was as undeniable as it was excusable in the burning sun or biting cold of their high plateaus.

Practically all the traffic between China and its great western dependency passes through Tachienlu, and the little town is full of bustle and stir. From Tibet are brought skins and wool and gold and musk, to be exchanged here for tobacco and cloth and miscellaneous articles, but tea, of course, forms the great article of trade, the quantity sent from Tachienlu annually amounting to more than twelve million pounds. Conspicuous in the town are the great warehouses where the tea is stored, awaiting sale, and there are numerous Tibetan establishments where it is repacked for the animal carriage which here replaces the carrier coolies from the east. Among the Chinese the trade is mostly in the hands of a few great merchants who deal with the women representatives of the Tibetan priesthood who practically monopolize the sale in their country, deriving a large income from the high prices they charge the poor people to whom tea is a necessity of life.

When I grew weary of the confusion and dirt of the narrow streets I was glad to escape to the hillside above my lodgings. The mission compound is small and confined, affording no room for a garden, although fine masses of iris growing along the walls brightened up the severity of the grey stone buildings; but a little climb behind the mission house brought me to a peaceful nook whence I could get a glorious view over the town and up and down the valley, here so narrow that it seemed possible to throw a stone against the opposite hillside.

The first fine morning after my arrival I made an early start for the summer palace of the King of Chala, situated about eight miles from Tachienlu in a beautiful, lonely valley among the mountains. This is the favourite camping-place of Chengtu missionaries, who now and then brave the eleven days' journey to and fro to exchange their hothouse climate for a brief holiday in the glorious scenery and fine air of these health-giving uplands. We were mounted, the interpreter and I, on ponies provided by the Yamen, one worse than the other, and both unfit for the rough scramble. After traversing the town, first on one side and then on the other of the river which we crossed by a picturesque wooden bridge, roofed in but with open sides, we passed out at the South Gate — Tachienlu has no West Gate — and found ourselves in a small suburb with a few meagre gardens. A mile farther along we crossed the river again by a striking single arch bridge, known as the "Gate of Tibet." We were now on the great trade route to Lhasa, but between us and the mysterious city lay many days of weary travel.

From time to time we met groups of Tibetans, men and women, rough-looking and shy, with the shyness of a wild animal. Generally after a moment's pause to reassure themselves, they answered my greeting in jolly fashion, seeming quite ready to make friends. Occasionally the way was blocked by trains of ox-like yaks, the burden-bearers of the snow-fields, bringing their loads of skins and felt and musk and gold. Astride of one was a nice old man who stuck out his tongue at me in polite Tibetan fashion.

After an hour's ride we left the highway and turned into a beautiful green valley, following a very bad trail deeper and deeper into the mountains, the soft meadows gay with flowers forming a charming contrast to the snow-peaks that barred the upper end of the valley. We came first to the New Palace, a large rambling building having no more architectural pretensions than an ordinary Chinese inn. As the king's brother, who makes his home there, was away, I saw nothing more of the place than the great court-

LAMA AND DOG AT TACHIENLU

THE GATE OF TIBET

yard filled with mangy, half-starved dogs and unkempt men. Not far off is one of the great attractions of the place, at least to the natives, — a hot sulphur spring. To the disappointment of my Tibetan guide I declined to visit it, preferring a leisurely cold lunch on the bank of a rushing stream which was vigorously turning a large prayer-wheel, a cylinder of wood inscribed many times over with the mystic words of the Buddhist prayer, "Om mani padme hum," oftenest repeated perhaps of all prayers. Each revolution of the wheel was equivalent to as many repetitions of the words as there were inscribed on the wood. So night and day, while the stream runs, prayers are going up for the king, — and truly he needs them, poor man, between the bullying of his Chinese overlords and the machinations of turbulent lamas. Other indications of the Buddhist's comfortable way of getting his prayers said for him are found all about Tachienlu. From temple roof and wayside rock flags bearing the same legend wave in the breeze, each flutter a prayer, and just outside the city we rode by a long stone wall, much like those of New England, only its top was covered over with inscribed stones. If you passed by, having the "mani" wall on your right hand, each inscribed stone would pray for you; hence the trail always forks to suit the coming and the going Buddhist, and I remember well the insolent pride with which my

Mohammedan servants always took the right hand when passing these walls in Ladakh.

A mile farther up the valley we came to the Old Palace, a collection of hovels banked with piles of manure. Far more attractive than the royal residence were some tents not far off, where a band of Tibetans, retainers of the prince, were encamped. They came out to greet us in friendly fashion, pointing out a blind trail up the valley where we could get better views of the snow-peaks; but we had to turn back, sorry though I was to leave the spot, parklike in its beauty of forest and meadow, a veritable oasis in a wilderness of rock and ice. It was more like home than anything I had seen in West China, for there were stretches of fine, grassy meadows where the royal herds of cattle were grazing, and all at once I realized that it was weeks since I had seen a field of grass or real cows. It is the great lack in this country. Pigs abound, and fowls, but there is no place for cattle, and the horses live on beans and corn, or more likely on leaves and twigs.

Priest-ridden Tachienlu boasts many temples and lamasseries, and the last day of my stay I paid a visit to one of the largest, not far from the South Gate. It was a wide, rambling, wooden building standing near a grove of unusually fine trees, a sort of alder. The approach was not unattractive, flowers growing under the walls and about the entrance. Once inside the portal, we found ourselves in a large courtyard paved with stone and surrounded by two-story galleried buildings. Facing us was the temple, scarcely more imposing in outward appearance than the others. On one side a group of half-naked lamas were gathered about an older man who seemed to be relating or expounding something, whether gossip or doctrine I could not tell, but I should judge the former from their expressions. They paid little attention to us, nor did others strolling about the yard, but the big dogs roaming loose were not backward in their greeting, although to my surprise they did not seem at all ferocious, and treated my imperturbable little dog with distant respect. Earlier travellers recount unpleasant experiences, but perhaps the lamas have learned better in late years, and fasten up their dangerous dogs if visitors are expected. Afterwards I saw in another inner courtyard a large, heavy-browed brute adorned with a bright red frill and securely chained. He looked savage, and could have given a good account of himself in any fight.

While I was waiting for permission to enter the temple, I inspected the stuffed animals — dogs, calves, leopards — suspended on the verandah. They were fast going to decay from dust and moth, but I was told that they were reputed sacred. The temple, which we were forced to enter from a side door, was large and high, hung with scrolls and banners and filled with images, but it was so dark that I found it difficult to discern much save a good-sized figure of Buddha, not badly done.

At the invitation of an old lama, a friend of our guide, I was invited to a large, disorderly dining- or living-hall on the upper floor, where we were very courteously served with tea, Chinese fashion. The old man had a rather nice face, and I tried to learn a little about the place, but conversation through two Chinese intermediaries, one speaking imperfect English and the other bad Tibetan, was not very satisfactory, and I soon gave up the attempt. I did succeed, however, in making the lama understand my wish to hire some one to cut for me a praying-stone, to which he replied that there were plenty outside, why did I not take one of them? I had thought of that myself, but feared to raise a storm about my ears. Now, acting on his advice, I made a choice at my leisure and no one objected. Under the double restraint of an unusually strong prince, backed by Chinese officials, the priests of Tachienlu are less truculent than farther west, but at best Lamaism rests with a heavy hand upon the Tibetans; it is greedy and repulsive in aspect and brutalizing in its effects; wholly unlike the gentle, even though ignorant and superstitious, Buddhism of China.

CHAPTER VII

THE LESSER TRAIL

AT Tachienlu I reached the western limit of my wanderings; not the western boundary of China, nor yet of my desire, but my time was nearly spent; in less than four months I had to be back in England; moreover, late summer was not a favourable season for descending the Yangtse. So with a longing glance up the great Lhasa trail I turned my face eastwards; but it is always wearisome to retrace one's steps, and a chance remark of Captain Bailey set me on the scent of an alternative route to Ya-chou. As far as Lu Ting Ch'iao there was no choice; all traffic across the Ta Tu must seek the great iron bridge both coming and going, but at that point there turned off to the north and east a shorter trail than the main packroad which we had struck near Ni T'ou. Although more direct, it was less travelled owing to the difficulties of the way, for there were two steep mountain-ranges to be crossed, and path and bridges were often insecure, calling for a sure foot and a steady head. It was not easy to get precise information as to the condition of the road. Captain Bailey knew little save the mere fact of its existence, and although Major Davies had taken this route, he notes in his book "Yünnan" nothing more than that it is much too steep for animals. Even the friendly postmaster failed us here; all he could tell was that an official who had attempted to take ponies through lost them all, swept away by the torrents. The interpreter wagged his head doubtfully when I suggested my plan, but his opinion did not matter, for, like all of his class in China, he was disinclined to active exertion. And when I called the fu t'ou into council I found he had once gone this way, and was not inclined to go again.

Ku Niang (my title): "I wish to go to Ya-chou by the Lesser Trail."

Fu t'ou: "It is impossible."

Ku Niang: "I intend to go all the same, and I expect you to go with me."

Fu t'ou: "Very well. I will guide the Ku Niang by the Lesser Trail, but the pony cannot go, nor the chairs, nor the men, for it is impassable for shoulder loads, and these are Ning-yüan men who know no other way of carrying."

Apparently the fu t'ou and the cook, Jack and I were the only ones equal to the trip, as I had already told the interpreter he might go by the main road. But persistence conquers most things in the East. The pony should be sent round by the longer way in charge of the ma-fu. As for the interpreter, when he found I was ready to get along without him, he decided to stay with me. I would not have the Ning-yüan men discharged if they wished to go on with me to Ya-chou and Chengtu, as first arranged but I was sure that by hiring two or three extra coolies, so as to lighten the loads, they could get along; nor did the chairs present any real difficulty. We would walk when the trail was bad, and surely they could be taken empty wherever pack-coolies went. So it proved, all was arranged as I planned, and in the end everything turned out satisfactorily.

Our departure from Tachienlu was attended with the usual noise and confusion; nothing is done quietly in China. Also there were the customary delays. As we had only a short stage before us, I sat serenely aloof on the steps of the mission house, enjoying for the last time the wonderful views over the town to the snow peaks above, while things gradually got themselves straight. After a long wait for the second soldier, who never turned up, we were at last off, and the descent of the valley was very enjoyable in the soft grey light of a misty day. As the river had risen appreciably during our stay in Tachienlu, it rushed along at a fine rate between the high, steep banks, and I held my breath as I watched people pulling themselves over by the perilous rope bridges. Half-way to Wa Ssu Kou we met a procession of six chairs, and from each looked out the fair, smiling face of a French sister bound to her mission station at

Tachienlu. Already in thought the town seemed purer and better for the presence of these noble women, who had probably left their homes for good, to take up a work which they would lay down only with life.

We found room in Wa Ssu Kou in the same "comfy" inn as before, and the welcome we received gave me a truly homelike feeling. Soon after starting the next morning we passed the funeral cortège of a Chinese official of Tachienlu, making his last long journey to his distant home two hundred li beyond Chengtu. The ponderous coffin in its red case, upon which stood the usual white cock to avert disaster, was preceded by men carrying flags and cymbals which they clashed in accompaniment to the almost continuous chanting of the eight bearers. As they stopped for frequent halts we had soon left them far behind, but late at night they arrived at Lu Ting and were given quarters in the same temple where we were lodged, for I had refused to try the inns again.

While it was still dark the next morning we were aroused by the sound of chanting and clashing cymbals in the court outside. The bearers of the dead were starting on another stage of their long journey, and at quarter-past six we too were off, after a last parting injunction to the ma-fu to take good care of the pony. Already the town was astir, the market-place, as we passed through, crowded with traders and their produce, chiefly good-looking vegetables and fruit. For a few miles we kept up the left bank of the Ta Tu, and then turned abruptly up the mountain-side. Here my chair-men halted for breakfast and I did not see them again until we reached our night's stopping-place. Alone with Jack I kept on along the steep trail, revelling in my freedom. At first we met few people, although later in the day the number increased, but wherever the way seemed doubtful there was always some one to put me straight by signs. After a little we dropped by a sharp descent into the valley of a small wild river flowing into the Ta Tu from the east. We kept up this, crossing the stream from side to side on planks and stepping-stones. After passing through two tiny hamlets embowered in walnut trees, we reached the head of the valley and faced a long, steep zigzag. The climb was hard, hot work, but I found some diversion in a friendly race with a good-looking woman going the same way; her unbound feet kept up with mine while our dogs romped along gaily. Women with unbound feet were far more common here than elsewhere in my travels, and they seemed exceptionally alert and intelligent, but the population of the region is scanty, many of the people being newcomers of Hakka stock. Arrived at the top of the cliff we found ourselves on a narrow ridge, and for the rest of the short stage our way led along the face of the mountain, from time to time topping a wooded spur. Everywhere azaleas made the air sweet and the steep slopes wonderful with colour. At length we dropped without warning into a little village at the head of a precipitous narrow ravine, where we spent the night in an unusually interesting inn. Save for two or three private rooms, the best of which was given to me, all life centred in a great hall open to the roof and with merely a suggestion of partition in a few rough railings. Through the open doors men, children, pigs and fowls, cats and dogs, strolled in from the rain. Up in the roof our chairs were slung out of the way. Each coolie, having secured a strip of matting, had found his place. Some were cleaning off the sweat and dirt of the day's work with hot water : not until they have done that can they obtain the quilts that are rented for twenty cash each ; others had already curled up for the afternoon pipe of opium, while still others were busy preparing the evening meal over the big semicircular range. In one pot bean-cake was being made, a long, complicated process ; in another, cakes were frying in oil ; in another, rice was boiling. One of my chair coolies seemed to be the *chef par excellence ;* brandishing a big iron ladle, he went from pot to pot, stirring, tasting, seasoning, and generally lording it over two others working under his orders. In full control of the whole was a good-looking woman with bound feet, apparently the proprietor of the inn ; at least I

A WAYSIDE REST HOUSE

A FORTIFIED POST

saw no man to fill the post. Every one was good-tempered and friendly, and I was glad to exchange the tiresome seclusion of the town inns for the bustling scene in which I was willingly included, tasting each dish, watching the men at their games, making friends with the children.

The pouring rain of the night gave way to a soft drizzle at dawn, and we were off before seven. As we ascended the valley we faced a solid green wall flushed with masses of pink azaleas and cherry-red rhododendrons, and broken by half a dozen streams which flung themselves over the lip of the cliff to dash in feathery cascades from rock to rock below. Our way led back and forth over rushing mountain streams. Riding was of course out of the question, and I had long since left my chair-coolies behind; but one of the Tachienlu men, a strong, active fellow with bits of coral adorning his black queue, was very alert in looking out for me, always waiting at a difficult place with a helping hand. We crossed the Ma-An Shan Pass, about ten thousand feet high, by the middle of the forenoon, having climbed more than five thousand feet since leaving Lu Ting Ch'iao. Just before reaching the top we descended into a cup-like hollow, a huge dimple lined with the rich greens and gay reds of the rhododendron, and merry with the babble of many tiny waterfalls. I exclaimed with delight at the vision of beauty, and even the coolies grinned appreciatively. It would have been a place to dream away a day had it not been as wet as a shower bath. Nearing the pass, we heard weird sounds above us, not unlike the cries of rejoicing uttered by the Ladakhis of Western Tibet when they have successfully surmounted a difficult height, and I wondered if I was to find the same custom here. But it turned out to be the lullaby with which two men were tooling ten black pigs over the pass. Again, a little way down on the other side, my path was suddenly barred by a man frantically gesticulating. I thought at first that he was mad, but it was merely that he feared Jack would attack a flock of geese that he was driving in the wake of the pigs, and when I picked the dog up, the man prostrated himself at my feet in gratitude.

We ought to have had a fine view from the pass over the trackless mountain tangle to the north, some of the peaks towering almost eighteen thousand feet into the sky, but again the clouds and mist veiled everything from sight. All the rest of the day we were making our way down the steep east side, picking our steps laboriously along the wet rocky trail. Our path led through a precipitous narrow gorge, its walls draped with wonderful vegetation, and as we descended it, it grew wetter and greener, and the thousand little brooks leaping down the sides of the ravine rapidly swelled the main stream to an impassable torrent. Now we crouched under overhanging ledges, now we slipped and sprawled down a rough rock staircase, constantly crossing the stream from side to side on planks placed from boulder to boulder, or on slippery logs with insecure handrails or none at all. I found the descent far more tiring than the climb on the other side. The soldier and the gallant coolie fortunately kept always with me, one in front and one behind, and I was often glad of a helping hand. At one time the path led straight into the torrent, but while I was wondering as to the depth of the water and the strength of the current, the coolie, hastily depositing his load, motioned to me to get on his back, and the sturdy fellow carried me safely around the projecting cliff. Still another time we were forced to take to the river, and as I could get no wetter than I was, I proposed to wade in, but again the man was at hand, insisting that I should ride, and the strength and agility with which he made his way over the slippery rocks, the swirling water rising above his knees, were really wonderful; but then my weight was less than one hundred and thirty pounds, while the ordinary load of the tea-carrier is two hundred. At our heels came the soldier carrying Jack, whose short legs could hardly have made headway against the strong current forcing him out into midstream.

About the middle of the afternoon we forerunners

of the caravan reached Chang-ho-pa, the night's stop. The whole village turned out to greet us, and their interest was not to be wondered at, as few Europeans and perhaps no European woman had ever before come this way. The interpreter did not arrive until two hours later, and what stories my two companions made up about me to satisfy the curiosity of the villagers, I can only imagine. As a rule, one stands to lose nothing in the mouths of one's followers in the East. Whatever reflected glory they may earn by exalting their masters is generally theirs. Years afterward I learned that on a journey I once made in Kashmir and Baltistan I travelled in the guise of King Edward's sister. How much I profited by the dignity thus thrust upon me I do not know, but I have often thought that my servants must have been hard put to it sometimes to account for the simplicity of my outfit.

The rest of the caravan straggled in toward the end of the afternoon, wet and tired, but all in good spirits over the successful day, no loads drenched, no one hurt. The great room of the rough little inn was noisy and gay with the men drying their clothes and cooking their dinner, the centre of an interested throng of village folk. I sat among them on a low bench by the fire, watching the fun. Every one was heedful of my comfort, poking the fire, bringing a fan to screen my face from the heat, drying my shoes, rubbing Jack. The thoughtfulness and good will of my men during all the journey were unfailing, and I never found that friendliness on my part diminished in any way my authority over them.

After dinner the chair-bearers gathered round and with the aid of the interpreter I took down as best I could some of their calls and responses, a sort of antiphonal chorus handed down from generation to generation of coolies. Thus the men in front cry, "Lao di!" — "Something in the road!" — and those behind call back, "Ti chi!" — "Lift higher!" or maybe it is "Chiao kao!" — "Something overhead!" — and then the answer comes, "Keo yao!" — "Stoop lower!" When the way is very uneven, you hear "Leo puh ping!" — "The road is not level!" — to which is replied, "Mon tien hsin!" — "There are stones like stars!" — followed by "Tien shan hsin To!" — "Many stars in the sky!" — with the response, "Ti hsia ken to!" — "Many holes in the ground." Or perhaps at a bridge, "Hsio mo lan chao!" — "Bridge bad, building for a thousand years!" — to which comes the proverbial answer, "Chien mien wan lao!" — "Must last for ten thousand." When there is a steep bit, one calls out, "Deo shan deo!" — "Steeper and steeper!" and the others retort, "Kuan shan kuan!" — literally, "Official upon official," but the meaning is plain, "As steep as the ladder of promotion." In the villages one hears constantly, "Yu ti kou yao!"—"There is a dog on the road,"—with the response, "Han lao-pan lai chi tao!"—"Call the owner to chain it"; or else, "Tso shou wahwah keo!"—"A child on the left hand,"—and then comes the answer, "Han ta ma lah pao!"—"Call his mother to tend him."[1]

Every hundred yards or so on the road comes the cry, "Fan keo!"—"Change shoulders!"—followed by a momentary stop to shift the pole. And you always cross a town to the tune of "Pei-a, pei-a, pei-a!"—"Mind your back, mind your back, mind your back!" And if a man does not mind, he is likely to get a poke in the back from the chair pole.

The next day's journey was much the same thing as the preceding. We started in the grey morning, and I and my two companions of the day before had soon distanced the others. At first the trail was rough and slippery, and all ups and downs. The vegetation was of almost tropical density, and the moisture underfoot and overhead was so great that it seemed to me I had never been wetter except in a bathtub. As we descended to lower levels the valley broadened out, and the going improved so that we

[1] An apology is due to those wise in Chinese for the blunders that must be found in this attempt by an American who knows no word of the vernacular and a Kiangsi man having a limited command of English to catch and translate the "dirt talk" of Szechuan coolies.

were able to make very good time. At one point, after passing through a little hamlet, — we came out on a high bluff overlooking a good-sized stream flowing in from the south. Fifty feet below roared the river, spanned at this place by a suspension bridge a hundred and fifty feet long, constructed of three iron cables held together by cross-chains at regular intervals. The footway was merely a single row of boards not more than twelve inches wide, and there was no handrail at all. The soldier at my side waved his hand significantly up and down. I understood quite too well, and was shaking in my shoes at the thought of walking that narrow, unsteady plank, when I espied my knightly coolie, who, having deposited his load on the opposite bank, was hurrying back to my assistance. Gripping Jack, who was as frightened as I, under one arm, I seized the man's hand, and slowly we inched across to safety. There we joined the people of a near-by hamlet, who apparently found their pastime in watching the traffic across the bridge, perhaps waiting for a chance to earn a few cash by carrying the loads of the less sure-footed coolies. My chair-men came over triumphantly, and Mercury almost ran with his baskets, but the interpreter was glad of the fu t'ou's aid, and two of the coolies balked, but were helped out by some of the others.

Later in the day we left the river, and crossing a

head ridge or pass affording beautiful views to the south, came out after a time in the same valley, but now wider and more open. Though the mountains still towered to left and right, we were getting down to lower levels, and the change was marked in the palms, bamboos, and peach trees that began to appear. But the villages were nothing more than hamlets, and the outlook for dinner at the first stopping-place was so poor that I, now riding in my chair, decided to go on to the next settlement; but here conditions were even worse, the only inn being dismantled and abandoned. Although it was getting late and the others were far behind, there was nothing left but to travel on. Our last hope for the night proved to be a group of four houses only with few supplies, but the people bade us welcome and did their best to make us comfortable. Fires were lighted and clothes were soon drying and rice a-boiling. After the arrival of the interpreter I learned that we had been taken for missionaries, and that it was expected we would hold a service.

The scenery grew even more beautiful as we descended the valley the next day. Our trail led through fine groves high on the hillside, while below us the river, now big enough to have a name, the Ya, turned and twisted in splendid green swirls. Seen from a distance the villages were very attractive, built usually of wood, their thatched roofs just putting forth green

A ROADSIDE TEA-HOUSE

TEA-COOLIE CROSSING A SUSPENSION BRIDGE

His load weighed about 160 lbs

shoots. A new feature in the landscape were tall spruce trees, reminding me in their outlines of the rock pines of Italy. As the road was now good, it was possible for me to ride in my chair once more, for which I was glad, as the hard climbs and still more wearying descents of the last three days had made me rather stale. The people along the way were much interested in me and still more in Jack, but it was the naïve curiosity of a simple folk, and I did not find it irksome like the hard stare of the townspeople. At one place where we halted for tiffin, a lame man with an interesting face attached himself to us, and presently I found myself and my belongings the subject of an explanatory talk he was giving the bystanders. He told them how I kept my eyeglasses on, expatiated on the advantages of my shoes, indicated the good points of my chair, the like of which had never been seen before in these parts, and finally expounded at length the character of my dog. If I wished him to be bad he would bite, but since I was kind I would desire him to be good, and he would be good. To illustrate, he patted Jack's head rather gingerly. Fortunately the dog appreciated pats from any quarter, so our characters did not suffer.

Toward the end of the day we were nearing Tien-chüan-chou, the one largeish town on this road. The approach was one of the finest things I have ever seen. We were now well down, having descended seven thousand feet since crossing Ma-an-Shan. Everywhere there was careful cultivation, the nearer hills being terraced to the top, and the well-paved trail traversed long stretches of rice-fields just beginning to show green above the mud. Here and there a group of farm buildings stood on little knolls above the surrounding marsh, each in a charming setting of trees. Do trees anywhere group themselves as picturesquely as in China? Unsympathetic people tell me that no Chinese ever plant trees save for severely utilitarian purposes. I am in no position to contradict the verdict of these overpowering persons, the old residents (fortunately they sometimes contradict each other); and yet why is it that most temples are set in fine groves, put to no purpose that I can see save to satisfy a sense of the beautiful, or why are so many Chinese towns, looked at from a height, bowers of green beauty, the trees serving neither for fuel nor for food? The truth is, it seems to me, that the needs of life press so hard on the Chinese that they are forced to look at things from a utilitarian point of view, but given the least chance and their appreciation of the beautiful shows itself.

Near the town we struck down to a good iron suspension bridge over the Ya, which here runs with a tremendous current, broken by curious reefs thrusting out into the stream some twenty or thirty feet and at right angles to the bank. Beyond the bridge we came in sight of the town, its staring red walls draped with green creepers. Entering through a fine stone gateway, we found ourselves in the single street, broad, well paved, and wonderfully clean. The inhabitants were apparently well used to foreigners, which is natural, as Ya-chou with its Roman Catholic and Protestant missions is only twenty miles away.

The country through which we passed the next day was very varied, and always beautiful. On leaving the town the path led along a low ridge given over to graves. Living and dead dwell side by side in China, and often it seems as though the rights of the one were sacrificed to the claims of the other. The Chinese saying, "For every man that Heaven creates, Earth provides a grave," takes on a new significance as one looks over the land, the dead are so many, the living so hard put to live. This was not an unattractive place, for the mounds of earth and stone were overgrown with grass and ferns, while many were decorated with a tuft of bamboo or a bush of wild roses. The free use of stone in this district was very striking; pavements, often in good condition, were general, the irrigating ditches were bridged by a single slab of the red sandstone of Szechuan, perhaps ten feet in length, while at every turn there were charming little stone shrines in place of the shabby wooden ones found farther south.

After a bit we turned away from the plain and river

and entered a more broken country, hills and valleys, ridges and dells, rushing brooks between banks of ferns, little tumbling cascades over mossy stones, groups and avenues of fine trees, picturesque stone bridges, everywhere painstaking tillage and ingenious irrigation. It was all charming, with the artificial beauty of a carefully ordered park. Resting in my chair in front of a tea-house where the coolies were refreshing themselves, I noticed my knight of the bridges suddenly throw himself on the ground before the interpreter, crying out something in beseeching tones, while the other coolies standing about laughed unsympathetically. The poor man was urging the interpreter to ask that I give him back his soul, of which apparently I had deprived him when I took his picture an hour back. Without his soul he would die, and then what would his mother, a widow, do? After some talk he was consoled, the other men assuring him that they had been photographed over and over again without suffering harm. If only I had known at the time, I could have consoled him with the information that there was no picture. Photographing in cloudy Szechuan has many drawbacks, and I was ready to bark with the proverbial dog of the province when I saw the sun. The feeling of the Chinese toward the camera seems to vary. Children were sometimes afraid. One boy old enough to carry a heavy load, having been induced by the promise of a reward to stand still, burst into tears just as I was about to snap him, and I had to send him off triumphant over his bits of cash, while I was left pictureless. Some, too, of the older people made objection, while on the other hand I was occasionally asked to take a picture.

Toward noon we found ourselves again in the valley of the Ya, sometimes following a well-paved trail above the river, the ups and downs carefully terraced in broad stone steps, occasionally threading our way among the huge rush mats with which the village streets were carpeted. The harvesting of the millet and barley crops was over, and the sheaves had been brought into the village to dry and were spread out in the only level space available, the highway. Men walked over the sheaves, children and dogs romped among them, and no one said them nay. Twice we were ferried across the river, and finally a short run over the low, wide reefs that here narrow the channel brought us to Ya-chou and to the end of the Lesser Trail. We had made the trip without any of the prophesied mishaps, and for me it was far more comfortable and more interesting than following the main track. To be sure, we took five days to it, but it would not have been difficult to have saved a day, only there was no object in doing it, for a wait at Ya-chou was inevitable that the ma-fu and pony might catch us up there.

My enforced stay of one day in Ya-chou gave me a chance to see something of the town. I had the good fortune to be entertained by members of the American Baptist Mission, Dr. and Mrs. Shields, and there as elsewhere I found the missionaries most helpful in giving the traveller an insight into local conditions. There is one limitation to this, however, in the gulf which seems fixed between Protestants and Roman Catholics in the East, cutting off the chance of learning what the latter are doing; and when one bears in mind that Rome has had her missionaries in China for three hundred years and numbers her converts by millions, one would like to know more of the work done.

But there is no doubt as to the reality of Protestant achievement. In Ya-chou the relations of missionaries and townspeople seemed very cordial and natural. Medical work is being carried on, and a hospital was shortly to be opened. But more valuable, perhaps, than any formal work may be the results from the mere presence in the town of Christian men and women living lives of high purpose and kindly spirit.

If you listen to the talk of the treaty ports you will hear much criticism of missionaries and their work, and since they are human it is reasonable to suspect that they sometimes make mistakes; but after all they are the only Europeans in China who are not there for their own personal interests, and the people are quite shrewd enough to see this. In spite of differences of views the Chinese who knows the missionary at all generally respects him. A Chinese gentleman in no way friendly to missions, speaking of the good relations that existed between Europeans and Chinese in Nanking, declared it was all because the missionaries came first. And Dr. Soothill tells the story of an Englishman who applauded the harsh criticism of mission work by a Chinese river captain, and met the retort, "That's all well enough, but if it were not for the missionaries we should not know there were any good men in your country."

The prefectural city of Ya-chou is the centre of a great tea-growing district, while in the town itself are large establishments where the article is made up for the Tibetan trade. The Szechuan tea for the most part does not rank very high, little being exported from the province save to Tibet, and for that market even the poorest is reckoned too good, as the so-called tea carried by the thousands of coolies whom we met bound for Tachienlu is everything save genuine tea leaves, being a mixture of which the leaves and twigs of scrub oak and other trees form the largest part. The Ya-chou tea, when gathered and dried, is bought up and brought into the towns to be made into the brick tea of Tibetan commerce. The preparation consists in chopping fine the tea and adulterating leaves and twigs. After adding a little rice-water the whole is packed in cylinders of bamboo matting, each package weighing from sixteen to eighteen catties. It is estimated that the cost to the manufacturers, exclusive of packing, is about thirty-two cash a catty, somewhat less than a cent and a half gold the pound. By the time the tea has reached Tachienlu it is sold at about five and a half cents a pound. At Batang the price is doubled, and at Lhasa quadrupled. Thus the stuff bought as tea by the Tibetans can scarcely be called cheap, and yet they consume great quantities of it. To them it is not a luxury, but a real necessity.

CHAPTER VIII

ACROSS CHENGTU PLAIN

THOROUGHLY set up by the day's rest in Ya-chou, my men were on hand at five o'clock on the morning of May 24, in good spirits for the rest of the trip. Even the ma-fu, whom we had left behind at Hua-lin-ping, turned up with the coolie and pony sent round from Lu Ting.

Two missionaries going down the river to Chia-ting, at the junction of the Min and the Ta Tu invited me to take a turn at rafting, and I was glad to go with them for a few li. The Ya Ho joins the Ta Tu just west of Chia-ting, the fall from Ya-chou being about six hundred and fifty feet in a distance of ninety miles. So swift is the current and so tortuous and rocky the bed of the stream that the only navigation possible is by means of bamboo rafts fifty or sixty feet long, with a curled prow. Amidships is a small platform partly roofed over with matting. In spite of the rapids, which at times make the trip vastly exciting, there is no danger save the certainty of getting wet. The scenery on either hand is very beautiful; the great mountains recede in the distance, fading out in the soft light, but the fine red sandstone cliffs, alternating with the brilliant green of bamboo groves and rice-fields on the lowland, afforded a charming picture at every turn.

My men were waiting for me at the appointed place, and ten minutes' precarious scrambling along the narrow dykes between the fields brought me to the great highway leading to the capital, four days' march away. All this day and the three succeeding ones we were travelling through a district park- or garden-like in its exquisite artificial beauty. The trail, which was at first fairly good, ran now along the top of an embankment some six feet broad constructed across the swimming paddy fields, then dropped into a little valley shaded with fine "namti" trees, and again it wound along a low ridge. Far off against the western horizon stretched the splendid snow-line of the Tibetan range from which I had just come, but now more than a hundred miles away. Every inch of land that could be irrigated was under cultivation, save where a substantial looking farmhouse set in groves of fine trees, bamboos, cypress, and namti, occupied a little knoll laboriously built up above the encircling marsh. Last year their crumbling walls testified to the security of the country, but I wonder what has been the fate of these solitary houses in the recent months of lawlessness. Toward the end of the day a soft mist settled down upon the earth, outlining the nearer hills and throwing up against the sky the distant peaks.

A FARMHOUSE IN CHENGTU PLAIN

We had tiffin at the little town of Ming Shan-hsien. About five miles west of here rises from the plain the Ming Shan, a small mountain famous throughout China for its tea, which is grown by the priests of a Buddhist temple on the summit. According to tradition the seeds from which this tea is produced were brought centuries ago from India by a Chinese pilgrim. Only a few pounds are gathered annually and these are always sent as tribute to Peking for the use of the imperial household. To whom will they now fall? There is a saying current in China that to make a first-rate cup of tea you must take "leaves from the Ming Shan and water from the Yangtse." No one believes for a moment that the turbid water of the Great River is meant here, and yet no one could explain what it did mean. But De Rosthorn, in his interesting pamphlet on "Tea Cultivation in Szechuan," gives what seems to him the true explanation. Crossing the bay at Chen-kiang he saw men in boats filling buckets with water. Asking what they were doing, he was told that there was a famous spring at the bottom of the river well known from the time when the river bed was dry land. Here, then, was the Yangtse water which, combined with leaves brought from Ming Shan two thousand miles away, made the best tea in the world.

We stopped for the night at the village of Paichang, where I spent a tiresome evening trying to arrange for a pony to take the place of mine, left behind at Ya-chou, as he seemed in need of a longer rest. The weather was now too hot for walking, but all day in the chair was unendurable, so I hoped here to hire a pony for half a stage. I refused to engage one without seeing its back, but nothing appeared to be inspected, why, I could not tell. The shifts and turns of the oriental mind are not our shifts and turns, so I finally gave up trying to find out, and went to bed, telling the fu t'ou he must have something ready in the morning, only if its back was sore I would not take it. But morning came and no pony. I was told it was waiting for me outside the town, and there it was, sure enough. Ordering off saddle and blanket I inspected its back to make certain that all was right, as it was. But the strange ma-fu seemed quite overcome with consternation at the sight of me, while the fu t'ou collapsed on a stone wall near by, doubled up with laughter. At last an explanation was made. When the fu t'ou tried to get a pony for me from the pony hong he was met by a refusal. No foreigner should ride one of their horses; they had let one to a foreign gentleman not long before, and he had abused it and gone so fast that the ma-fu could not keep up, and nearly lost the pony; nor were they to be moved. Anyway, the fu t'ou told them, he must have one himself. When it was brought to the inn at dawn he mounted and rode outside the town. There, finding he had forgotten something,— me,— he went back for it, while pony and ma-fu waited. In true Chinese fashion the ma-fu accepted the inevitable and walked quietly at my side, but he had an anxious expression at first, as though he expected me at any moment to whip up my steed and vanish. I am not wise in horseflesh, but at least I try to be merciful to my beasts. When I got off, as I did now and then, to save the horse over a particularly bad place, the man began to cheer up, and finally when, according to my custom, I took the pony outside the village to graze a bit while the men had their breakfast, — a very unsuitable proceeding, I was later told, — his surprise broke forth. "What sort of a foreign woman was this?" At noon I sent the pony back, paying for the half day one hundred and forty cash, about seven cents gold.

Just before reaching Cheung-chou, where we were to spend the night, we crossed the Nan Ho by a fine stone bridge of fifteen arches. The Nan is one of the lesser waterways of West China connecting this corner of Szechuan with the Great River, and many cumbersome boats laden with produce were slipping down with the rapid current on their way eastwards.

I entered the gate of the town with some doubt as to my reception. Baron von Richthofen, who passed through here a generation ago, wrote of the place: "All the men are armed with long knives and use them frequently in their rows. I have passed few cities in China in which I have suffered so much molestation from the people as I did there; and travellers should avoid making night quarters there as it was my lot to do." Time enough has elapsed since the good baron went this way to have changed all that, but the missionaries at Ya-chou had also cautioned me against the temper of the people, relating some unpleasant experiences of recent date. They had kindly given me a note of introduction to two missionaries who had their headquarters at Cheung-chou who would make me safe and comfortable in their house. I had sent this ahead only to learn that the mission was closed, as the people were touring in the district; and so there was nothing to do but go to the inn as usual.

In the narrow streets of the town there was of course the everlasting pushing, staring crowd, but I saw no signs of unfriendliness, and Jack's gay yaps in response to pointing fingers and cries of "K'an yang kou! k'an yang kou!" ("Look at the foreign dog! look at the foreign dog!") brought the invariable grins of delight. Later in the day, wearying of the confinement of the inn, and not unwilling to test the temper of the people a bit, I went marketing with the cook. Of course a crowd of men and boys dogged my steps, but it was a good-natured crowd, making way for me courteously, and when they found that I was looking for apricots they fairly tumbled over each other in their eagerness to show us the best shop.

Cheung-chou lies on the southwestern edge of the great plain of Chengtu, which, although only some ninety miles long by seventy miles wide, supports a population of four millions, so kindly is the climate, so fertile the soil, and so abundant the water supply. Two of these blessings are the gift of nature, but the last is owed to the ingenuity of Li Ping and his nameless son, known only as the "Second Gentleman," two Chinese officials who worked and achieved and died more than two thousand years ago. At Kwan-hsien there is a temple, perhaps the most beautiful in China, erected in their memory, but their truest monument is this beautiful plain, blossoming like a Garden of Eden under the irrigation system which they devised, and which will endure so long as men obey their parting command engraved on a stone in the temple, "Dig the channels deep; keep the banks low."

The people of the plain were as friendly as the mountain folk I had been travelling amongst, but they displayed less of the naïve curiosity of the out-of-the-way places. Evidently the foreigner was no novelty, nor the camera either. At one village I stopped to photograph a fine pailou, not to the "virtuous official" this time, but to the "virtuous widow."

A little group of villagers gathered to watch, and would not be satisfied until I had taken a picture of another local monument, a beautiful three-storied stone pagoda rising tall and slender above the flat rice land. These picturesque structures add much to the charm of the level plain which tends to become monotonous after a while. As far as one can see stretches the paddy land in every stage of development. Some fields are hardly more than pools of water mirroring the clouds overhead. Others are dotted over with thin clumps of rice through which the ducks swim gaily, while still others are solid masses of green, and transplanting has already begun.

Although we were now approaching the largest city of West China, and the capital of the empire's richest province, the roads went steadily from bad to worse. Made with infinite labour centuries ago, they had been left untouched ever since, and weather and wear had done their work. For long stretches the paving was quite gone; elsewhere you wished it were. The people have their explanation of these conditions in the saying, "The hills are high and the emperor far." It remains to be seen if that will hold good of the new government. Certainly nothing will mean so much in the development of the country as good roads. We were now once more on the line of wheeled traffic, and the wheelbarrow was never out of sight or hearing. Enormous loads were borne

MEMORIAL ARCH TO A "VIRTUOUS WIDOW," CHENGTU PLAIN

along on the large flat-bottomed freight barrow, while on every hand we saw substantial looking farmer folk, men, women, and children, going to town in the same primitive fashion.

To save the journey a little for my chair-men, and also for the fun of a new experience, I bargained with a barrow-man to carry me for a few miles. My coolies took it as a fine joke, and after starting me off trotted on behind, but my military escort looked troubled. No longer striding proudly in front, he showed a desire to loiter behind, although so long as my grand chair kept close at my heels he could save his face by explaining my strange proceeding as the mad freak of a foreigner. But finally, when I bade the chair-men stop for a smoke at a rest-house, knowing they could easily overtake my slow-moving vehicle, he too disappeared, and only took up his station again at the head of the procession when I went back to my chair after dismissing the barrow with a payment of eighty cash for a ride of twenty-five li. Barrow travelling is not as bad as it seems, for there is a chair-back, and rests for the feet are fixed on either side of the wheel. But in spite of the dexterity with which the coolie trundled me over the rough places and through the deep ruts, an upset into an unsavoury rice-patch seemed unpleasantly possible, and more than all, you can never lose consciousness of the straining man behind.

I thought the last stage into Chengtu would never end; the passing of people became more and more incessant and tiring, while the hot-house temperature of this rich lowland was most exhausting, and the occasional downpours only made the roads more impassable without cooling the air. My coolies, coming from higher altitudes, were almost used up. They stopped often to rest, and hardly one was doing his own work, making an exchange with another man, unless he had given up entirely, sweating out his job to some one hired on the way. So we straggled along, a disorderly, spiritless crowd, showing a little life only when Jack, whom nothing daunted, created a diversion by chasing the village dogs along the narrow earth balks between the fields, their favourite resting-places. Then the whole party waked up, cheering the little dog on with gay cries, and laughing impartially when hunter or hunted slipped into the muck of a rice-patch, while the toilers by the roadside thought we had all gone mad until they saw what it was, and then they too joined in with chuckles of delight. There is something quite childlike in the way in which this old Chinese people welcomes any little break in the grey days of grinding drudgery.

As the day wore on, one could guess that a great centre of government and trade was near at hand; the traffic was continuous, — coolies bent almost double under their heavy burdens, laden barrows creaking dolefully as they moved, foot travellers plodding wearily along, groups of wild Tibetans from the distant frontier, gorgeous mandarins returning from an inspection tour, all were hurrying towards the capital. Yes, we were nearing Marco Polo's "large and noble" city of Sindin-fu and it is to-day again a "large and noble" city, only now it is known as Chengtu, and the days are not so very far in the past when it was hardly a city at all.

Szechuan's later history begins with the troubled times that marked the fall of the Ming dynasty. While the Manchus were busy establishing themselves at Peking, the outlying provinces of the empire were given over to brigandage and civil strife. Here in Chengtu an adventurer calling himself the Emperor of the West succeeded in getting the upper hand for a short time, and when his end came there was little left to rule over save ruins and dead men, which was hardly to be wondered at, seeing his idea of ruling was to exterminate all his subjects. Baber has made from De Mailla's "History of China" the following summary of his measures: "*Massacred:* 32,310 undergraduates; 3000 eunuchs; 2000 of his own troops; 27,000 Buddhist priests; 600,000 inhabitants of Chengtu; 280 of his own concubines; 400,000 wives of his troops; everybody else in the province. *Destroyed:* Every building in the province. *Burnt:* Everything inflammable."

Since that time Szechuan has been repeopled and to-day the capital has a population of quite three hundred and fifty thousand, although the walls, that in the thirteenth century extended twenty miles, are now no more than twelve in length and enclose a good deal of waste land. The wonderful bridges described by Marco Polo, half a mile long and lined with marble pillars supporting the tiled roof, no longer exist, but the city still abounds in bridges of a humbler sort, for it is crossed by the main stream of the Min as well as by many smaller branches and canals, all alive with big and little craft. Chengtu is proud of its streets, which are well paved and broader and cleaner than common, and on the whole it is an attractive, well-built city.

The viceroy of the province has his seat here, and Szechuan shares with the metropolitan province of Chihli the honour of having one all to itself, and he is more truly a viceroy than the others, for the Mantzu and Tibetan territories lying to the west are administered through the provincial government and are in a way tributary to it. Even from far Nepal on the borders of India come the bearers of gifts to the representative of the emperor.

Ser Marco speaks of the "fine cloth and crêpes and gauzes" of Chengtu, and still to-day the merchants unroll at your feet as you sit on your verandah exquisitely soft, shimmering silks and wonderful embroideries. It was these last that caught my fancy, and the British Consul-General, himself a great collector, kindly sent to the house his "second-best" man and then his "first-best," and between the two I made a few modest purchases at even more modest prices. Imagine getting two strips of wonderful silk embroidery for twenty cents gold, or two silk squares ingeniously ornamented and pieced with gold for the same contemptible sum. That was what the men wanted at the missionary house where I was staying; at the Consul-General's they asked me twenty-five cents: that is the price of being an official.

I liked even better to go to the shops, and Chengtu is so progressive that that is quite possible. One section is given over to brass and copper dishes, another to furs, another to porcelains, and so on. Indeed, the town seems to be a very good place for "picking up" things, for hither come men from the far distant Tibetan lamasseries, and patient effort is often rewarded with interesting spoil, while Chinese productions of real value sometimes drift into the bazaar from the collections of the ever-changing officials.

But I did not spend all my days bargaining for curios, although they were tempting enough, for there were other things to do more worth while. The European community of Chengtu is surprisingly large for so far inland. In numbers, of course, the missionaries lead, and besides the Roman Catholic mission there are representatives of English, American, and Canadian churches, all working together to give to this out-of-the-way corner of the empire the best of Christian and Western civilization. Their latest and most interesting undertaking is a university on Western lines, the outcome of the combined effort of the Friends', Baptist, and Methodist societies of Chengtu. The economy and efficiency secured by coöperation must be of even less value than the force of such a lesson in Christian harmony to the keen-witted Chinese. Indeed, all over China one is impressed by the wisdom as well as the devotion of most of the mission work. And however it may be in the eastern seaports, where I did not spend much time, inland there seems to be the best of feeling between the different elements of the European community, official, missionary, and merchant. Perhaps because they are a mere handful in an alien people they are forced to see each other's good points, and realize that neither side is hopelessly bad nor impossibly good.

There is quite a large Tartar population in Chengtu, and the Manchu quarter is one of the most picturesque parts of the city, with the charm of a dilapidated village set in untidy gardens and groves of fine trees. Loafing in the streets and doorways are tall, well-built men and women, but they had a rather down-at-heel air, for their fortunes were at a low ebb when I was in Chengtu. The military service they once rendered had been displaced by the new modern trained troops, and three years ago their monthly rice pension of four taels, about $2.50, was cut down by a viceroy bidding for popular support. Although Chengtu is two thousand miles from the sea, it is one of the most advanced cities of China, and has no mind to put up with outgrown things, such as Manchu soldiers and Manchu pensions. It boasts to-day a mint turning out a very respectable coinage, a large arsenal, and a university of more promise, perhaps, than achievement; and the pride of the moment was a new arcade of shops where the goods were set out with all the artifice of the West in large glazed windows. Although Japanese and Europeans are employed, yet these are all truly native undertakings, and that, to my mind, is the best part of Chengtu's progress; it shows what the Chinese can do for themselves, not simply following Western leadership. And on the whole they seemed last year to be doing a number of things very well. It argued real efficiency, I think, that the officials at Chengtu knew at every moment the whereabouts of the travelling foreigners in a province larger than France. To be sure, we were only two, Captain Bailey and myself, but all the same they could not have done it save by a very up-to-date use of the telegraph. And again, the Chengtu police are really guardians of the peace. I had a chance to see the order that was kept one night when my chair-men lost their way taking me to a dinner at the house of the French Consul-General, quite across the city from where I was staying. For more than an hour we wandered about, poking into all sorts of dark corners, finally reaching the consulate at half-past nine instead of an hour earlier, and nowhere, either in thoroughfare or alley, was there any rowdyism, and this though it was the night of the Dragon Festival when all the people were making holiday. But then under ordinary conditions the Chinese is a peaceable man; he has his own interpretation of the rule of life: in order to live, let others live. I met an example of that in Peking. Opposite the hotel door stood a long line of rickshaws. You soon had a favourite man, and after that the others never thrust themselves forward, but, instead, at once set up a shout for him if he failed to note your appearance. However, the Chinese individual is one thing, the Chinese mob another. It was not many years since an infuriated crowd stormed through the streets of Chengtu seeking the lives of the foreigners, and in even fewer weeks after my visit other crowds would besiege the viceroy's yamen demanding justice for their wrongs. For even when I was there the undercurrent of discontent in the province was visible. The students of the university, like those in Yunnan-fu, had more than once got out of hand; people complained that the new educational system lacked the discipline of the old, and indeed Young China seems to outdo even Young America in self-assurance, and in the spring of 1911 the university was just beginning to recover from the turmoil of a strike of the students for some real or fancied slight by the Government.

And there was more serious trouble afoot. The Szechuan merchants and gentry, wealthy and enterprising, had contributed generously (for China) to the building of a railway connecting the western capital with Wan-hsien and Ichang, but now they were hearing that the money had been squandered and the railway was to be built with foreign capital. It was bad enough to lose their money, but the evil that might come in the trail of the foreigner's money was worse. So people were talking hotly against the new "railway agreement," and it proved in the end the proverbial straw, for three months later the Railway League of Szechuan set in motion the revolution which overthrew the Manchus and the empire.

But these things were still on the knees of the gods, and my stay in Chengtu was altogether delightful, save for the thought that here my out-of-the-way journeying ended. Henceforth I should go by ways often travelled by Europeans. And then I was leaving so much behind. Of my caravan only three would go on with me, the interpreter, the cook, and the Yunnan coolie, who was ready to stay by me a little longer. The rest I had paid off, giving to all a well-earned tip, and receiving from each of my chair-men in turn a pretty, embarrassed "Thank you," learned from hearing me say it. The pony, too, would go no farther, for most of the next month my travelling would be by water, so I handed him over to a horse-loving missionary, and I only hope he proved worthy of his master. My chair, which had been such a comfort for so many weeks, was left in Chengtu waiting a chance to be sent to Ning-yüan-fu, where I trust it arrived in time to serve Mrs. Wellwood on her hurried journey to Yunnan-fu at the outbreak of the Revolution. Even the little dog came nigh to ending his travels at Chengtu, for the Post Commissioner put forward a claim of common Irish blood, which I could hardly deny because of the many kindnesses received from him. But I could not make up my mind to part with my little comrade, and I said a determined nay.

It was early June when I started on the next stage of my journey, a three days' trip down the Min River to Chia-ting. The sun was sinking as I went on board the "wu-pan" or native boat lying in the stream outside the South Gate, and after carefully counting heads to make sure that the crew were all there, and that we were carrying no unauthorized passengers, we pushed off and the current took us rapidly out of sight of Chengtu.

The trip to Chia-ting was very delightful. I was tired enough to enjoy keeping still, and lying at ease under my mat shelter I lazily watched the shores slip past; wooded slopes, graceful pagodas crowning the headlands, long stretches of fields yellow with rape, white, timbered farmhouses peeping out from groves of bamboo and orange and cedar, it was all a beautiful picture of peaceful, orderly life and industry. Each night we tied up near some village where the cook and boat people could go a-marketing, generally coming back after an hour with one vegetable or two. As the river was high, we made good speed, and on the morning of the third day after starting, the picturesque red bluffs opposite Chia-ting came in sight.

CHAPTER IX

OMEI SHAN, THE SACRED

THE rose-red city of Chia-ting lives in my memory as a vision of beauty, the most charming (at a distance) of the many charming (always at a distance) Chinese towns that I have seen. Built on a sandstone ledge at the junction of the Ta Tu and Ya with the Min, its crenellated red walls rise almost directly from the water, which, when in flood, dashes high against the foundations. On the northwest the city rises to nearly three hundred feet above the level, and standing on the wall one looks down upon a sea of living green from which rise temple and pagoda, or west across Chia-ting plain, perhaps the loveliest and most fertile spot in the Chinese Eden, and then farther west still to where on the horizon towers Omei Shan, the Holy of Holies of Buddhist China, often, alas, shrouded in mist from base to summit, for this is a land of clouds and rain and floods.

Looking across the river to the great cliffs opposite the town, one discerns dimly, carved on the face of the rock, the wonder of the region, a colossal Buddha more than three hundred feet in height, sitting serenely with his hands on his knees, and his feet, or what ought to be his feet, laved by the rushing water of the Ta Fo Rapid. As the tale runs, this was the work of a good monk of the eighth century, who spent his life over the undertaking in the hope that by this pious act he might avert the terrible floods that devastated the region. A mighty task boldly conceived and patiently carried out, but still the rain pours down, and still the rivers rise and drown the land.

Baber tells the dramatic story of one of the greatest of the floods. It occurred in 1786 when the fall of a cliff in the Ta Tu dammed the river completely for a time. Warnings were sent to the villages along the banks, and many fled to the hills, but the people of Chia-ting, trusting to their open plain over which the water could spread itself, scouted the warning, and the cry, "Shui lai-la" ("The water is coming"), became the catchword of the hour. Let Baber tell the rest:—

"It was holiday in Chia-ting some days after the receipt of the notice, and the light hearted crowds which gathered on such occasions were chiefly attracted by a theatrical representation on the flat by the water-side. One of the actors suddenly stopped in the middle of his rôle, and gazing up the river, screamed out the now familiar by-word, 'Shui lai-la!' This repetition of the stock jest, with well-simulated terror, as it seemed to the merry-makers, drew shouts of laughter; but the echoes of the laugh were drowned in the roar of a deluge. I was told how the gleeful faces turned to horror as the flood swept on like a moving wall, and overwhelmed twelve thousand souls."

While in Chia-ting I crossed the river one day to see the great Buddha from near by, but it is very difficult to get a good view of the image. The river runs at the foot of the cliff at such a rate that it was all the boatmen could do to keep us off the rocks, and looking down from above, the overhanging shrubs and grasses almost hide it from sight. There is an interesting monastery on the summit of the hill, called the "Monastery of the Voice of the Waters." Here I spent a delightful hour wandering through the neglected garden and looking over the treasures of the place, a rather remarkable collection of drawings and inscriptions engraved on slate, the work of distinguished visitors of past times, some dating back even to the Sung period. There were landscapes extremely well done, others were merely a flower or branch of a blooming shrub, but all bore some classic quotation in ornamental Chinese character. I bought of the priest for a dollar a bundle of really fine rubbings of these engravings. At another monastery a gallery full of images of the "Lo-han," the worthiest of Buddha's disciples, was being tidied up. The variety of pose and expression in these fifty-odd life-size images was extraordinary, and some of them were wonderfully good, but the workmen handled them without respect as they cleaned and painted. It is a Chinese proverb that says, "The image-maker does not worship the gods; he knows what they are made of."

There is one drawback to the delights of Chia-ting, and that is the climate. To live and work in the damp heat that prevails much of the time must test the strength, and I imagine the Europeans stationed here find it so. Chia-ting boasts two strong Protestant missions, American Baptist and Canadian Methodist, well equipped with schools and a hospital, and they are hard at work making Chia-ting over, body and soul. At the time of my visit they were engaged in a strenuous contest with the representatives of the British American Tobacco Company, and both sides were placarding the town with posters setting forth the evils or the benefits of cigarette-smoking.

Chia-ting is the great point of departure for Mount Omei, thirty miles away, and I stayed only long enough to rearrange my kit and hire coolies for the trip. Again I had a chance to see the strength that the Chinese have through organization. Each quarter of Chia-ting has its coolie hong, and woe betide you if you fall out with your own; you will have difficulty in getting served elsewhere. Fortunately my host was on good terms with his proper hong, and after a good-humored, long-drawn-out discussion I secured the men I wanted.

It was raining when we started from Chia-ting and it kept on all day. Nevertheless, as soon as I was outside the West Gate of the city I exchanged my closed chair for one specially devised for the mountain climb, simply a bamboo chair furnished with a swinging board for a foot-rest. It gave of course no protection against sun or rain, but there was nothing to cut off the view. The closed chair affected by the Chinese seemed to me intolerable, a stuffy box half closed in front, and with mere loopholes on the sides. But fifteen years ago no European woman could ride in anything else without danger of being mobbed.

All the first day we were crossing the beautiful Chia-ting plain, seamed and watered by many rivers and streams. The path wound in and out among splendid fields of maize and fine fruit orchards, and the comfortable looking villages were densely shaded with oak and mulberry trees. It ought to be a prosperous district, for not only is it rich in natural resources, but the throngs of pilgrims that pass through here on their way to the Sacred Mountain must bring a lot of money into the towns.

At the start we kept above the Ta Tu, but later we crossed the Ya, now a strong-flowing tranquil river, and farther along still at the little town of Süchi ("Joyous Stream"), famous for its silk, we came to the Omei, which has its sources on the lower slopes of the Great Mountain. After this the country was more broken, but everywhere there was the same careful cultivation, and on all sides we heard the plash of falling water and the soft whirr of the great Persian wheels busily at work bringing water to the thirsty land; and occasionally we saw men working with the foot a smaller wheel by which the next higher levels were irrigated.

Chen Chia Ch'ang, a small market-town a few miles east of Omei-hsien, made a charming picture, its walls shining white against the dark background of the mountain as we approached it across the green rice-fields. Entering its broad, crowded street we found a theatrical performance going on in an open hall opposite the temple. While my coolies were drinking tea I joined the crowd in front of the stage, which was raised several feet above the street. The play, which was in honour of the village idol, was beyond my comprehension, but the pantomime of the actors was very good. This sort of thing is dearly liked by the Chinese. The players are usually maintained by the village, and a good deal of the unpopularity of the Christian converts arises, I am told, from their unwillingness to contribute because of the so-called idolatrous character of the performance.

The town of Omei where we spent the night seems to exist chiefly for the sake of the thousands of pilgrims who make a last halt here before they begin the ascent of the mountain. Mindful of the many

Tibetans who pass through here in the spring, I made a raid upon the shops, but in vain; all that I found was two good pieces of Chinese bronze. The owner and I could not agree on a price, so I left him to think it over until I came by again, and then he was away and his wife did not dare unlock his cases, although I offered her what he had asked. The rain poured down, but a crowd gathered to offer sympathy and suggestions, while my men and I argued with her. Would she not fare worse if her husband found she had missed a sale than if she disobeyed orders? All to no purpose, so I went away empty-handed. That evening it rained brass pots, but alas, nothing that I wanted.

Usually in these small places the woman seems a very active member of the establishment, and I am told that a man often wishes to consult his wife before making a large deal. The Chinese woman, perhaps, lacks the charm of the Japanese or Indian, but in spite of her many handicaps she impresses the outsider with her native good sense and forcefulness, and I should expect that even more than the other two she would play a great part in the development of her people when her chance came.

It was again raining when we started the next morning; indeed, it seemed a long time since I had felt really dry, but the grey day harmonized perfectly with the soft English beauty of the country that lies between Omei-hsien and the foot of the mountain, wooded lanes and glens, little brooks rippling between flowery banks, fine stone bridges spanning the swift green Omei, red temples overhung by splendid banyan trees, and over all the dark mysterious mountain, lifting its crown ten thousand feet above our heads. Did ever pilgrim tread a more beautiful path to the Delectable Mountains? And there were so many pilgrims, men and women, all clad in their best, and with the joy of a holiday shining in their faces. There were few children, but some quite old people, and many were women hobbling pluckily along on their tiny feet; the majority, however, were young men, chosen perhaps as the most able to perform the duty for the whole family. They seemed mostly of a comfortable farmer class; the very poor cannot afford the journey; and as for the rich—does wealth ever go on a pilgrimage nowadays? All carried on the back a yellow bag (yellow is Buddha's colour) containing bundles of tapers to burn before the shrines, and in their girdles were strings of cash to pay their way; priests and beggars alike must be appeased.

After an hour or so we left behind the cultivation of the valley, and entered the wild gorge of the Omei, and after this our path led upwards through fine forests of ash and oak and pine. The road grew steeper and steeper, often just a rough staircase of several hundred steps, over which we slipped and scrambled. Rain dripped from the branches, brooks dashed down the mountain-side. We had left behind the great heat of the plain, but within the walls of the forest the air was warm and heavy. But nothing could damp the ardour of the pilgrim horde. A few were in chairs; I had long since jumped out of mine, although as Liu complained, "Why does the Ku Niang hire one if she will not use it?" He dearly loved his ease, but had scruples about riding if I walked, or perhaps his bearers had. Some of the wayfarers, old men and women, were carried pick-a-back on a board seat fastened to the coolie's shoulders. It looked horribly insecure and I much preferred trusting to my own feet, but after all I never saw an accident, while I fell many times coming down the mountain.

The beginnings of Mount Omei's story go back to the days before writing was, and of myth and legend there is a great store, and naturally enough. This marvel of beauty and grandeur rising stark from the plain must have filled the man of the lowlands with awe and fear, and his fancy would readily people these inaccessible heights and gloomy forests with the marvels of primitive imagination. On the north the mountain rises by gentle wooded slopes to a height of nearly ten thousand feet above the plain, while on the south the summit ends in a tremendous precipice almost a mile up and down as though slashed off by the sword of a Titan.

Perhaps in earliest times the Lolos worshipped here, and the mountain still figures in their legends. But Chinese tradition goes back four thousand years when pious hermits made their home on Omei. And there is a story of how the Yellow Emperor, seeking immortality, came to one of them. But Buddha now reigns supreme on Omei; of all the many temples, one only is Taoist. According to the legend, at the very beginning of Buddhist influence in China, P'u-hsien Bodhisattva revealed himself to a wandering official in that wonderful thing known as "Buddha's Glory," and from this time on, Mount Omei became the centre from which the light of Buddhist teaching was spread abroad over the entire country.

The land now belongs to the Church, and there are not many people on the mountain besides the two thousand monks scattered about in the different monasteries which occupy every point where a flat spur or buttress offers a foothold. Each has its objects of interest or veneration, and I believe that to do one's duty by Omei, one must burn offerings before sixty-two shrines. Judging by the determined look on some of the pilgrims' faces, they were bent on making the grand tour in the shortest time possible; in fact, they almost raced up the breakneck staircases. To save expense, some make the whole ascent of one hundred and twenty li from Omei-hsien in a day. Even women on their bound feet sometimes do this, I am told. I would not believe it on any authority had I not seen for myself the tramps these poor crippled creatures often take.

As I was in no hurry, we stopped for the night at Wan-nien Ssu, or the "Monastery of Ten Thousand Years," one of the largest on the mountain and with a recorded history that goes back more than fifteen hundred years. We were made very welcome, for the days have passed when foreigners were turned from the door. Their patronage is eagerly sought and also their contributions. After inspecting our quarters, which opened out of an inner court and were spacious and fairly clean, I started out at once to see the sights of the place, for daylight dies early in these dense woods. Like all the rest Wan-nien Ssu is plainly built of timbers, and cannot compare with the picturesque curly-roofed buildings one sees in the plains below. Indeed, it reminded me of the Tibetan lamasseries about Tachienlu, and it is true that thousands of Tibetans find their way hither each spring, and the hillsides reëcho their mystic spell, "Om mani padme hum," only less often than the Chinese, "Omi to fo."

Behind the building where I was quartered is another, forming part of the same monastery, and within is concealed rather than displayed the treasure of the place, and indeed the most wonderful monument on the mountain, a huge image of P'u-hsien enthroned on the back of a life-size elephant, all admirably cast in bronze. Although dating from the ninth century, the wonderful creation remained unknown to the "outside barbarian" until Baber came this way a generation ago. He speaks of it as probably the "most ancient bronze casting of any great size in existence." It is a sad pity that no one has succeeded in getting a good picture of this notable work, but not merely is it railed about with a stone palisade, but the whole is enclosed in a small building of heavy brick and masonry with walls twelve feet thick, which secure it against wind and rain, but also keep out most of the light.

Wan-nien Ssu boasts another treasure more readily displayed, a so-called tooth of Buddha weighing about eighteen pounds. The simple pilgrims looked on reverently as the priests held it before me, but the latter had a knowing look when I expressed my wonder at the stature of the being who had teeth of such size. Probably they knew as well as I that it was an elephant's molar, but they were not above playing on the credulity of the ignorant folk.

Out of respect for the feelings of the monks I had brought up no fresh meat, and of course there is none to be obtained on the mountain, so I dined rather meagrely. Although the people generally do not hesitate to eat meat when they can get it, the priests hold stiffly to the Buddhist discipline which forbids the taking of life, and it is only unwillingly that they have acquiesced in foreigners' bringing meat into the monastic precincts or even onto the mountain. But at least they did their best to make good any lack by sending in dishes of Chinese sweetmeats, candied seeds, ginger, dried fruits. After dinner one of the younger priests sat for a long time by my brazier, amusing himself with Jack, the like of whom he had never seen before, and asking many simple questions. What was I writing? How did I live? Where would I go when I went away? Where was my husband? — the same questions asked everywhere by the untutored, be it in the mountains of Kentucky or on the sacred heights of Mount Omei.

On leaving the next morning the "Yuan-pu," or "Subscription Book of the Temple," a substantial volume in which one writes one's name and donation, was duly put before me. Being warned beforehand I knew what to give, and I was not to be moved even though my attention was called to much larger sums given by other visitors; but I had also been told of the trick practised here of altering the figures as served their purpose, so I was not moved even by this appeal.

The next day brought us to the summit after a wearying pull up interminable rock staircases as steep as the steepest attic stairs, and hundreds of feet high. Most of the time we were in thick woods, only occasionally coming out into a little clearing, but even when the trees fell away, and there ought to have been a view, nothing was to be seen, for the thick mists shut out all above and below. We passed by innumerable monasteries, most of them looking prosperous and well patronized; they must reap a rich harvest in cash from the countless pilgrims. Everywhere building was going on, indicating hopeful fortunes, or, more likely, recent disaster, for it is the prevailing dampness alone that saves the whole mountainside from being swept by fires, and they are all too frequent as it is.

It is one of the many topsy-turvy things in topsy-turvy China that this prosaic people is so addicted to picturesque and significant terms. I found the names of some of the monasteries quite as interesting as anything else about them. From the "Pinnacle of Contemplation" you ascend to the "Monastery of the White Clouds," stopping to rest in the "Hall of the Tranquil Heart," and passing the "Gate to Heaven" you enter the "Monastery of Everlasting Joy."

Toward the summit the forest dwindled until there was little save scrub pine and oak, a kind of dwarf bamboo, and masses of rhododendron. At last we came out into a large clearing just as the sun burst from the clouds, lighting up the gilded ball that surmounts the monastery where I hoped to find shelter, the Chin Tien, or "Golden Hall of the True

Summit," a group of low timbered buildings, quite without architectural pretensions. Entering the open doorway I faced a large shrine before which worshippers were bending undisturbed by our noisy entrance. Stairs on either hand of the shrine led to a large grassy court surrounded on all four sides by one-story buildings, connected by a broad corridor or verandah, and back of this, steep steps led to a temple perched on the very edge of the great cliff.

A young priest came to meet me and very courteously showed me the guest-rooms, allowing me to choose two in the most retired corner, one for myself and another for the interpreter and cook, while the coolies found comfortable quarters near by. View there was none, for my room, though adorned with real glazed windows, looked out on a steep bank, but at least it had an outside door through which I might come and go at will. The furniture was of the usual sort, only in better condition than ordinarily; heavy beds, chairs, tables, but everything was surprisingly clean and sweet-smelling.

Here in this Buddhist monastery on the lofty summit of China's most sacred mountain I spent three peaceful days, happy in having a part in the simple life about me. Chin Tien is one of the largest and most prosperous of Omei's monasteries, and it is also one of the best conducted. Everything was orderly and quiet. Discipline seemed well maintained, and there was no unseemly begging for contributions as at Wan-nien Ssu. It boasts an abbot and some twenty-five full-fledged monks and acolytes. All day long pilgrims, lay and monastic, were coming and going, and the little bell that is rung to warn the god of the presence of a worshipper tinkled incessantly. Some were monks who had come long distances, perhaps from farthermost Tibet, making the great pilgrimage to "gain merit" for themselves and for their monastery. Many of the houses on Omei gave to these visitors crude maps or plans of the mountain, duly stamped with the monastery seal, as proof that the journey had been made, and on my departure one such, properly sealed with the Chin Tien stamp, was given to me.

One day was like another, and all were peaceful and full of interest. I expect the weather was as good as one could look for at this season of the year; although the mists rolled in early in the forenoon shutting out the plain, yet there was little rain, and the night and dawn were glorious. Each morning I was out before sunrise, and standing on the steps of the upper temple saw the whole western horizon revealed before my enchanted eyes. A hundred miles away stretched the long line of the Tibetan snow-peaks, their tops piercing the sky. It seemed but a step from earth to heaven, and how many turn away from the wonderful sight to take that step. Two strides back and you are standing awestruck on the edge of the stupendous precipice. The fascination of the place is overpowering, whether you gaze straight down into the black depths or whether the mists, rolling up like great waves of foam, woo you gently to certain death. No wonder the place is called "The Rejection of the Body," and that men and women longing to free themselves from the weary Wheel of Life, seek the "Peace of the Great Release" with one wild leap into the abyss below.

At every hour of the day pilgrims were standing at the railed-in edge of the cliff, straining their eyes to see into the uttermost depths below, or looking skywards for a sight of "Buddha's Glory," that strange phenomenon which has never been quite explained; it may be akin to the Spectre of the Brocken, but to the devout Buddhist pilgrim it is the crowning marvel of Mount Omei.

Looking off to the north and east one saw stretched out, nearly ten thousand feet below, the green plains and silver rivers of Szechuan. Southward rose the black peaks and ranges of Lololand, buttressed on the north by the great, table-shaped Wa Shan, second only to Omei in height and sacredness.

Before the first day was past every one had become accustomed to my presence, and I attracted no attention as I came and went. My wants were looked after, and one or the other of the little acolytes spent

THE "REJECTION OF THE BODY"
Cliff a mile high. Mount Omei, West Szechuan

many hours in my room, tending the fire in the brazier, or playing with Jack, or munching the sweetmeats with which I was kept supplied. They were nice little lads and did not bother me, and rarely did any one else disturb my quiet; it was such a comfort after the living in public of the last month.

The second morning of my stay I attended an early service in the lower temple near my room. Some twelve monks took part; one, the abbot, was a large, fine-looking man, and all had rather agreeable faces, quite unlike the brutal, vicious look of the lamas of Tachienlu. There was much that recalled the ritual of the Roman Catholic Church, — processions, genuflexions, chanting, burning of incense, lighting of candles, tinkling of bells, — all centring round a great figure of Sakyamuni. The words I could not understand, but the reverent expression on the monks' faces, their orderly bearing as they circled slowly round, keeping always the bared right shoulder toward the image, made the service very impressive in spite of the pranks of the little acolytes and the loud talk of passing men and women.

In turn I visited the near-by temples, but few were of any special interest. The hilltop has been burnt over several times, the last time within a generation, and all the buildings on the summit are of recent date. The most famous of all, the great bronze temple dating from the fifteenth century, which after being struck by lightning several times was finally destroyed, has never been restored, thus giving the lie to the popular belief that what the lightning destroys the gods will replace. The fragments of castings that are left are really fine, and it is a marvel how they ever were brought from Chengtu where they were made, for many are of great weight. A little below the trail by which we came was the pewter-roofed monastery, very appropriate here, as pewter is the only metal the Buddhist pilgrim is supposed to use or possess.

But after all, the charm of the place lay not in this or that building or relic, but in the beauty of the surroundings and in the peace of spirit that seemed to abide here. No need to cast one's self over the precipice to secure freedom from the body. Here on the high mountain-top among these simple minds, the cares and bothers of the life of the plain seemed to fall off. If I came as a sight-seer I went away in the mood of a pilgrim. Turning my back upon the crowded paths I spent long hours of quiet under the pines on the western slope, facing always toward the mountains. Sometimes the clouds concealed them wholly, at other times just one peak emerged, and then perhaps for a moment the mists rolled away, and the whole snowy line stood revealed like the ramparts of a great city, the city of God.

And the best of all was not the day, but the night.

The monastery went early to bed, and by ten o'clock bells had ceased to ring, the lights were out. Then came my time. Slipping out of my room I stole up the slope to the overhanging brow of the cliff. The wind had died down, the birds were still, not a sound broke the great silence. At my feet were the depths, to the west rose height on height, and on all lay the white light of the moon. Close by hundreds of weary pilgrims were sleeping heavily on their hard beds. Day after day and year after year they climbed these steeps seeking peace and help, pinning their hopes to burning joss stick and tinkling bell and mystic words, and in Western lands were other pilgrims entangled likewise in the mazes of dogma and form. But here among the stars, in the empty, soundless space of the white night, the gods that man has created seemed to vanish, and there stood out clear the hope that when time has ceased, —

> "When whelmed are altar, priest, and creed;
> When all the faiths have passed;
> Perhaps, from darkening incense freed,
> God may emerge at last."

Finally the day came when I was forced to turn away from the miracles of Omei. Our stores were almost gone, and the coolies had burnt their last joss sticks; so I took farewell of the kindly monks of Chin Tien and started down the mountain. The sun shone as we set off, but as we descended, the clouds gathered and the rain fell in torrents. Each steep, straight staircase was a snare to our feet. Sprawling and slithering we made our way down. No one escaped, and the woods resounded with gay cries, "Have a care, Omi to fo! Hold on tight, Omi to fo! Now, go ahead, Omi to fo!" There was no going slowly, you stood still or went with a rush. Women tottering along on crippled feet pointed cheerily at my big shoes. I dare say the difference in size consoled them for all their aches and pains.

It was almost dark when we reached Omei-hsien, soaked to the skin. I had a big fire made for the coolies and we all gathered round in companionable fashion for the last time. The return journey the next day across the plain was as charming as ever, but the steamy heat of the low level was very depressing, and we were all glad to take to a boat for the last twenty-two li.

I had one more day in Chia-ting, visiting one or two temples and making the last arrangements for the trip down the river to Chung-king. Wisely helped by one of the American missionaries I secured a very comfortable wu-pan, for which I paid twenty-five dollars Mexican. It was well fitted out, and equipped with a crew of seven, including the captain's wife, and a small dog known as the "tailless one." We started down the river late in the afternoon. There was just time for one look at the Great

Buddha as the current hurled us almost under his feet, then a last glance at the beautiful town, all rose and green, and a wonderful chapter in my journeying had come to an end. Only three months later and Chia-ting was aflame with the fires of revolution, for it was the first city in all Szechuan to declare for the Republic, and there was many a fierce contest in its narrow, winding streets.

CHAPTER X

DOWN THE YANGTSE

AFTER the toilsome life of the last three months it was good to look forward to ten days or so of laziness, for surely river travel may be the most luxurious of any sort of journeying, and even a humble native boat on the Yangtse affords many delights. You make yourself comfortable with your own bed and chair, stop at your pleasure, go as you choose, without hurry and without noise through charmingly varied scenery, now soft and cultivated, now wild and grand.

My own little apartment occupied the middle of the boat, screened off with mats and curtains from the ends occupied by the boat people and my men, and though it was necessarily a thoroughfare, my privacy was always respected and no one attempted to enter without permission. By an ingenious arrangement of the mat roof I could lie at ease on my camp-bed and watch the shores slip past, but toward evening when the sun was setting, I often sat out on the extreme prow of the boat where I could enjoy the full sweep of the view up and down. Liu, the cook, had provided himself with a little cement cooking arrangement on which he prepared me very savoury messes. He and the Yunnan coolie and the interpreter and the boat people all chummed together very amicably, and I was impressed again, as so many times before, by the essential democracy of China. The interpreter was several pegs above the others, socially, but he showed no objection at going in with them, and more than once, when the inns were crowded, took up his quarters with the coolies, but — he always got well waited upon. Nor was the captain's wife kept in seclusion (it would have been hard, indeed, to get it in a thirty-foot wu-pan), but all day long I could hear her chatting with the men in cheerful give-and-take fashion.

By the way, the name which Europeans give to the river down which I was floating, the Min, is quite unknown to the Chinese, and it may have originated with the Jesuits, the first men from the West to make their home in Szechuan. By the natives the river is sometimes called the "Fu" because of the three "fu" towns on its banks, Chengtu, Chiating, and Suifu, and sometimes they speak of it as the Ta-kiang, regarding it as the upper waters of the Yangtse.

Below Chia-ting the river, by whatever name called, flows through a smiling, open country, with gently varied scenery. The soft slopes on either hand were richly cultivated with maize and rape, and nameless little villages, picturesque with black timbered houses and red temples, peeped out of groves of banyan and bamboo and orange. Then the hills closed in on the river and the current ran like a millrace. Often a promontory was crowned with one of the many-storied white "chuman" pagodas of Szechuan, while in the face of a cliff I could now and then discern openings which I knew were the famous, mysterious cave-dwellings of a bygone time and an unknown people found all about Chia-ting. I visited one that had been converted into a miniature temple, and there are several in one of the mission compounds. I believe they are known only in this region. They have been excavated by an expert hand, showing traces, it is thought, of Indian influence. Much conjecture has been expended upon them, and as yet there is no advance upon Baber's conclusion "that these excavations are of unknown date, and have been undertaken for unexplained purposes, by a people of doubtful identity."

As the river was now high, the current carried us along at a good speed, but I was in no hurry and we made many stops, when I got out to stretch my legs along the bank. At night we always tied up, and it took some effort to secure a place to the liking of us all. I wanted air and quiet, but the desire of my boat people was set on a chance to go a-marketing or to do a little visiting. Sometimes I got what I wished, sometimes they did, but they did their best, I think, to gratify my strange whims.

One night when they had their way and we were tied up to a shingle alongside some forty or fifty junks and small craft, we had all to turn out on a grand hunt for the "tailless one" who had gone astray. As soon as the plank was down, I went ashore followed by the dogs. As it grew dark I sat down on a rock not far away, and Jack curled up by me, but the other one went back to the boat. Presently I saw the men come ashore and walk up and down swinging their paper lanterns and sending out long, loud cries. The little dog was missing, and they were afraid he was being kept concealed on one of the other boats, for, so they said, people liked to steal little dogs. I asked if they thought it would help if I went with them along the beach and they called out that I was looking for the dog. They were sure it would, so we paraded up and down the long line of junks, flashing out our lanterns while the men called, not to the junk people, for "face" must be saved, but to the little dog himself, "O tailless one, come home, O tailless one, come home, the foreign devil is seeking thee." And presently there was a joyful shout from our boat. The "tailless one" had come walking up the gangplank, quietly returned under cover of darkness. The men were immensely pleased, and said it was all due to me; the people were afraid to steal from a foreigner.

Three days after leaving Chia-ting, we came in sight of Suifu, most picturesquely set on a rocky slope at the junction of the Min and the Yangtse. But how changed was the Great River since I crossed it at Lung-kai, four hundred miles to the west. There it dashed furiously along, dammed in between precipitous cliffs and fretted to foam by rocky reefs. Now it flowed broad and deep and quiet between soft wooded banks, bearing many craft on its strong current.

The streets of the prosperous city of Suifu, the starting-point of all overland traffic to Yunnan, are broad and attractive, and there was a great display of fruit and vegetables in the open shops, but it needs much faith in the cleansing power of boiling to overlook the sights of the river front where vegetables and feet are washed side by side, while as to the fruit, that had been gathered green, as is so often the case in China, why I could not learn. Some said the Chinese preferred it so, others that if it were kept on the trees it would be stolen long before it ripened. But to tell the truth, the goodness of Chinese fruit seems to be all on the outside. I never saw finer-looking peaches than in Szechuan, but they proved worm-riddled and tasteless. Apparently all that the Chinese can teach themselves has been learned, in fruit-growing as well as in other things. Now if they are to advance they must begin to borrow, and much else besides money. I was glad to learn that one of the American missionaries at Ya-chou is in close touch with the Department of Agriculture at Washington on a basis of give and take that ought to be to the advantage of both sides.

We covered the distance of nearly two hundred miles between Suifu and Chung-king in good time; the weather was favourable, and the river now ran so high that the troublesome rapids had disappeared. The scenery was charming as ever, but I was wearying of inactivity and it was a relief to see the crenellated walls of Chung-king come in sight. I paid off my boatmen, who had lived up to their agreement (not written this time) in every particular, and in an hour I had ferried across the river and found myself once more being carried over the steep hills that here form the south shore of the Yangtse, to meet a kind welcome from the friends of friends to their charming summer refuge high above the depressing heat of the Yangtse valley.

Chung-king, which has been dubbed the Chicago of West China,— Hankow claims the name in East China,—is one of a trio of cities that cluster around the junction of the Chia-ting and the Yangtse, and it is easily the chief, with a population of close on half a million. The approach from upstream is very striking, a grey city perched on a huge grey reef and enclosed in a strong, crenellated grey wall. The narrow strip of shore outside the walls is filled with poor, rickety buildings easily removed when the river rises or as easily swept away if not taken down in time. Broad, steep flights of steps lead up from the river to the city gates, and over these stairs all the water used by hundreds of thousands is carried in buckets.

In 1895 Chung-king was declared open as a treaty port, and since then its commerce has grown in true modern fashion by leaps and bounds, and there seems no limit to its development, for it is in a position to control the up-country trade. The fleets of junks lie closely packed three deep along the shore, and within the walls the multiplying thousands are even more densely crowded, for the room to expand is set by the limits of the great rock on which Chung-king stands, and apparently every square foot of land within or without the city is already occupied by the living or the dead. Nowhere did I see such crowded streets, and nowhere missionaries living in such cramped quarters as in Chung-king, a confinement all the more unendurable because of the long months of damp heat.

The large foreign community of Chung-king has many elements, missionary, merchant, and officials of the customs, post-office, and consular services. And lying in the river opposite the city are generally English, French, or German gunboats. The relations between all these seem more cordial and helpful than in some treaty ports. So, too, Europeans and Chinese are on an unwontedly friendly footing in Chung-king; perhaps something may be due to the fine standard set in the mercantile community by that pioneer trader, Archibald Little, who boldly established himself here eight years before the town was made a treaty port. And on the Chinese side there seemed readiness to appreciate what the West has to offer; in fact the town has a distinctly go-ahead air. It has already held one commercial exhibition on Western lines, and is planning another, and it is now lighted by electricity, boasting the best plant west of Shanghai, which it sets up against Chengtu's mint and arsenal. There is, in fact, a real Western flavour about the rivalry of the two Szechuan cities, recalling the relations of Chicago and St. Louis.

As a purely trading centre Chung-king lacks some of the interest of the capital, but the merchant class, the backbone of China, is well represented here, and is famed for its intelligence and initiative. Through the kindness of Mr. Warburton Davidson, of the Friends' Mission, I was given a chance to meet members of this class, and also to see something of a very interesting experiment he had recently started. Realizing the importance of making known to this influential element the best that Christian civilization has to offer, but well aware of the difficulty, indeed, the impossibility, of meeting them through the ordinary channels of missionary effort, Mr. Davidson hit upon the idea of starting a social club where men of standing, Christian and non-Christian, European as well as Chinese, might mingle on an equal footing. The plan proved successful from the start. Largely through the interest of a Chinese gentleman of Chung-king an attractive house has been put up and equipped with newspapers, books, games, and the beginnings of a museum, and here in the reading and recreation rooms some of the best business men of the city meet for social intercourse, discussions, and occasionally a lecture on such up-to-date subjects as X-rays, tuberculosis, and, very recently, the American Constitution. It is now open every day and evening except Sunday, and already it is making itself felt in the life of the city.

Mr. Davidson kindly planned for me to visit the Friends' Institute, as the club is called, and to meet some of the Chinese committee by which it is managed, for very wisely things are left as far as possible in the hands of the natives. For two hours or more I had the pleasure of talking with these gentlemen, and I was much impressed with their keen interest in outside matters. All were of a type new to me, quiet, dignified, interested, with the fine manners of the Chinese gentleman, but without the rather lackadaisical superciliousness of some officials, nor was there anything Western about them; they were not copying Europe, but learning how to be a new, fine sort of Chinese. Among those whom I met were Mr. Yang, president of the Institute, and a prominent business man of Chung-king, and Mr. Cheo, the elderly head of the Chinese Imperial Telegraph, who has now been succeeded by another member whom I also met. When I left they all escorted me most courteously to my chair, the passers-by stopping to gape with surprise. So far as I know the club is a new departure in mission work, and most worthy of support as a rational and hopeful method of presenting the best of Christian civilization to a class often repelled by missionary propaganda.

In Chung-king I parted with the faithful coolie who had come with me all the way from Yunnan-fu. As carrier or as cook's helper he had worked well; indeed, on more than one occasion he had cooked my dinner when Liu was under the weather, and he had become so dexterous in waiting on the table that he had grown ambitious and was now looking out for a place in a restaurant. I wrote him a "chit," or letter of recommendation, which I hope served his purpose if he could get any one to read it. At least I made it look as imposing as possible. How would the wheels go round in the East without "chits"? You are called upon to write them for every sort of person and every kind of service or none. On one occasion the recovery of a stolen necklace brought upon my head demands for a whole sheaf of letters, every one concerned, no matter how remotely, wanted one, — hotel proprietor (it was at a hotel that the affair occurred), hotel manager, clerk, servants, chief of police, ordinary policemen. Finally in desperation I offered one to the thief for allowing himself to be caught so promptly. But I think the strangest one I was ever called upon to write was for a tiger-tamer in the employ of an Indian rajah. I protested I knew nothing about such things, but he would not take no, and as he had reduced the big brute that he brought to my bungalow to the point of drinking milk from a china bowl that I put before him, I agreed to recommend him as a trainer of tigers. But for my Yunnan coolie I wrote a good letter most willingly in spite of the fact that he was a confirmed opium-smoker; in all the long journey that he made with me I could not see that it weakened his wits or his muscles. I was told that such journeyings were not at all uncommon, the coolies taking work wherever offered, and going on and on as new jobs turned up. With all its shortcomings the Manchu Government did not make the blunder of imposing artificial restraints upon the movements of the people, and since no passports were required within the empire, men could come and go at their own will. The part of the commercial traveller in creating the American nation has been noted. Who can tell what the Chinese coolie is doing in the same way?

At Chung-king I had to arrange for the trip down the river. I might take passage on the wonderful new steamer plying with some regularity between the city and Ichang; but that went too fast for my liking, besides giving me no chance to go ashore. Or I might engage a houseboat; but at this season of the year the charges were high, as it might be weeks before the return trip could be made, and one hundred taels was the best rate offered. So in spite of the fact that "nobody travelled that way," or perhaps because of it, I, being a nobody, decided to try the humble wu-pan again, and through the efforts of one of the Christian helpers in the Friends' Mission I secured a very comfortable boat to take me and my reduced following to Ichang for twenty-five dollars Mexican. The boat was all that could be desired, and the captain, or "lao-pan," proved skilful and obliging, but unfortunately he was not, as is usually the case, the owner of the boat, and still more unfortunately, one of the owners, a rather old man, was serving with the crew. Nothing happened, but I had at times an uncomfortable feeling that nobody was in authority over any one.

I started down the river at noon on a fine day at the end of June, and a little over forty-eight hours brought us to Kwei-fu at the head of the gorges. For the most part it was a country of soft undulating slopes and comfortable farmhouses, with here and there a little hamlet or a bustling town, framed the last part of the way by strange-looking pyramidal hills. On we went, hurried along by the strong current, stopping for an hour's marketing at Foo-chou at the mouth of the Kung-tan Ho, navigable for one hundred and fifty miles by boats of strange shape known as the "Crooked Sterns," and again at Wan-hsien, famous for its cypress-wood junks, then on past the City of the Cloudy Sun, attractive with broad streets and lovely temples, past the Mountain of the Emperor of Heaven, where for a few cash you may have a pass direct to Paradise, past Precious Stone Castle, a curious rock three hundred feet high standing out boldly from the shore and surmounted by a temple which contains gruesome paintings of the horrors of hell, through the Goddess of Mercy Rapid and the Glorious Dragon Rapid, and several smaller ones that I did not even know were rapids, for with the high water these tend to disappear, while wicked-looking bays of swirling water showed the peculiar danger of the summer, the great whirlpools. The nights were very hot, and all our efforts did not avail to get the air which alone could make sleep possible. Before this the mosquitoes had given little trouble, but now they sang outside my net all night long, while the poor, unprotected boatmen, robbed of their hard-earned sleep, kept up an accompaniment of slapping on the other side of the curtain. The river was falling again, leaving long stretches of mudbank over which I had to clamber if I tried to leave the boat for a little change, but I always managed to go on shore for a while when the men were cooking and eating their supper. They took an interminable time over it, and I never could see why they did not burn us all up, for their cooking was done in the tiny hold in an unprotected brazier. In fact, we did catch fire one day, but of course there was plenty of water at hand.

The third day about noon we tied up for a short time to cook some sort of a meal, and the rain coming on, the captain thought it best to wait. To escape the bad air of the boat, where all the mattings were down, I sat under an umbrella on the bank. A huge junk slowly pulling upstream moored close at hand, and I watched with interest the trackers making fast. They were men of all ages and sizes, but mostly young and well grown. Their naked bodies were well developed and muscular, but often cut or scarred with falling on the rocks. Having made all secure they too got under cover on the junk, and fell to eating, naked and wet as they were. It seemed to me that I sat for hours on that mudbank while the rain fell in torrents and the river rose higher and higher, for the changes in level are extraordinarily rapid. It was almost dark before we could set off again, and then we got no farther than Kwei-fu, the trackers' Paradise. Perhaps that was the reason why we could not start the next morning, but I fancy it was the truth that the water was too high to be safe, for there were double rows of junks moored under the walls of Kwei-fu, and I saw no boats starting down. When the water covers the great rock at the mouth of the Windbox Gorge, two miles down the river, the authorities forbid all passing through. And anyway there was nothing to do but make the best of it.

Kwei-fu is a pleasant-looking town set in maize-fields which grow quite up to the walls. A few years ago it was notorious for its hostility to foreigners. No missionaries were admitted, and when Mrs. Bird Bishop came this way in 1897 she did not attempt to go inside the town. Now all is changed; the China Inland Mission has a station here, and I went about freely. But I did not see much of Kwei-fu, as I preferred to enjoy that Paradise from afar; so we pulled a little way downstream, tying up near some maize-fields in which I promptly got really lost, so tall and thick was the growth.

The next morning dawned clear, and the lao-pan declared we could start, as the water was falling, but he professed unwillingness to take me through the dreaded Hei Shi Tan, or "Black Rock Rapid," near the western end of the first gorge; so I carried two two-carrier chairs for myself and the interpreter, paying one thousand cash for thirty li. At starting, the road made a bend away from the river, passing through a succession of hamlets, the homes of the trackers. Leaving my men at a tea-house I walked on, following a well-made path which led me finally into the White Emperor's Temple, beautifully set on the very edge of an angle of the cliff, affording wonderful views down the gorge. It was clean and light, and the priests who came to greet me in the usual kindly Buddhist fashion had rather nice faces. It was a place to dream away a glorious day. At our feet the rippling water just revealed the dreaded Goose-tail Rock, now almost submerged, but in winter standing like a sentinel forty feet tall at the mouth of the gorge; and over our heads towered, on both sides the narrow waterway, grey vertical cliffs, fifteen hundred to two thousand feet high. I hated to leave, but as I had plainly lost my way there was nothing to do but go back and seek to overtake the men who were pounding along on the right path, trying to come up with me.

It is here that the great Szechuan road begins, a pathway galleried into the solid rock for the whole length of the gorge at about one hundred and fifty feet above the winter level of the river. It is a fine piece of road, the gift, I believe, of a rich Kwei-chou merchant. The surprising thing, of course, is not that it is good — the Chinese have built many good roads — but that it is new. At present it stops at the Szechuan frontier, but there is talk of extending it across Hupeh.

The day and a half that I spent in going through the gorges of the Yangtse were the most exhausting part of my whole trip; from the mere strain of seeing and feeling, one's senses were all the time on the rack. Scenes of overpowering savagery and grandeur that held one spellbound, were relieved by beautiful bits of cultivation, little hamlets of brown houses and red temples half concealed in groves of golden bamboo and the glossy green of orange trees; moments when the boatmen lounged on the deck or hung exhausted over their oars were followed by brief, fierce struggles against the dreadful force of a whirlpool that threatened to engulf us.

But, after all, that which most often comes back to me as I recall those days is the feeling of the ruthless human will grappling with nature and winning the mastery. Who can call China aged and in decay face to face with her success in conquering a passage up these gorges? Who can question the vitality of the Chinese, that has watched the trackers at work pulling a huge junk against a current like the rapids of Niagara, clambering over wet, rough boulders, creeping like cats along a thread of a trail overhanging the

R. J. Davidson.

IN THE YANGTSE GORGES

gulf, clinging to the face of rocks that do not seem to offer a foothold to a mountain goat, and all the time straining with every muscle at a thousand-foot rope. An inhuman task where men take great risks for a pittance, where death by drowning or by being dashed to pieces on the rocks confronts them at every turn, and where, at best, strains and exposure bring an early end. In my dreams I see them, the long lines of naked men, their strong bodies shining with wet and bleeding from many a cut, keeping time in a wild chant as they tug at the taut line; a rope breaks and the toil of hours is lost; one misstep and a life has ended.

But this is the sole highway to Szechuan; all the trade of China's largest province, the one best endowed by nature, must pass up and down here. Any people less prodigal of their strength, less determined and less resourceful than the Chinese, would have given up the struggle before it was begun, and Szechuan would have slumbered undeveloped and forgotten, instead of being as it is now the richest and most advanced part of the empire.

And the next step is assured; before many years have passed, a railway will connect the western capital with Wan-hsien and Hankow, the deserted gorges will no longer reëcho the cries of the trackers, and the upward trip that now takes six weeks will be a matter of two or three days. It will be a different

Szechuan then, with its resources exploited, with mines and factories, good roads and fine hotels, a power in the world's market, the goal of the tourist, and — I am glad I saw Szechuan before the railway came.

CHAPTER XI

FROM THE GREAT RIVER TO THE GREAT WALL

AT Ichang, a thousand miles from Shanghai, I met the West, modern comforts, bad manners, and all. Situated at the eastern end of the gorges, this town of thirty thousand Chinese inhabitants and a handful of Europeans is just where all the merchandise going upstream must be shifted from the light-draft steamers of the lower Yangtse to the native junks of forty to a hundred tons which are still the only freight boats that venture regularly through the rapids and whirlpools of the upper waters of the Great River. So the water front of Ichang is a busy scene at all times, and in the winter season the boats are packed together sardine fashion. When the railway is put through, all the river traffic will cease, but Ichang proposes to control the new route as it has the old, and already an imposing station has been completed, even though only a few miles of iron rail have been laid down.

I shifted my belongings directly from the wu-pan to the Kweilu, a Butterfield & Swire boat leaving the same evening. It was very comfortable, although crowded, as everything seems to be in China. Ichang stands at the extreme eastern edge of the tangle of mountains that stretch across Szechuan to the Tibetan plateau, and just below this point the scenery changes, the hills dwindle, and the valley opens into the wide flat plains of the lower Yangtse. It is a merciful arrangement, allowing the eyes and brain a chance to recover their tone after the strain of trying to take in the wonders of the gorges, and I was glad for the open, vacant land, thankful that there was nothing to look at.

The second morning in the early dawn we moored off Hankow, where I planned to stay a day or two before turning northward. Hankow, Hanyang, Wuchang, these three cities lie at the junction of the Han and the Yangtse, having, all told, a population of some two millions. Located on the Yangtse, at the mouth of the Han, one of the great waterways of China, halfway between Shanghai and Ichang, and a little more than halfway from Peking to Canton, and at present the terminus of the Peking railway, which in good time will be extended to Canton, the future of these cities is assured. Each of the three has some special claim to preëminence, but the greatest of them is Hankow. Hanyang's chimneys are preparing to rival those of Bombay, and it boasts the largest iron-works in China. Wuchang is the provincial capital, and the seat of the viceroy or governor, as it happens, and its mint and arsenal are the most important in the south, while Hankow is the trading centre, and the headquarters of the great banking and shipping concerns.

When I was there in early July of last year I noticed only the look of substantial prosperity about the place, and the comfortable bustle and stir in the streets. Chinese and Europeans alike seemed intent on making money, pound-wise or cash-wise. The one matter of concern was the high water in the river, here nearly a mile wide. Already it was almost up to the top of the "bund"; a few inches more and it would flood the lowland, destroying life and property, and stopping all business. There were no outward signs of commotion underneath, but in about three months the viceroy's yamen was in flames, shops and offices were looted, and the mint and arsenal in the hands of the Revolutionary party. One stroke had put it in possession of a large amount of treasure, military stores, and a commanding position.

I planned to stay in Hankow just long enough to pack a box for England, and efface a few of the scars of inland travel before confronting whatever society might be found in Peking in midsummer, but rather to my dismay I found the weekly express train left the day after my arrival. It was out of the question to take that, and apparently I would have to wait over a week unless I dared try the ordinary train that ran daily, stopping two nights on the road. But there seemed many lions in the way. It would be quite impossible to go by this train unless I could take all my things into the carriage with me; nothing was safe in the luggage van. It would be a long and tedious journey, and I could get nothing to eat on the way, and of course it would be impossible to put up at Chinese inns at night. But face the Eastern lions and they generally turn to kittens. Travelling by way trains had no terrors for me, it would give me a chance to see the country, and it was for that I had come to China, and I knew I could manage about my things; but the Chinese inn was something of a difficulty, as I was leaving interpreter and cook in Hankow. I jumped into a rickshaw and by good luck found the genial superintendent, M. Didier, at the station. *Mais oui*, I might stop in the train at night; *mais oui*, the little dog could be with me; *mais oui*, I could certainly manage a trunk in my compartment. And he did even better than his word, wiring ahead to the nights' stopping-places, Chu-ma-tien and Chang-te-ho, and when the train pulled in at each place, I was charmingly welcomed by the division superintendent with an invitation from his wife to put up with them; and so instead of two nights in the stuffy sleeping-compartment of the express train, I had two enjoyable evenings in French homes, and long nights in a real bed. It was indeed a bit of France that these delightful Frenchwomen had created in the plain of Central China; books and journals, dogs and wines from home, and French dishes skilfully prepared by Chinese hands. But the houses where they lived opened out of the strongly walled station enclosure; it would not take long to put it in condition to stand a siege. No one in China forgets the days of 1900.

The train was of the comfortable corridor sort. Most of the time I was the only European, and the only person in the first class, but the second and especially the third were crowded full, although the passengers did not seem about to flow out of the windows, feet foremost, as so often on an Indian railway. The Chinese is beset by many fears, superstitious fears or real mundane ones, but he has the wit to know a good thing when he sees it, and it does not take him long to overcome any pet fear that stands in the way of possessing it. In 1870 the first Chinese railway was built by the great shipowners of the East, Jardine, Mattheson & Co. It was only twelve miles long, connecting Shanghai with Woosung. At first there was no trouble, then certain native interests, fearing the competition, stirred up the people by the usual methods, finally clinching the opposition by a suicide (hired) under a train; so in the end the Government bought out the English firm and dismantled the railway. That was forty years ago, and to-day all that stands in the way of gridironing China with iron highways is the lack of home capital and the perfectly reasonable fear of foreign loans. The Chinese want railways, and they want to build them themselves, but they have not got the money, and for the moment they prefer to go without rather than put themselves in the power of European capitalists and European governments. And who can blame them?

The Six Power Railway Loan of 1908 proved the undoing of the Manchus, and the inevitable sequence, the appointing of European and American engineers, — to the American was assigned the important section between Ichang and Chengtu, — was bringing matters to a head before I left China. The Changsha outbreak in the early summer was directed against the Government's railway policy, represented for the moment in the newly appointed Director of Communications, the Manchu Tuan Fang, who visited the United States in 1906 as a member of the Imperial Commission. Many will remember the courteous old man, perhaps the most progressive of all the Manchu leaders. I had hoped to meet him in China, but on inquiring his whereabouts when in Shanghai I was told that he had been degraded from his post as Viceroy of Nanking and was living in retirement. A few weeks later the papers were full of his new appointment, extolling his patriotism in accepting an office inferior to the one from which he had been removed. But delays followed, and when the rioting occurred in Changsha he had not yet arrived at headquarters in Hankow. It was said openly that he was afraid. On my way north the train drew up one evening on a siding, and when I asked the reason I was told a special train was going south bearing His Excellency Tuan Fang to his post. He had just come from a conference at Chang-te-ho with Yuan Shih Kai, who was living there in retirement nursing his "gouty leg." If only one could have heard that last talk between the two great supporters of a falling dynasty.

And one went on his way south to take up the impossible task of stemming the tide of revolution, and before four months were past he was dead, struck down and beheaded by his own soldiers in a little Szechuan town, while the other, biding his time, stands to-day at the head of the new Republic of the East.

The Lu-Han railway, as the Peking-Hankow line is called, crosses three provinces, Hupeh, Honan, and Chihli. Save for low hills on the Hupeh frontier, it runs the whole way through a flat, featureless country, cultivated by hand, almost every square foot of it. Seven hundred miles of rice- and millet-fields and vegetable gardens unbroken by wall or hedge; nothing to cast a shadow on the dead level except an occasional walled town or temple grove! And the horrible land was all alive with swarming, toiling, ant-hill humanity. It was a nightmare.

On the second day we reached the Hoang Ho, China's sorrow and the engineer's despair. The much-discussed bridge is two miles long, crossing the river on one hundred and seven spans. As the train moved at snail's pace there was plenty of time to take in the desolate scene, stretches of mudflats alternating with broad channels of swirling, turbid water; and, unlike the Yangtse, gay with all sorts of craft, the strong current of the Yellow River rolled along undisturbed by sweep or screw.

Once across the Hoang Ho and you enter the loess country, dear to the tiller of the soil, but the bane of the traveller, for the dust is often intolerable. But there was little change in scenery until toward noon of the following day, when the faint, broken outlines of hills appeared on the northern horizon. As we were delayed by a little accident it was getting dark when we rumbled along below the great wall of Peking into the noisy station alive with the clamour of rickshaw boys and hotel touts. In fifteen minutes I was in my comfortable quarters at the Hôtel des Wagons Lits, keen for the excitement of the first view of one of the world's great historic capitals.

Peking is set in the middle of the large plain that stretches one hundred miles from the Gulf of Pechihli to the Pass of Nankow. On the north it is flanked by low hills, thus happily excluding all evil influences, but it is open to the good, that always come from the south. So from a Chinese point of view its location is entirely satisfactory, but a European might think it was dangerously near the frontier for the capital city of a great state. Years ago Gordon's advice to the Tsungli Yamen was, "Move your Queen Bee to Nanking." And just now the same thing is being said, only more peremptorily, by some of the Chinese themselves. But for the moment lack of money and fear of Southern influences have carried the day against any military advantage, and the capital remains where it is. Perhaps the outsider may be permitted to say she is glad, for Nanking could never hope to rival the Northern city in charm and interest.

The most wonderful thing in Peking is the wall. That is what first holds your attention, and you never for a moment forget it. There it stands, aloof and remote, dominating the city it was set to defend, but not a part of it. Huge, massive, simple, it has nothing in common with the gaudy, over-ornamented, unrestful buildings of the Chinese, and as you enter its shadow you seem to have passed into a different world.

Often before breakfast I climbed to the top of the wall beyond the Water Gate for a run with Jack before the heat of the day set in. It was a glorious place for a morning walk. The wall is some forty feet high, and along the top runs a broad path enclosed by crenellated parapets. From here your vision ranges north and south and east and west; no smoke, no tall chimneys, no towering, hideous buildings to break and spoil the view.

North you look over the Tartar City, which is really three cities, all walled, and one within the other like the boxes of a puzzle, the Tartar City enclosing the Imperial City, and that in turn the Forbidden City. If you stand under the many-storied tower that surmounts the Chien-Men, you look straight along the road that leads through the vermilion walls, right into the Purple City, the heart of Peking. In Marco Polo's time the middle door of the great portal was never opened save to admit the emperor, and that was still true a few months ago, but last winter a day came when the bars rolled back, and there entered no emperor, no ruler, but the representative of the People's Assembly, and then a placard was posted announcing that hereafter the door was open to every one, for all China belonged to the people. For a matter-of-fact man the Chinese has a very dramatic way of doing things.

Turning southwards from the top of the wall you look beyond the Chinese City, which is nothing but a walled suburb, to the gleaming white walls of the Temple of Heaven, half buried in the trees. There each year the emperor comes to offer sacrifices to his

Underwood & Underwood

TARTAR WALL, PEKING

Underwood & Underwood

CARAVAN OUTSIDE THE TARTAR WALL

ancestors, the crowning expression of China's truest religion, ancestor worship. In a few months only, Prince Ch'un, the Regent, whom you have just met driving in state through the Imperial City, standing among his ministers, and acting for the baby emperor, will take the oath, not to the people of China, nor to any representative assembly, but to the imperial ancestors to accept and obey the new constitutional principles. "I, your descendant, P'u Yi," he will say, "have endeavoured to consummate the constitutional programme, but my policy and my choice of officials have not been wise. Hence the recent troubles. Fearing the fall of the sacred dynasty I accept the advice of the National Assembly, and I vow to uphold the nineteen constitutional articles, and to organize a Parliament. . . . I and my descendants will adhere to it forever. Your Heavenly Spirits will see and understand."

There is unfailing charm and interest in the view over Peking from the top of the wall. Chinese cities are generally attractive, looked down upon from above, because of the many trees, but here the wealth of foliage and blaze of colour are almost bewildering; the graceful outlines of pagoda and temple, the saucy tilt of the roofs, yellow and green, imperial and princely, rising above stretches of soft brown walls, the homes of the people, everything framed in masses of living green; and stretching around it all, like a huge protecting arm, the great grey wall. You sigh with satisfaction; nowhere is there a jarring note; and then — you turn your eyes down to the grounds and buildings of the American Legation at your feet, clean, comfortable, uncompromising, and alien. Near you paces to and fro a soldier, gun on shoulder, his trim figure set off by his well-fitting khaki clothes, unmistakably American, unmistakably foreign, guarding this strip of Peking's great wall, where neither Manchu nor Chinese may set foot. And then your gaze travels along the wall, to where, dimly outlined against the horizon, you discern the empty frames of the wonderful astronomical instruments that were once the glory of Peking, now adorning a Berlin museum, set up for the German holiday-makers to gape at. After all, there are discordant notes in Peking.

Down in the streets there is plenty of life and variety. Mongol and Manchu and Chinese jostle each other in the dust or mud of the broad highways. The swift rickshaws thread their way through the throng with amazing dexterity. Here the escort of a great official clatters by, with jingling swords and flutter of tassels, there a long train of camels fresh from the desert blocks the road. The trim European victoria, in which sits the fair wife of a Western diplomat, fresh as a flower in her summer finery, halts side by side with the heavy Peking cart, its curved matting top framing the gay dress and gayer faces of some Manchu women. And the kaleidoscopic scene moves against a background of shops and houses gay with paint and gilding. The life, the colour, the noise are bewildering; your head begins to swim. And then you look away from it all to the great wall. There it stands, massive, aloof, untouched by the petty life at its foot. And you think of all it has looked upon; what tales of men and their doings it could tell. And you ask the first European you meet, or the last, — it is always the same, — about the place and its history, and he says, "Oh, yes, Peking is full of historical memorials which you must not fail to see"; but they always turn out to be the spots made famous in the siege of the legations. To the average European, Peking's history begins in 1900; you cannot get away from that time, and after a while you tire of it, and you tire, too, of all the bustle and blaze of colour. And you climb again to the top of the wall that seems to belong to another world, and you look off toward the great break in the hills, to Nankow, the Gate of the South. On the other side the road leads straight away to the Mongolian uplands where the winds blow, and to the wide, empty spaces of the desert.

So you turn your back upon Peking, and the railway takes you to Kalgan on the edge of the great plateau. It is only one hundred and twenty-five miles away, but you spend nearly a whole day in the train, for you are climbing all the way. And time does not matter, for it is interesting to see what the Chinese can do in railway building and railway managing, all by themselves. The Kalgan-Peking railway was the first thing of the kind constructed by the Chinese, and the engineer in chief, Chang-Tien-You, did the work so well (he was educated in America, one of the group that came in the early seventies) that he was later put in charge of the railway that was to be built from Canton northwards. It seems to be an honest piece of work; at any rate, the stations had a substantial look.

At the grand mountain gateway of Nankow you pass under the Great Wall, which crosses the road at right angles, and as you slowly steam across the plateau on the outer side, you see it reappearing from time to time like a huge snake winding along the ridges. Old wall, new railway; which will serve China best? One sought to keep the world out, the other should help to create a Chinese nation that will not need to fear the world.

My first impression of Kalgan was of a modern European station, and many lines of rails; my last and most enduring, the kindness of the Western dweller in the East to the stray Westerner of whose doings he probably disapproves. Between these two impressions I had only time to gain a passing glimpse of the town itself. It is a busy, dirty place, enclosed in high walls, and cut in two by the rapid Ta Ho. A huddle of palaces, temples, banks lies concealed behind the mud walls that hem in the narrow lanes, for Kalgan has been for many years an important trading centre, and through here passes the traffic across the Gobi Desert. In the dirty, open square crowded with carts are two or three incongruous Western buildings, for the foreigner and his ways have found the town out. Of the small European community, missionaries of different nationalities and Russians of various callings form the largest groups. The energetic British American Tobacco Company also has its representatives here, who were my most courteous hosts during my two days' stay.

Kalgan stands hard-by the Great Wall; here China and Mongolia meet, and the two races mingle in its streets. Nothing now keeps them in or out, but the barrier of a great gulf is there. Behind you lie the depressing heat and the crowded places of the lowlands. Before you is the untainted air, the emptiness of Mongolia. You have turned your back on the walled-in Chinese world, walled houses, walled towns, walled empire; you look out on the great spaces, the freedom of the desert.

CHAPTER XII

THE MONGOLIAN GRASSLAND

MY stay in Peking was not all pleasure and sight-seeing, for it was necessary to decide there upon the next steps. Within a few weeks I would have to be on the Siberian railway homeward bound. Should I spend the time left me in seeing Shantung, the Sacred Province, with all it had of interest to offer, or should I make a hurried run through the debatable land of Manchuria? One or the other seemed the natural thing to do, but I had an uneasy feeling that either would mean conventional travel, so far as that is possible in China, railways, and maybe hotels. Then Shantung is now a much-visited country, while Manchuria, dominated by Russia and Japan, was hardly likely to offer "an open door" to anything more than the most cut-and-dried guide-book travel.

But Mongolia seemed to afford a way out of my doubts. Post-roads and trade-routes crossed the country from the Great Wall, sooner or later striking the Siberian railway near Lake Baikal. That would set me forward some five days on the overland journey to Moscow, cutting off just so much of railway travel, and as far as I could learn there were no hotels, not even Chinese inns, in Mongolia, so I would not need to fear being too comfortable. But above all, there was the charm in the very word Mongolia. Out of that great, little known plateau, almost as large as all of China proper, had come in days past horde upon horde of savage warriors, the scourge of God, the terror of the West, carrying north and south, from Peking to Budapest, from the Volga to the Hugli, their victorious banners. What was the land that bred such a race? What of the Mongols nowadays? Even a few weeks would tell me something.

Having made up my mind to go, I set about learning the how and the where, with the usual results; much advice asked and unasked of a very contradictory sort. The American Legation with fine courtesy offered no counsel, but gave every possible help, securing for me the proper visés for my passports, even speeding the wheels of the slow-moving Wai-wu-pu so that I might not be delayed. The matter of getting a servant proved rather difficult. One who was proposed declined to go with a lady, for he "would have to be braver than she"; others were daunted by the sound of Mongolia; but finally, through the kind help of Captain Reeves, the American military attaché, I got hold of my invaluable Wang, interpreter, cook, and general factotum in one, and faithfullest of Chinese. Dr. Morrison, the famous *Times* correspondent, gave me much-needed encouragement at just the right moment. He had long hoped to do it himself, he said, and of course I could do it; and speaking of his own recent extended trip the length of Mongolia and Chinese Turkestan, he flung out a remark which was very comforting to my soul: Did I not hate to have people tell me that I could not do a thing, that it was too difficult or too dangerous? If they would only stop with giving you the facts as they knew them, and keep their opinions to themselves. Well, I thought, if people dare to tell Dr. Morrison what he can and cannot do, I must not mind if I am treated in the same way.

But I needed to take that comfort to my heart more than once in those days. A request for some bit of information so often met with no facts, but simply the stern remark that it was not a thing for a woman to do. And when I did get precise statements they could not all be facts, they were so very contradictory. I could go from Kalgan to Urga in eighteen days; I must allow twenty-four or thirty; it usually took thirty days to the railway; I must not expect to do it under forty-five. I must buy ponies to cross from Kalgan; camels were the only thing to use; no camels could be had in summer. Beyond Urga I must hire a droshky; the only way to travel was by steamer; I could never stand a cart; I could never sit so many hours in the saddle. There would be no water; I could not drink it if there were. The weather would be intolerably hot; I must expect snowstorms and sandstorms; there would be heavy rains making going impossible. My transport would give out; my men would desert me; brigands would waylay and rob my caravan.

One gentleman to whom I wrote began his reply by saying that he answered my inquiries "with much pleasure"; and then continued, "Frankly, I do not think the trip from Kalgan to Urga should be taken by a lady alone at any time." Then followed ten good reasons why I should not go, and first and foremost that I should have to leave behind me all inns, and would have to camp out.

That settled it. There was nothing I should be so glad to leave behind as inns, and for months I had been longing to sleep in a tent. So I fell to making my preparations with good heart. But the enemy had not reached the end of his resources (the enemy was usually a well-bred, intelligent European or American with charming manners and the kindest intentions.) An English officer just returned from Mongolia assured me I could never get my dog across, the savage Mongol brutes would tear him in pieces; but I knew my dog and he did not, so I put that aside. The last shot was the hardest to meet: "It will not be worth while." Almost I gave in, but I had reached the pig-headed stage, and I could not, though I wanted to.

And now the crossing of Mongolia is a thing of the past, and I am not prepared to deny anything that any one asserted about the journey, only somehow I managed to slip through between all the dangers and difficulties. I did the trip from wall to railway, not counting the stops I made for my own pleasure, in twenty-eight days; the weather was generally a joy, and I bade my Mongols good-bye in Urga with real regret. I had no troubles, I met with no accidents, and it was worth while — for once.

It is surprising how well one gets on with makeshifts. As Peking is not a treaty port there are few European shops, and it would seem as unsatisfactory a place for making up a camping-outfit as Hong Kong was satisfactory, but with the help of kind friends I managed to get together something that would pass muster. There were the usual stores, but with much more in the way of tinned meat and smoked fish than I took in West China, for there would be no handy fowls along our road across Mongolia, only now and then a sheep; and, as always, I laid in a fair supply of jam. I understand now why England sent tons of jam to the army in South Africa; the fruitiness of it is most refreshing when fresh fruit and vegetables are short. But of all my supplies, nothing proved so comforting as two bottles of lime juice and a tin of so-called grape nuts. The latter mixed with milk helped out the early starts when the fuel was so damp that a fire was out of the question, while the lime juice made drinkable the roiliest and warmest water. The only time when I felt like losing my temper with good Wang was when he smashed the last bottle. I had to gallop off to keep from saying things. By good luck I succeeded in hiring an old American army saddle, and it proved just what I wanted. There is nothing like that sort of saddle for long tours on horseback, easy for rider and beast.

The question of money required careful planning; it always does in out-of-the-way travel; but finally, through the kindness of the officials of the Russo-Asiatic Bank, everything was arranged. I would use little money in crossing the desert, and of course the less I carried the better, but a good sum must be forthcoming when I reached Urga and the railway, so the bank furnished me with drafts on the native banks and their own branches, and I had no difficulty, while from Peking I carried dollars and taels to meet expenses at the start. I felt like Pilgrim freed from his burden, to be quit of carrying a lot of small change, for a dollar's worth of cash is almost twenty pounds in weight.

Fortunately my arrangements were so complete when I arrived in Kalgan that during my two days' wait for letters I had little to do, for my various activities in Peking, combined with the damp heat, had rather done me up, and I was glad to take my ease while my kind young host of the British American Tobacco Company turned the place upside down in his efforts to provide for the comfort of my journey. My saddle was overhauled, a charming saddle-cloth of Mongolian work was supplied, a great package of cigarettes put up to cheer my men on the road, and for me a box of soda water.

One very important thing had been omitted from my stores. I had neglected to bring onions and potatoes from Peking, most desirable supplies in the country for which I was starting, a land where nothing is grown; and neither potatoes nor onions were to be had in Kalgan. Even my host could not help; he was out of them himself. But when I bewailed the omission to resourceful Wang he looked wise and said quietly, "Madam wants potatoes and onions; she shall have potatoes and onions"; and I had, a good bag of each, and such fine ones that a missionary lady, seeing my supplies, asked if she might inquire of my "boy" where he had got them; never had she seen the like in Kalgan. I hope she found out; I did not. Most likely it was one of those back-stair arrangements common in the East, and I hope no Chinese official or Russian merchant had to go short because of it, but I am sure my need was greater than his. They tell a delightful story in Peking of an occasion when a group of young men attached to a certain legation, as student interpreters, wishing to give a dinner party found themselves short of silver, but the servants rose to the situation, and when the night came the dinner table was resplendent with massive silver decorated with the armorial bearings of — another legation.

Just before I left Kalgan my larder was enriched from another and unexpected source. Thanks to the friendly introduction of an American gentleman in Peking, His Excellency, Hou Wei Têh, the Senior Vice-President of the Wai-wu-pu, most courteously sent instructions to Chinese officials along my route, especially at Kalgan and Urga, to give me every assistance. And soon after my arrival in Kalgan three officials of the Bureau of Foreign Affairs made me a formal call, and the next day they came again, followed by a coolie bearing a basket of stores which proved to be of great value before my journey was over. One feels rather shabby at accepting courtesies for which one can make no return. I did my best by writing appreciative letters to all concerned, beginning with His Excellency, the Senior Vice-President. I hope he got the letter, but the next thing I heard of His Excellency was his sudden appearance over the wall of the American Mission Compound at Peking, fleeing before the mutinous soldiers.

On the morning of July 26, I was rumbling over the broken pavements of Kalgan streets in a Peking cart guided by the trusty Mongol of a friend, and escorted by soldiers sent by the Foreign Office. My kit was packed in around me, or I should certainly have whacked my brains out against the sides of the cover. As it was, my hair came down, my hat rolled from side to side, and it was a miracle that anything stayed in the cart. And I did not long, for as soon as we were outside the walls and making our way along the dry bed of the Sha Shin Ho, I jumped out, and for most of that day I either walked or rode the Mongol's pony. A Peking cart may have other and better uses, but as an instrument of torture it is unrivalled. Just as the thing was in Marco Polo's time, so it is to-day. You crawl in on hands and knees, and then painfully screw yourself round, and so sit cross-legged, or with feet outstretched if there is room, your head only escaping the top as you crane your neck to catch the view or to get a bit of fresh air. The driver sitting on the shafts has much the best of it, and more than once I joined him, — very unsuitable, of course.

The main trails that cross Mongolia from Kalgan to Urga are two. One, the longer and better known, tends a little to the west, and is called by various names, the "Mandarin Road" or "Relay" or "Cart Road." Along its course are markets and Mongol settlements, and there are post or relay stations at regular intervals. Hence it is preferred by the Chinese caravan men as well as by the great, or those in a hurry, who use relays. The other, known as the

"Camel Road," turns northward from Kalgan and after a hundred miles takes a northwestward course to Urga. There are no Mongol settlements after you have passed the fringe of villages bordering the Great Wall, and wells are few and far between, but it is one hundred miles shorter than the more western route, and by so much the better for those who go through with the same animals. Much of the way is marked by the telegraph wire that now stretches its many miles across the desert, but it would be rather unwise to trust entirely to this guidance, for at times it leads where only winged things can follow, and above all it never swerves to point out the wells along the way, and missing one you might not reach another for twenty-four hours, or perhaps never. As I was neither hurried nor privileged, I chose this road.

Over one or the other of these trails pass thousands of carts and camel trains each year, carrying north or south tea and cloth and notions and hides and furs, to the value of many millions of taels. But most of Mongolia's exports go on their own feet, ponies or cattle or sheep.

Under the treaties of 1858 and 1860 a post-route between the Russian frontier and Kalgan was established, and in spite of the competing railway through Manchuria, a horse-post still crosses the desert three times a month each way. The Mongols who are employed for the work go through from city to city in seven days, galloping all the way, with frequent changes of horses and, less frequent, of men. And once a month a parcels-post makes its slow way across, guarded by Cossacks.

Just why the Russians persist in this costly and slower method of forwarding mails when the railway would do it in about half the time, I cannot understand. One reason given me was that they might not care to trust their mails to the Japanese, who control the southern section of the Manchurian railway. And in case of trouble between the two powers the Russians might find it convenient to have a connection of their own with China. It seemed to me more like a part of Russia's plan of "peaceful penetration," of extending her influence over Mongolia even to the Great Wall. Kalgan seems already an outpost of Russia, with its groups of Russian merchants, its Russian church, bank, post-office, and consulate, one as much as the other representative of the White Tsar.

Toward the end of the first day from Kalgan we passed under the towers which are all that is left here of the Great Wall, save the pile of stones which marks the line where it stood. Built of mud faced with stone, it has crumbled away, leaving the solid masonry towers standing like giant sentinels to guard the road.

Here I stood face to face with another world. China lay behind me and below, for we had risen some fifteen hundred feet since leaving Kalgan. Before me stretched the great Mongolian plateau. The wind that cooled my face had blown over thousands of miles of prairie and desert. The long lines of stately, shambling camels, the great droves of sheep herded by wild-looking men on sturdy little ponies told of an open country. Each mile led deeper and deeper into the rolling grassland and the barren waste of Gobi, and between me and the next town lay nearly seven hundred miles of treeless plain and barren sand.

For four days we were crossing the grassland, wide stretches of gently undulating country covered with thick rich grass; wave upon wave it rolled like a great ocean up to the ramparts of China. As far as the eye could reach there was nothing but living green untouched by plough or spade, unbroken save where little lines of settlement stretched like clutching fingers into the sea of grass, the menacing advance of the Chinese, the tillers of the soil.

Much of the time I walked; the air of the uplands almost carried me along, and it was joy to feel my feet on real grass once more. Over the open country short cuts were easy to find, and I generally kept in advance of the others. The groups of Mongols hurrying to the town greeted me in friendly fashion; the look of the desert was in their faces, bold, hardy, burnt, and lined by sun and wind and biting cold.

Like and yet unlike the Tibetans I had seen in Tachienlu, they were slighter of build and gayer and more open of expression; they attracted me as the others had repelled me. Scrambling over the grassy slopes, I more than once lost my way, but some Mongol always turned up to put me straight.

Our first stops at noon and at night were at wayside inns built much like a Turkish khan on two or three sides of an enclosure of mud and stones, and furnished with a strong gate. At one, the small private room off a large common hall was given to me and to a neat-looking Chinese woman who apparently was travelling alone and on horseback. Two thirds of the room was taken up by a "kang," or plaster furnace, raised some three feet above the floor, and on this our beds were spread. But that was my last sight of a house for many a day; henceforth there was nothing but tents and "yurts."

Our stop the next night was at a small Mongol settlement of several yurts. One of these was vacated for me. Judging from those I stayed in later, it was unusually large and clean.

Here I was in the unchanging East, if it be anywhere to-day. More than six centuries ago an observant Venetian passed this way, and his brief description of a Mongol abode fits as well now as it did then. "Their huts or tents," says Marco Polo, "are formed of rods covered with felt, and being exactly

A POOR MONGOL FAMILY AND YURT

round and neatly put together, they can gather them into one bundle." But since his description is so brief, it may be supplemented by a more modern traveller, genial Abbé Huc, whose visit dates back only sixty-five years: —

"The Mongol tent, for about three feet from the ground, is cylindrical in form. It then becomes conical, like a pointed hat. The woodwork of the tent is composed below of a trellis-work of crossed bars, which fold up and expand at pleasure. Above these, a circle of poles, fixed in the trellis-work, meets at the top, like the sticks of an umbrella. Over the woodwork is stretched, once or twice, a thick covering of coarse linen, and thus the tent is composed. The door, which is always a folding door, is low and narrow. A beam crosses it at the bottom by way of threshold, so that on entering you have at once to raise your feet and lower your head. Besides the door there is another opening at the top of the tent to let out the smoke. This opening can at any time be closed with a piece of felt, fastened above it in the tent, which can be pulled over it by means of a string, the end of which hangs by the door. The interior is divided into two compartments; that on the left, as you enter, is reserved for the men, and thither the visitors proceed. Any man who should enter on the right side would be considered excessively rude. The right compartment is occupied by the women, and there you find the culinary utensils: large earthen vessels of glazed earth, wherein to keep the store of water; trunks of trees, of different sizes, hollowed into the shape of pails, and destined to contain the preparations of milk, in the various forms which they make it undergo. In the centre of the tent is a large trivet, planted in the earth, and always ready to receive the large iron, bell-shaped cauldron that stands by, ready for use."

And that is just what I found, but the tent covering was always of felt, not linen, and there were often two tents, one for the men and one for the women, instead of a tent with two divisions; and alas, more often than not, the hollow tree trunk was replaced by Standard Oil tins. But as the Mongol lived in Marco Polo's time, and Huc's, so he does still, and so he will continue to live until Chinese colonization or Russian rule forces him to give up his nomadic ways and settle down and cultivate the soil.

Around the yurt gathered women and children, dogs and calves. They were friendly, almost too much so, and the women interested me as much as I did them. All alike were clad in long, shapeless woollen garments that might have been any colour, so grimy were they, but the dirt and rags of their dress only set off the more the splendour of their headgear; a broad bandeau, elaborately fashioned of silver and set with bright stones, turquoise, and coral, encircled the head, and from this hung long chains and pendants falling to the shoulders. This is the woman's dowry, with which she never parts, wearing it apparently day and night. The women themselves, in spite of the dirt, were good-looking; fine eyes, rather good though heavy features, a skin darkened by the sun and wind, gave them the look of peasants of southern Europe. In bearing they were much gayer and more unconstrained than the Chinese.

Mongolia, the land of many names, with a great past and perhaps with a future, but to-day merely a pawn in the world's game, is a great plateau rising some four thousand feet above the sea, the eastern extension of the T'ien-Shan, or "Heavenly Mountains." It stretches east and west nearly two thousand miles, but its north and south width is only about nine hundred. In the central part of the plateau is a huge depression which the Mongol calls Gobi, the "Desert," or Shamo, the "Great Sand," and the Chinese, Han-Hai, or "Rainless Sea." To the north the high land rises and breaks into the wooded hills and mountains of the Altai Range, and there are many streams, most of them finding their way sooner or later into the Amur. To the south the land rolls in great grassy waves up to the foot of the mountain barrier along the Chinese frontier, but the forests have all been swept away, and the few streams quickly lose themselves in the ground. Over most of the seven hundred miles between Kalgan and Urga there are no trees save half a dozen scrub elms, and the only rivers are the Sha Ho, or "Rivers of Sand." But the grassland, after the summer rains have set in, is like the rolling prairies of the West, and even in Gobi there are only about fifty miles quite without vegetation. Elsewhere there is a sparse growth of coarse scrub broken by stretches of rock and sand.

In crossing Gobi one sees here and there a marsh or shallow salt lake, telling of a different climate in a bygone time, but to-day the passing caravan depends on wells of varying depth, and found at irregular intervals, — ten, twenty, even fifty miles apart. They date back beyond the tradition of living men, and each has its name and character. In some the water is never-failing, in others it quickly runs dry. Occasionlly it is slightly brackish, but usually it is clear and cold. Without these wells the three hundred miles of Gobi would impose an almost impassable barrier between North and South Mongolia. As it is, the desert takes its toll from the passing caravan; thirst, hunger, heat, and cold count their victims among the animals by thousands, and the way is marked by their bleaching bones.

This great, featureless, windswept plateau keeps

but a scanty population of less than three millions. On the northern and southern borders a few among the people have adopted the settled ways of the Chinese; but elsewhere they live as their fathers lived before them, their fields the land where the flocks are grazing, their home the spot where the yurts are temporarily set up. Nomads they are, but within definite limits, moving no long distance nor very often. Over them rule their native princes or khans, subject, up to last year, nominally to China; but Chinese interference has mostly been confined to the exaction of a tribute — and a good part of that stuck to the fingers of the princes through whose hands it passed — and to occasional demand for police or military service. The head of the Chinese administration is or was the Amban at Urga, and his duties seemed to consist in looking after the Chinese traders there and keeping a watchful eye on the Living Buddha, the spiritual and maybe now the political head of Mongolia. But in spite of his many rulers, or perhaps because of them, the Mongol seems to know little of the evils or benefits of government. It is far away, it does little for him, but in turn its demands are small.

The Mongol's wealth consists in his herds; horses, cattle, sheep, camels. In our sense he owns no land, but if he digs a well, which, I believe, he rarely does, he has certain rights over it, and his claims to the water and grass near his yurt should be respected.

His friends have to admit that the Mongol is lazy. His chief duty is to keep an eye on his herds, but mostly they take care of themselves. Each drove of horses is in the charge of a stallion which looks sharply after the mares, fighting savagely with any other stallion which attempts to join the herd. I am told that the owner only needs to count his stallions to be sure that all the mares have come home. There is almost nothing of Mongolian manufacture, — just rugs and felt and saddles; and most of the work is done by the women. Nor does the Mongol till the soil; nothing is found growing near his yurt. Unlike the rice-eating people just across the Great Wall, his diet is almost wholly meat, and milk in some form or other, — cheese, curds, koumiss. The tea which he drinks in enormous quantities, so that even my "boy" opened his eyes, is brought by the Chinese traders.

The Mongol has great endurance; days in the saddle are nothing to him, and he sleeps as soundly on his camel as on the ground. Nor does he seem to mind heat or cold. I have seen them wearing sheepskin coats in the blazing summer sun, and at night the men on the march would throw themselves down without a rug or mat under the open sky, and the nights were often cold. If he must, the Mongol can go a long time without eating, but when the chance comes he is a great glutton, bolting enormous quantities of half-cooked meat. Drunkenness, I am told, is a Mongol failing. By preference he gets drunk on whiskey; failing that, on a sort of arrack of soured mare's milk. On the other hand, the opium habit does not seem to have crossed the frontier. Very rarely is a Mongol addicted to that. But they all smoke tobacco, — men, women, and children, — just as they all ride. To appreciate the Mongol you must see him on horseback, — and indeed you rarely see him otherwise, for he does not put foot to ground if he can help it. The Mongol without his pony is only half a Mongol, but with his pony he is as good as two men. It is a fine sight to see him tearing over the plain, loose bridle, easy seat, much like the Western cowboy, but with less sprawl.

The Mongol of to-day is the degenerate son of the conquering warriors of a thousand years ago. Once his name carried terror to the shores of the Midland Sea. Now those who do not like him can say with some truth that he lives the life of an animal, mating rather than marrying, his warlike spirit gone, his home a lair, his chief pleasures gorging and getting drunk; but those who do like him — and they are the ones who know him best — declare he is a good fellow, gay, good-tempered, independent, hospitable.

CHAPTER XIII

ACROSS THE DESERT OF GOBI

TOWARD the end of the third day from Kalgan we were following a blind trail among low, grass-covered hills, all about us beautiful pasture-land dotted over with herds of horses and cattle. A sharp turn in the road revealed a group of yurts like many that we had passed, but two khaki tents a little at one side showed the European, and in a few minutes I found myself among the new friends that so speedily become old friends in the corners of the world.

Here I was to make the real start for my journey across the desert, and by good luck it turned out that one member of the little settlement, a man wise in ways Mongolian, was leaving the next morning for a trip into the heart of Mongolia, and if I went on at once we could journey together for the two or three days that our ways coincided. There was nothing to detain me, fortunately, and by noon the next day I was again on the road.

I looked with some complacency at my compact but wholly adequate little caravan. My luggage, including a capacious Chinese cotton tent, was scientifically stowed away in a small Russian baggage cart, a strong, rough, two-wheeled affair drawn by two ponies, and driven by the Mongol who was to guide me to Urga. My boy bestrode rather gingerly a strong, wiry little Mongol pony, of the "buckskin" sort, gay with Western saddle and red cloth. Wang bravely said he would do his best to ride the pony when I did not care to use him, but he added pathetically that he had never before mounted anything save a donkey. As for me, I sat proudly in an American buggy, a "truly" one, brought from the United States to Tientsin and then overland to Kalgan. It was destined for a Mongol prince in Urga, and I was given the honour of taking it across the desert. There are various ways of crossing Mongolia, in the saddle, by pony, or camel cart; one and all are tiring; the desert takes its toll of the body and the spirit. But here was a new way, and if comfort in Gobi is obtainable it is in an American buggy; and with a pony for change, no wonder I faced the desert without dismay.

The combined caravans looked very imposing as we moved off. All told, we were one Swede, one American, one Chinese, seven Mongols, one Irishman (Jack), and twelve horses. Three of the Mongols were lamas, the rest were laymen, or "black men," so called from their unshorn black hair worn in a queue. They were all dressed much alike, although one of the lamas had clothes of the proper red colour, and all rode their sturdy ponies well, mounted on high-peaked saddles.

After the first day we fell into our regular course, an early start at six o'clock or so, long halt at noon, when tents were set up, and all rested while the horses grazed, and then on again until the sun went down below the horizon. During the hotter hours I took my ease in the buggy, but in the early morning, and at the end of the day I rode. The Mongols were gay young fellows, taking a kindly interest in my doings. One, the wag of the party, was bent on learning to count in English, and each time he came by me he chanted his lesson over, adding number after number until he reached twenty. The last few miles before getting into camp was the time for a good race. Then, riding up with thumbs held high in greeting, they would cry to me "San?" ("All right?") and answering back "San!" I touch my horse and we are off. Oh, the joy of those gallops with the horsemen of the desert! For the moment you are mad. Your nomad ancestors — we all have them — awake in you, and it is touch and go but you turn your back forever on duties and dining, on all the bonds and frills that we have entangled ourselves in — and then you remember, and go sadly to bed.

The weather was delightful; whatever there might be in store for me, the present was perfect. A glori-

JACK AND HIS LAMA FRIEND

MY CARAVAN ACROSS MONGOLIA

ous dawn, no severe heat but for a short time in the middle of the day, which cooled off rapidly in the late afternoon, the short twilight ending in cold, starlit nights. The wonder of those Mongolian nights! My tent was always pitched a little apart from the confusion of the camp, and lying wrapped in rugs in my narrow camp-bed before the doors open to the night wind, I fell asleep in the silence of the limitless space of the desert, and woke only as the stars were fading in the sky.

At first we were still in the grassland; the rolling country was covered with a thick mat of grass dotted with bright flowers, and yurts and men and herds abounded. Happenings along the road were few. The dogs always rushed out from the yurts to greet us. They looked big and savage, and at first, mindful of warnings, I kept close guard over Jack; but he heeded them as little as he had the Chinese curs, and hardly deigned a glance as he trotted gaily along by the horses who had captured his Irish heart. Once we stopped to buy a pony, and secured a fine "calico" one, unusually large and strong. Again a chance offered to get a sheep, not always possible even though thousands are grazing on the prairie, for a Mongol will sell only when he has some immediate use for money. The trade once made, it took only a short time to do the rest, — to kill, to cut up, to boil in a big pot brought for the purpose, to eat.

Two hundred miles from Kalgan we passed the telegraph station of Pongkiong manned by two Chinese. It is nothing but a little wooden building with a bit of a garden. The Chinese has his garden as surely as the Englishman, only he spends his energy in growing things to eat. At long intervals, two hundred miles, these stations are found all the way to Urga and always in the charge of Chinese, serviceable, alien, homesick. It must be a dreary life set down in the desert without neighbours or visitors save the roving Mongol whom the Chinese look down on with lofty contempt. Indeed, they have no use for him save as a bird to be plucked, and plucked the poor nomad is, even to his last feather. It is not the Chinese Government but the Chinese people that oppress the Mongol, making him ready to seek relief anywhere. Playing upon his two great weaknesses, lack of thrift and love of drink, the wandering trader plies the Mongol with whiskey, and then, taking advantage of his befuddled wits, gets him to take a lot of useless things at cut-throat prices — but no bother about paying, that can be settled any time. Only when pay-day comes the debts, grown like a rolling snowball, must be met, and so horses and cattle, the few pitiful heirlooms, are swallowed up, and the Mongol finds himself afoot and out of doors, another enemy of Chinese rule.

Whenever we halted near yurts, the women turned

out to see me, invading my tent, handling my things. They seemed to hold silk in high esteem. My silk blouses were much admired, and when they investigated far enough to discover that I wore silk "knickers," their wonder knew no bounds. In turn they were always keen to show their treasures, especially of course their headdresses, which were sometimes very beautiful, costing fifty, one hundred, or two hundred taels.

A wife comes high in Mongolia, and divorce must be paid for. A man's parents buy him a wife, paying for her a good sum of money which is spent in purchasing her headgear. If a husband is dissatisfied with his bargain he may send his wife home, but she takes her dowry with her. I am told the woman's lot is very hard, and that I can readily believe: it generally is among poor and backward peoples; but she did not appear to me the downtrodden slave she is often described. On the contrary, she appeared as much a man as her husband, smoking, riding astride, managing the camel trains with a dexterity equal to his. Her household cares cannot be very burdensome, no garden to tend, no housecleaning, simple cooking and sewing; but by contrast with the man she is hard-working. Vanity is nowise extinct in the feminine Mongol, and, let all commercial travellers take note, I was frequently asked for soap, and nothing seemed to give so much pleasure as when I doled out a small piece. Perhaps in time even the Mongol will look clean. Asiatics as a rule know little about soap; they clean their clothes by pounding, and themselves by rubbing; but sometimes they put an exaggerated value upon it. A Kashmir woman, seeing herself in a mirror side by side with the fair face of an English friend of mine, sighed, "If I had such good soap as yours I too would be white."

But there is a good deal to be said against washing, at least one's face, when crossing Gobi. The dry, scorching winds burn and blister the skin, and washing makes things worse, and besides you are sometimes short of water; so for a fortnight my face was washed by the rains of heaven (if at all), and my hair certainly looked as though it were combed by the wind, for between the rough riding and the stiff breezes that sweep over the plateau, it was impossible to keep tidy. But, thanks to Wang, I could always maintain a certain air of respectability in putting on each morning freshly polished shoes.

Of wild life I saw little; occasionally we passed a few antelope, and twice we spied wolves not far off. These Mongolian wolves are big and savage, often attacking the herds, and one alone will pull down a good horse or steer. The people wage more or less unsuccessful war upon them and at times they organize a sort of battue. Men, armed with lassoes, are stationed at strategic points, while others, routing the wolves from their lair, drive them within reach. Sand grouse were plentiful, half running, half flying before us as we advanced, and when we were well in the desert we saw eagles in large numbers, and farther north the marmots abounded, in appearance and ways much like prairie dogs.

At first there were herds on every side. I was struck by the number of white and grey ponies, and was told that horses are bred chiefly for the market in China, and this is the Chinese preference. Cattle and sheep are numbered by thousands, but I believe these fine pasture lands could maintain many more. Occasionally we saw camels turned loose for the summer grazing; they are all of the two-humped Bactrian sort, and can endure the most intense winter cold, but the heat of the summer tells upon them severely, and when used in the hot season, it is generally only at night.

From time to time we passed long baggage trains, a hundred or more two-wheeled carts, each drawn by a bullock attached to the tail of the wagon in front. They move at snail's pace, perhaps two miles an hour, and take maybe eight weeks to make the trip across the desert. Once we met the Russian parcels-post, a huge heavily laden cart drawn by a camel and guarded by Cossacks mounted on camels, their uniforms and smart white visored caps looking very comical on the top of their shambling steeds. Most of the caravans were in charge of Chinese, and they thronged about us if a chance offered to inspect the strange trap; especially the light spider wheels aroused their interest. They tried to lift them, measured the rim with thumb and finger, investigated the springs, their alert curiosity showing an intelligence that I missed in the Mongols, to whom we were just a sort of travelling circus, honours being easy between the buggy, and Jack and me.

We were now in the Gobi. The rich green of the grassland had given way to a sparse vegetation of scrub and tufts of coarse grass and weeds, and the poor horses were hard put to get enough, even though they grazed all night. The country, which was more broken and seamed with gullies and rivers of sand, Sha Ho, had taken on a hard, sunbaked, repellent look, brightened only by splendid crimson and blue thistles. The wells were farther apart, and sometimes they were dry, and there were anxious hours when we were not sure of water for ourselves, still less for the horses. One well near a salt lake was rather brackish. This lake is a landmark in the entire region round; it seems to be slowly shrinking, and many caravans camp here to collect the salt, which is taken south. The weather, too, had changed; the days were hotter and dryer, but the nights were cool and refreshing always.

For eleven days we saw no houses but the two

telegraph stations, save once early in the morning when we came without warning upon a lamassery that seemed to start up out of the ground; the open desert hides as well as reveals. It was a group of flat-roofed, whitewashed buildings, one larger than the rest, all wrapped in silence. There was no sign of life as we passed except a red lama who made a bright spot against the white wall, and a camel tethered in a corner, and it looked very solitary and desolate, set down in the middle of the great, empty, dun-coloured plain.

I had now separated from my travelling companions, cheering the friendly Mongols with some of my bountiful supply of cigarettes. As they rode off they gave me the Mongol greeting, "Peace go with you." I should have been glad to have kept on the red lama to Urga, for he had been very helpful in looking after my wants, and had befriended poor Jack, who was quite done up for a while by the hot desert sands; but I let him go well pleased with a little bottle of boracic acid solution for his sore eyes. The Mongols, like so many Eastern peoples, suffer much from inflammation of the eyes, the result of dirt, and even more of the acrid argol smoke filling the yurts so that often I was compelled to take flight. I expect the stern old Jesuit would say of them as he did of the Red Indian, "They pass their lives in smoke, eternity in flames."

For about eight days we were crossing the desert, one day much like another. Sometimes the track was all up and down: we topped a swell of ground only to see before us another exactly like it. Then for many miles together the land was as flat and as smooth as a billiard table, no rocks, no roll; and we chased a never-ending line of telegraph poles over a never-ending waste of sand. Another day we were traversing from dawn till sundown an evil-looking land strewn with boulders and ribs of rock, bleak, desolate, forbidding.

Nowhere were there signs of life, nothing growing, nothing moving. For days together we saw no yurts, and more than one day passed without our meeting any one. Once there appeared suddenly on the white track before us a solitary figure, looking very pitiful in the great plain. When it came near it fell on its face in the sand at our feet, begging for food. It was a Chinese returning home from Urga, walking all the seven hundred miles across the desert to Kalgan. We helped him as best we could, but he was not the only one.

An old red lama, mounted on a camel and bound for Urga, kept near us for two or three days, sleeping at night with my men by the cart, and sometimes taking shelter under my tent at noon, where he sat quietly by the hour smoking my cigarettes. He was a nice old fellow with pleasant ways, nearly choking himself in efforts to make me understand how wonderful I was, travelling all alone, and what splendid sights I should behold in Urga.

And so time passed; tiring, monotonous days, refreshing, glorious nights, and then toward the end of a long, weary afternoon I saw for a moment, faintly outlined in the blank northern horizon, a cloud? a mountain? a rock? I hardly dared trust my eyes, and I looked again and again. Yes, it was a mountain, a mountain of rocks just as I was told it would loom up in front of me for a moment, and then disappear; and it disappeared, and I rejoiced, for at its base the desert ended; beyond lay a land of grass and streams.

We camped that evening just off the trail in a little grassy hollow. In the night rain fell, tapping gently on my tent wall, and for hours there mingled with the sound of the falling rain the dull clang of bells, as a long bullock train crawled along in the dark on its way to Urga.

The next day rose cloudless as before. My landmark could no longer be seen, but I knew it was not far off, "a great rock in a weary land," and already the air was fresher and the country seemed to have put on a tinge of green.

In the afternoon a little cavalcade of wild, picturesque-looking men dashed down upon us in true Mongol style, trailing the lasso poles as they galloped. With a gay greeting they turned their horses about, and kept pace with us while they satisfied their curiosity. This was my first sight of the northern Mongol, who differs little from his brother of the south, save that he is less touched by Chinese influence. In dress he is more picturesque, and the tall, peaked hat generally worn recalled old-time pictures of the invading Mongol hordes.

The great mountain had again come in sight, crouching like a huge beast of prey along the boulder-strewn plain. But where was the famous lamassery that lay at its foot? Threading our way through a wilderness of rock, heaped up in sharp confusion, we came out on a little ridge, and there before us lay Tuerin, — not a house but a village, built in and out among the rocks. It was an extraordinary sight to stumble upon, here on the edge of the uninhabited desert. A little apart from the rest were four large temples crowned with gilt balls and fluttering banners, and leading off from them were neat rows of small white plastered cottages with red timbers, the homes of the two thousand lamas who live here. The whole thing had the look of a seaside camp-meeting resort. A few herds of ponies were grazing near by, but there was no tilled land, and these hundreds of lamas are supported in idleness by contributions extorted from the priest-ridden people. A group of them, rather repulsive-looking men, came out to meet us, or else to keep us off. As it was growing

HORSEMEN OF THE DESERT, NORTH MONGOLIA

late, and we had not yet reached our camping-place, I did not linger long.

We camped that night in the shadow of the mountain. The ground was carpeted with artemisia, which when crushed gave out a pungent odour almost overpowering. Before turning in we received a visit from a Chinese trader who gave us a friendly warning to look out for horse-thieves; he had lost a pony two nights back. Here, then, were the brigands at last! For the next three nights we kept sharp watch, camping far off the road and bringing the ponies in around my tent before we went to sleep. One night, indeed, the two men took turns in sitting up. Fortunately my Chinese boy and the Mongol hit it off well, for the Mongol will not stand bullying, and the Chinese is inclined to lord it over the natives. But Wang was a good soul, anxious to save me bother, and ready to turn his hand to anything, putting up tents, saddling ponies, collecting fuel, willing always to follow the Mongol's lead — save only in the matter of getting up in the morning. Then it was Wang who got us started each day, lighting the fire before he fell upon Tchagan Hou and pulled him out of his sheepskin; but once up, the Mongol took quiet and efficient control.

At Tuerin country and weather changed. There was now abundance of grass, and the ponies could make up for the lean days past. Thousands of cattle and sheep again gladdened our eyes, and the pony herds were a splendid sight; hundreds of beautiful creatures, mostly chestnut or black, were grazing near the trail or galloping free with flowing mane and tail.

We had been warned that the rainy season was setting in early, and for three days we met storm after storm, delaying us for hours, sometimes keeping us in camp a day or more. We stopped for tiffin the first day just in time to escape a drenching, and did not get away again until six o'clock. As some Chinese pony traders had encamped alongside of us, and there were two or three yurts not far away, I did not lack amusement. The Mongolian women camped down in my tent as soon as it was up, making themselves much at home. One was young and rather good-looking, and all wore the striking headdress of North Mongolia. Like that of the south, it was of silver, set with bright stones, but it was even more elaborate in design, and the arrangement of the hair was most extraordinary. Parted from brow to nape of the neck, the two portions were arranged in large plastered structures like ears on either side of the head; these extended out almost to the width of the shoulder, and were kept in place by bars of wood or silver, the two ends of hair being braided and brought forward over the breast. This is the style of head-dressing adopted at marriage and rarely meddled with afterwards. The dress, too, of these northern Mongol women was striking. Over their usual loose, unbelted garment (the Mongol for "woman" means "unbelted one") they wore short coats of blue cotton with red sleeves, and the tops of these were so raised and stiffened that they almost raked the wearer's ears. On their feet they had high leather boots just like their husbands', and if they wore a hat it was of the same tall, peaked sort. The sight of a Mongol woman astride a galloping pony was not a thing to be forgotten; ears of hair flapping, high hat insecurely poised on top, silver ornaments and white teeth flashing.

It was nine o'clock before we camped that night, but we did not get off the next day until afternoon because of the rain, and again it was nine in the evening when we pitched our tent in a charming little dell beautiful with great thistles, blue with the blue of heaven in the lantern light.

The next day I was getting a little desperate, and against Tchagan Hou's advice I decided to try bullying the weather, and when the rain came on again I refused to stop. As a result we were all soaked through, and after getting nearly bogged, all hands of us in a quagmire, I gave it up and we camped on the drenched ground, and there we stayed till the middle of the next day — spending most of our time trying to get dry. The argols were too wet to burn, but we made a little blaze with the wood of my soda-water box. For two days we had tried in vain to buy a sheep, and the men's provisions were running short. If it had not been for the generous gift of the Kalgan Foreign Office, we should have fared badly, but Mongols and Chinese alike seemed to be free from inconvenient prejudices, and my men, whom I called in to share the tent with me, feasted off tins of corned beef, bologna sausage, and smoked herring, washed down by bowls of Pacific Coast canned peaches and plums; and then they smoked; that comfort was always theirs, and if the fire burned at all, it smoked, too, and occasionally a drenched traveller stopped in to be cheered with a handful of cigarettes. And then all curled up in their sheepskins and slept away long hours, and I also slept on my little camp-bed, and outside the rain fell steadily.

But at last a morning broke clear and brilliant; the rain was really over. The ponies looked full and fit after the good rest, and if all went well we should be in Urga before nightfall. We were off at sunrise, and soon we entered a beautiful valley flanked on either hand by respectable hills, their upper slopes clothed with real forests of pine. These were the first trees I had seen, except three dwarfed elms in Gobi, since I left behind the poplars and willows of China. Yurts, herds, men were everywhere. Two Chinese that we met on the road stopped to warn us that the river that flowed below Urga was very high and rising fast, hundreds of carts were waiting until the water went down, and they doubted if we could get across. This was not encouraging, but we pushed on. It was plain that we were nearing the capital, for the scene grew more and more lively. At first I thought it must be a holiday; but, no, it was just the ordinary day's work, but all so picturesque, so full of *élan* and colour, that it was more like a play than real life.

Now a drove of beautiful horses dashed across the road, the herdsmen in full cry after them. Then we passed a train of camels, guided by two women mounted on little ponies. They had tied their babies to the camels' packs, and seemed to have no difficulty in managing their wayward beasts. Here a flock of sheep grazed peacefully in the deep green meadows beside the trail, undisturbed by a group of Mongols galloping townwards, lasso poles in hand, as though charging. Two women in the charge of a yellow lama trotted sedately along, their quaint headdresses flapping as they rode. Then we overtook three camels led by one man on a pony and prodded along by another, actually cantering, — I felt I must hasten, too, — but unhurried, undisturbed, scarcely making room for an official and his gay retinue galloping towards the capital, a bullock caravan from Kalgan in charge of half a dozen blue-coated Celestials moved sedately along, slow, persistent, sure to gain the goal in good time, — that was China all over.

And then the valley opened into a wide plain seamed by many rivers, and there before us, on the high right bank of the Tola and facing Bogda Ola, the Holy Mountain, lay Urga the Sacred, second to Lhasa only in the Buddhist world.

But we were not there yet; between us and our goal flowed the rivers that criss-cross the valley, and the long lines of carts and horses and camels and bullocks crowded on the banks bore out the tale of the Chinese. We push on to the first ford; the river, brimming full, whirls along at a great rate, but a few carts are venturing in, and we venture too. Tchagan leads the way, I follow in the buggy, while the boy on the pony brings up the rear, Jack swimming joyously close by. The first time is great fun, and so is the second, but the third is rather serious, for the river gets deeper and the current swifter each time. The water is now almost up to the floor of the buggy, and the horse can hardly keep his footing. I try to hold him to the ford, cheering him on at the top of my voice, but the current carries us far down before we can make the opposite bank.

Four times we crossed, and then we reached a ford that seemed unfordable. Crowds are waiting, but no one crosses. Now and then some one tries it, only to turn back, and an overturned cart and a drowned horse show the danger. But we decide to risk it, hiring two Mongols, a lama and a "black man," to guide our horses. One, on his own mount, takes the big cart horse by the head; the other, riding my pony, leads the buggy horse. Wang comes in with me and holds Jack. The crowds watch eagerly as we start out; the water splashes our feet. First one horse, then another, floundering badly, almost goes down, the buggy whirls round and comes within an ace of upsetting, the little dog's excited yaps sound above the uproar. Then one mighty lurch and we are up the bank. Four times more we repeat the performance, and at last we find ourselves with only a strip of meadow between us and Mai-ma-chin, the Chinese settlement where we plan to put up. Clattering along the stockaded lane we stop before great wooden gates that open to Tchagan's call, and we are invited in by the Mongol trader who, warned of our coming, stands ready to bid us welcome.

CHAPTER XIV

URGA, THE SACRED CITY

URGA the Sacred City, the home of the Gigin, the Living God, third in the Buddhist hierarchy, is not so much one city as three, all located on a high ridge above the Tola. Each is distinct, separate, entrenched. Arriving from the south, the one you reach first is Mai-ma-chin, the Chinese trading settlement, a tangle of small houses and narrow lanes hemmed in by stockades of wooden slabs and unbarked fir trees. Here are the eight or ten thousand Chinese who control the trade of North Mongolia. Apparently they make a good living, for there is a prosperous bustle about the place, and as you pick your way over the mud and filth of the streets, through open doorways you catch glimpses of courts gay with flowers and gaudily decorated houses such as the well-to-do Chinese build. But for the most part dull blank walls shut you out — or in. The Chinese is an unwelcomed alien in Mongolia, and he knows it.

A strip of waste, treeless land, bare of everything save a group of "chortens," that look like small pagodas, and a few yurts and sheds, separates Mai-ma-chin from the Russian settlement which occupies the highest part of the ridge, dominating everything in a significant way. It centres in the consulate, a large white building surrounded by high walls, but more prominent is the tall red Russo-Asiatic Bank close by. Other buildings are a church and a few houses and shops. The Russian Consulate also is well fortified, with the last contrivances for defence, — walls, ditches, wire entanglements, — and it looks fit to stand a siege.

Before reaching Urga proper, the Mongol or lama city, which lies about three miles farther west, shut off from the others by a branch of the Tola, you pass the headquarters of the Chinese governor, and he, too, has entrenched himself behind strong earthworks. Ta Huren, the "Great Encampment," as the Mongols call Urga, which is not a Mongol word at all, but merely a modification of the Russian "urgo," a camp or palace, is a network of palisaded lanes enclosing, not comfortable houses and offices and banks, as in Mai-ma-chin, but temples and lamasseries. And well within these is the most sacred spot of all, the lamassery where dwells enthroned Bogdo or the Gigin, the Living Buddha ranking after the Dalai Lama and the Tashi Lama only.

To Bogdo the Mongol millions look up as a god; he is the living representative of the divine one; and the city where he lives is the goal of thousands of pilgrims each year. And what do they see? — until late years, just a feeble, untaught child. When the Bogdo dies, his soul is reincarnated in the body of a newly born male child. For a hundred years or more that child has been always Tibetan, not Mongolian; probably the Chinese Government knows why. And the lamas who swarm the sacred encampment, debased representatives of a debased religion, probably could tell, if they would, why, in the past, the child has never lived to be a man. Furthermore, the Russian Consul-General at Urga probably knows the secret of the long life of the present incumbent, who is well past the time that has proved so fatal to his predecessors.

Politics sordid and gruesome are active within the gaily decorated walls of the sacred lamassery. But all that the outsider sees is a weak, debased-looking man whose vices should soon end his days even if he escapes the lamas' villainy. Formerly he amused himself with Western toys, photography, and especially motor-cars. It is true the millions of Mongols look to the Gigin as their divine leader, but after all there are ranks even in divinityship, and when the Dalai Lama, fleeing from Lhasa before the Younghusband expedition in 1904, took refuge here, they promptly forgot the smaller god to worship at the shrine of a first-rate one, and the Gigin's nose was put out of joint, and stayed so until his distinguished guest had

A LAMA BOUND FOR URGA

A MONGOL BELLE, URGA

departed. It was to appease his wounded vanity that a Russian official presented him with a motor-car which had been brought to Urga at vast expenditure of effort and money. When I asked what he could have been expected to do with it, for roads there were none, the answer was that to the divine one with fifteen thousand lamas to do his bidding, anything was possible. A road was, indeed, constructed to the Bogdo's summer retreat, a few miles away, but alas! no chauffeur was supplied with the motor-car, and it would not run of itself. When I passed through Urga last year I was told that the undaunted Bogdo had ordered a second car, fully equipped with chauffeur and all, from America, which was even then at Tientsin, so by now he may be getting stuck in the muddy lanes of the Sacred City, — unless he has put away such childish things to take up the farce of governing Mongolia under Russian guidance.

For more than three hundred years Lamaism has held Mongolia in its grip, checking the development of the country, sapping the vitality and self-respect of the people. More even than every other man you meet is a lama, for it is estimated, by those who know the situation best, that five eighths of the men are lamas, red or yellow, and the evil is on the increase. At least, two generations ago Abbé Huc placed the proportion at one in three. But lamas are not all of one sort. There are those who live in community, permanently attached to some one of the hundreds of lamasseries. They represent probably the abler or more ambitious in the priesthood, and are better versed and more regular in the observances of their order, living a life perhaps not unlike that in Western monasteries in their period of decline. It is this class that rules Mongolia — under Russia. Still another group might be compared to the begging friars when their brief, glorious day was past; they wander about the country, east, west, south, to Lhasa, to Omei Shan, to Peking, with little purpose or plan. As Huc says, "vagabondizing about like birds of passage," finding everywhere food and a tent corner, if not a welcome. They neither teach nor heal, and represent the most worthless though perhaps not the most vicious among the lamas.

A third class, and the largest, has no parallel, I think, in any Western church at any period. These are the lamas who, sent like the others to the lamasseries at an early age, after having received the prescribed training, — taking their "degrees," as Huc calls it, — return to their homes to live the life of the ordinary Mongol, in no wise to be distinguished from the "black man" save by their shorn heads and the red and yellow dress, which they do not always wear. They marry after a fashion, at least they take wives, though without even the ordinary scanty formalities, and probably the tie is as enduring as the "black man's" marriage. In Southwest Mongolia I was told a lama marries just like other people, while in some northern districts he has no right to his wife, and if a "black man" takes her away he has no redress. The Mongol who attended me on the first stages from Kalgan was a lama with wife, children, and home, faithful and hard-working, at least for a Mongol, and a useful member of society.

The question one naturally asks is, Why do these men become lamas; do they do it willingly or under compulsion? Apparently the matter is decided for them by their parents, who send them when boys to some lamassery where they are duly and meagrely trained; but they do not seem to chafe at their condition when they grow up, for the advantages are very real. The parents save in not having to buy wives for their sons, while the lama himself is always sure of support if he goes back to his lamassery, and he is free from all demands by the Government for military service.

It is said that the Chinese Government has encouraged Lamaism with the idea of keeping down the population; in this way it would avert the danger of Mongol invasion. But Lamaism has already done that in another way, by killing the vigour and warlike temper of the people. The memory of Genghis Khan still lives in the land where he was born; tradition holds that the Great Conqueror lies buried on the summit of Bogda Ola, the mountain that towers over Urga, and no one may climb the height lest his sleeping be disturbed. But it is the vicious weakling who holds uncertain sway in the Sacred City, not the spirit of the mighty warrior, that dominates the Mongol of to-day.

Buddhism takes on many forms. On one side you have the gentle, intelligent monk of Burma, and the kindly superstitious bonze of China. But that black travesty of Buddhism, Lamaism, seems to offer no redeeming feature; brutish in Ladakh, vicious and cruel in Tibet, it is debasing and weakening in its effects upon the Mongol, who comes of finer and stronger stock than either Ladakhi or Tibetan. But he sometimes succeeds in being a good fellow in spite of his religion.

The first day of my stay in Urga I devoted to repairing the damages of the journey across the desert. Oh, the luxury of plenty of hot water, of leisure, of privacy. I scrubbed and I mended, but above all I rested. And if I tired of that, there was always plenty to see just outside my door. The house where I was so kindly entertained was the home of a rich Mongol trader, a man of many deeds and few words. It was built around a large courtyard enclosed in a strong stockade some twelve feet high, the buildings forming part of the enclosing wall. On the long side of the court was a roofed-over space where carts and horses and fuel were kept. To the right hand and to the left were kitchen, godowns, servants' quarters, while on the side facing the great entrance gates boldly decorated with the swastika symbol were the family and guest rooms. Along this front was a narrow verandah roofed by the overhanging eaves of the one-story buildings. Most of the windows were of the ordinary Chinese style, — wooden lattices covered with paper, — but a few were glazed. My room was about fourteen feet by ten in size, one half or more of the space being taken up by a platform some three feet high, on which were a large gaudy rug and two or three tiny tables and chests of drawers. The rest of the furnishing was a rough bench and two decorated cabinets. The ceiling of the room was covered with a gaily flowered European paper, and on the walls hung some cheap Chinese kakemonos.

The state rooms, which were next to mine, were evidently held in great esteem, and my hostess displayed them with the reverent pride of a good New England woman showing her parlour. There were three of them, opening one into the other. In each there was the invariable platform covered by rugs, and big Chinese vases stood about on small tables.

The life that went on in the courtyard was simple and rather patriarchal. Servants, children, horses, everything was under the eye of the master, a good-looking, dignified man. I found it rather difficult to distinguish servants and family; everybody seemed to be on a familiar footing. But the joy of the place was a small boy, the son and heir, who played with Jack or sat in my room inspecting my things by the half-hour. According to Western ideas children in the East are not "brought up," and it is true they are abominably spoiled, but at least one's heart is not often wrung by seeing them slapped and beaten.

One of my first rides abroad was to the Russo-Asiatic Bank where I met much courtesy and helpfulness. Thanks to the bank officials in Peking I was expected, and I found a warm welcome, and a house ready prepared for me, which, however, I could not use, as I was already settled where I was. There is a community of about five hundred Russians in Urga, mostly traders and officials, and a fifth as many soldiers protecting them. The look of the Russian quarter takes you across the sea, for many of the houses are of logs set in a grass yard, the whole surrounded by a high board fence, almost a stockade in strength. Far East and Far West have met, and the homes of the Russian pioneer and American frontiersman are much alike.

For many decades Russia has been extending her influence into North Mongolia, patiently and persistently, and now through trade and employment she has the country in her grasp. Almost the only

MY MONGOL HOSTESS

THE MONGOL HOUSE WHERE I STAYED IN URGA

foreign people the Mongol knows are the Russians, and as a rule he seems to get on with them rather well, although a Russian official told me he doubted if there was much to choose between the Chinese and the Russian traders; both fleeced the poor nomad. However, European onlookers, who know Mongolia well, declare that if it came to war between China and Russia, the Mongols would take sides, — and with the Russians.

When I was in Urga there was much talk among the Chinese about the railway that was surely coming, and the Kalgan officials said the same thing. One only wonders that it was not done half a dozen years ago; there are no serious difficulties. Once outside the Great Wall, the rails could be laid down on the top of the ground almost as fast as a man could walk. Only as you approach Urga, north of the desert, would there be much in the way of bridging and embanking. And it would soon pay for itself, for the millions of taels' worth of trade done between North Mongolia and China would easily be doubled if once freed from the handicap of the costly and uncertain journey of to-day. But more important than all else is the political side of the question. The Chinese Government must have known for years that its hold on North Mongolia was insecure; it has pushed forward colonization by the Chinese with much more than its usual vigour, and, given time, that would have settled the matter. But it had no right to count on having time, while a railway across the desert, taking not long to build, would have bound all Mongolia to the empire with bands truly of steel, that even the Russians could not break. And now — is it too late?

The hours were quite too short which I had to spend in Urga, the Urga of the Mongols; the other settlements were merely frontier posts, one Chinese style and the other Russian, new and uninteresting. But Urga, Ta Huren, was another story. To reach it we forded the river, the strong current washing my feet as we rode through. There may be some other way, but that sort of thing is part of the ordinary day's work with the Mongol, and I believe he is rather shy of the one or two bridges the Russians have built.

Ta Huren has a temporary look that suits its name; fire or flood could easily sweep it away. And there is nothing of any architectural interest save two or three temples and lamasseries, and having seen one you have seen all, for there is little of beauty or fine workmanship about them. The broad main street and the open spaces above the river were much more attractive, for there the life of the settlement had gathered, and again you had the impression of a holiday. There was too much leisure, too much jollity, and too much colour for the work-a-day crowd of the West or of China. People came and went, stopped to talk, stopped to stare. No one seemed in a hurry except one or two self-important officials and their white-jacketed retinue. Only in the horse-market was there any real business going on. There the crowd seemed really intent on something, but buying and selling horses is a serious matter the world over, in Kentucky or in Mongolia. Indeed, the whole scene reminded me of nothing so much as "Court Day" in Kentucky, done in colour. But the colour made all the difference. Everywhere there were lamas, of course, — lamas in red dress and red hats, or lamas with blue-black shaven heads set off by yellow or flame-coloured garments. Women came and went on foot or on horseback, alone or in groups, just as much at home in the motley crowd as the men. Some of them were gorgeously attired, and the flashing of their silver headgear was quite dazzling. Now and then I caught sight of one more soberly clad and with a shaven head, a widow, perhaps, or an old woman who had become the family priest to the extent of performing the daily simple observances.

Mingling with the gay, happy-go-lucky throng of Mongols were two alien elements: one, the quiet, purposeful, observant, blue-gowned Chinese, each intent on his business; the other, the blue-eyed Cossacks in white caps and the big, bearded, belted Mujiks, looking tremendously substantial as they lounged heavily along, lazily watching the shifting crowd. I thought of the Afghan Amir Abdur Rahman's comparison of Russia to an elephant, "who examines a spot thoroughly before he places his foot down upon it, and, when once he puts his weight there, there is no going back and no taking another step in a hurry until he has put his whole weight on the first foot and smashed everything that lies under it." But the Chinese are like the tide, coming in noiselessly, gently, filling each hole and crevice, rising unnoticed higher and higher until it covers the land. Will it sweep away the elephant?

CHAPTER XV

NORTH TO THE SIBERIAN RAILWAY

ONE should spend weeks, not days, in Urga, but alas, time pressed and I had to be "moving on." Just how to move on was a question, for the ponies and buggy with which I had crossed Gobi could go no farther. I finally arranged with a Russian trader for a tarantass and baggage cart to take me the two hundred and twenty-five miles to the head of river navigation beyond Kiakhta. Innumerable cigarettes were smoked while the discussion went on in my room, and at times there seemed much more smoke than progress, for the trader knew only his own tongue and Mongolian, but one of the two Russians who were to go with me spoke a very few words of German, so he and I made shift to understand each other. My Mongol host was on hand, looking after my interests, but he could talk with me only through the medium of Tchagan Hou, who spoke a little Chinese, and Wang, who knew even less English.

My spirits were rather low as I said good-bye to my kind hosts one bright morning in August. I was sorry to leave Urga with so much unseen, sorry to see the last of Tchagan Hou, who had piloted me so skilfully across the desert — blessings on his good face! I hope luck is with him wherever he is — and I was sorry to part with my Chinese tent, my home for weeks, and with my little camp-bed, on which I had slept so many dreamless nights. A few days and nights in a tarantass were all that now lay between me and the uninteresting comforts of Western hotels and trains.

With great inward objection I climbed into the tarantass, like nothing so much as a huge cradle on wheels, drawn by three horses, one, the largest, trotting between the shafts, and the other two galloping on either side. At the very outset I had a chance to realize the difference between dealing with the Asiatic pure and simple, and the Asiatic disguised as a European. We had been told that it would be necessary to make an early start to cover the first day's stage before dark. I was on hand, and so was Wang, but it was afternoon before we were finally off. Luggage had to be packed and repacked, wheels greased, harness mended, many things done that ought to have been attended to the day before. Now of course that happens in China, — though nowhere else in my journeyings did I encounter such dawdling and shiftlessness, — but there at least you may relieve your feelings by storming a bit and stirring things up; these people, however, looked like Western men, and one simply could not do it.

So I kicked my heels for hours in the Russian merchant's lumberyard, drinking innumerable cups of tea and refusing as many more, and getting light on several things. I had been told that the Russians have little of the Anglo-Saxon's race pride, but I did not suppose they ignored all other distinctions. I was drinking a last glass of tea with the merchant in his pleasant little sitting-room, attractive with many blossoming plants, when Wang came in to collect my things. He was at once boisterously urged to draw up to the table between us. He refused, but the Russian insisted, trying to force him down into a chair. I watched without saying anything as my boy quietly took a glass of tea and a chair and withdrew to the other side of the room. He understood what was suitable better than the Russian.

Passing out of the little Russian trading settlement, like nothing so much as a thriving, hideous Western village, we drove through the main street of the Mongolian quarter, where all the life of Lama-town seemed to have drifted, for the gaiety and colour were intoxicating. Half an hour took us away from the river and into the hills. The track was rough and boggy and often blocked by interminable trains of bullock carts laden with logs or dressed lumber, Urga's important exports. Toward the end of the day the way became steeper and wilder, ascending between slopes well wooded with spruce and pine and larch and birch. It was a joy to be in a real forest again. The flowers that grew in great profusion were more beautiful than any I had seen before in North Mongolia, especially the wonderful masses of wild larkspur of a blue so intense that it dazzled the eyes.

A storm was gathering and we pushed on as fast as we could; but the road was too rough for speed and we were a long way from our camping-place when a tremendous downpour burst upon us, and in the twinkling of an eye our path was a rushing mountain torrent. Dry under my tarpaulin I could enjoy the scene, splendid masses of blue-black clouds shot with vivid flashes of lightning that served only to show the badness of the way and the emptiness of the country. I will say for Ivan, the tarantass driver, that he knew his business and kept the horses on their feet and in the road better than most men could have done.

We drove on until nine, when the driver declared he could go no farther, and proceeded to make camp by the roadside, not far from a couple of yurts. A light shone out, and there was the sound of angry voices and wrangling, but I could not find out what was the matter. Nicolai's German always gave out, as the Indian babu said his presence of mind did, "in the nick of time." Finally, the Russians sulkily turned their horses loose and set up the little shelter tent where the three men were to sleep. Apparently there was no fuel to be had, and we all went supperless to bed.

My first night in a tarantass was very comfortable. The body of the cart, made soft with rugs and sheepskins, was long enough for me to stretch out at full length if I lay cornerwise, and the hood protected me against rain and wind. When I waked in the morning the whole land was drenched, but the sun shone brilliantly. I started out on my own account to get a a little dry fuel from the Mongols, but was rather brusquely repulsed. And I now found out what was the matter. The people had objected the night before to our camping near the yurts, for it was their hayfield, theirs by the custom which forbids encroaching on the land near a settlement, but the Russians had persisted, and now, in their helpless anger, — they were an aged lama and an old woman, — they refused to sell us wood. They stood aloof looking ruefully at their trampled meadow as we made ready to start, hardly brightening up at all when I tried to make good their loss. An Englishman or an American would scarcely have asked my boy to sit at table with us, but on the other hand he would have spared the Mongol's poor little hayfield.

The experience of the first day was repeated all the following days; a late start in the morning, tedious halts at noon, getting into camp long after dark. Indeed, I do not know when we should have been off in the morning had it not been for Wang. He it was who roused the men, and did his best to get a fire started, collecting fuel for the whole camp. Although it rained every day, I do not think it ever occurred to the Russians to avail themselves of a chance to get dry wood against the next meal, and Wang remarked sadly that the Russians spent even more time than the Mongols in drinking tea.

After the first day we left behind the wooded hills and were again in rolling grassland like South Mongolia, but there was much more water; indeed, the streams and bogs often forced us to make long détours, and finally we came to a deep, strong-flowing river that could not be forded; but there was a ferry-boat made of four huge, hollowed logs securely lashed together and covered with a loose, rough flooring. The horses were taken out and made to swim across, while the Mongol ferrymen, all lamas and big fellows, went back and forth, taking us and the carts over.

The second morning we started again without our breakfasts, — there was no dry wood. Ivan, the tarantass driver, and the only one of the party who knew the road, cheered us with the prospect of something hot at a Russian colonist's house an hour farther on, but it was four hours' hard driving before we reached the place, which then, however, more than made good all he had claimed for it.

The two families that formed the little settlement

were engaged in cattle raising, and seemed prosperous and contented. Their houses and sheds were built of timber and mud, and looked substantial and well suited to stand the cold and winds of North Mongolia. We were given a hearty welcome and taken at once into a large whitewashed room, kitchen, living-room, and bedroom in one. Everything was spotlessly clean ; even under the bed there was no dust. I can testify to that, for I pursued Jack there. The mistress of the house was a very good-looking, dark-browed woman in a neat red gown with a red kerchief tied over her head. She promptly served us with delicious tea from the invariable samovar, and the freshest of eggs and good black bread, while a chicken, for me to take away, was set roasting on a spit before the fire. Two little tow-headed boys, put out of the way on the bed, stared stolidly at us as they munched raw parsnips, and a baby cradled in a basket suspended by a rope from the ceiling was kept swinging by a touch from the mother as she went to and fro. The people seemed to be on friendly terms with their Mongol neighbours, two or three of whom came in while I was there, but it must be a lonely life, a day's ride away from the nearest Russian family. When I asked Nicolai what the children did for school, he laughed scornfully. "Why should they learn to read? Their father and mother cannot."

Such homes as these are Russia's advance posts in Mongolia, but given a fair field and she would stand no chance, for the Chinese colonists must outnumber the others a hundred to one. From this time on we saw more and more signs of cultivation, the pasture land was broken by great fields of rye and barley, and the yurts of the Mongol were often replaced by Chinese houses, looking on the outside much like the one just described, save that the window openings were filled with paper instead of glass.

Board signs, not unlike "Keep off the grass" ones of the West, were set up here and there, showing a Chinese holding. With or without government aid the Chinese are coming in. They get land from the Mongols very much, I imagine, as did the first English settlers in America, buying for a song what the owner does not know he is selling. And once established they are not easily dislodged, for they are good farmers, thrifty and untiring. In the end they will oust the Mongol from the best lands as sure as fate, unless Russia first ousts them, as apparently she is doing. I am sorry for the Mongol; he is a happy-go-lucky, likeable fellow, but it is all nonsense for the Russian Government to talk about the way the Chinese settlers are wronging him, taking away the tillable lands. He does not want them to till, but to pasture his herds, and that is just the difficulty. It is not China but civilization that is driving the Mongol to the wall, just as the Red Indian was driven. Nowadays the people that will not make the best use of the land must give it up to those who will.

The next day promised to be a long, hard one, and proved even harder than I had expected. First the little dog was run over by my own baggage cart. I thought surely he was dead, and then I feared the first use of the revolver I had brought from America would be to end his gay little life. The Russians shook their heads dolefully and gave no help, but Wang lent a hand with his cheerful "all right," and in twenty-four hours Jack was able to bark at the horses, even though he was too much bunged up to stand.

My other trouble was the behaviour of the man Ivan. He was in fact a thoroughly bad sort, lazy, stupid, sullen, and brutal to his horses. He was supposed to take orders from the other Russian, but he refused to obey him or any one. Only when by signs I could make clear what I wanted could I do anything with him; then I could sometimes put enough peremptoriness in my voice to bring him to heel. Added to the natural bad temper of the man he was drinking constantly, and was quite beyond control.

The country where we now were was a succession of beautiful valleys watered by many streams and enclosed by barren, treeless hills, — a rich, uninteresting district. We stopped for tiffin by a broad stream bordered by willows. The grass was good, but the flies were so maddening that the poor ponies hardly grazed at all. Hot as it was, I thought they were better off moving than in this pestilential spot, but it was impossible to get Ivan started. For hours he slept and drank, while the horses twitched their skins and switched their tails and stamped their feet, and between times tried to snatch a bite. Poor-looking women and boys from some yurts crept over to our camp, and sought eagerly through the grass for any finds in the way of tins or bottles. They were quite the most miserable natives that I saw on my trip. As for me, I sat on the ground, comforting Jack and longing for a Chinese or a Mongol or anything that had learned to obey.

Finally at half-past five the driver roused from his drunken doze and we started off again. On and on we go, over a tedious, uninteresting stretch; the sun goes down, the twilight deepens into night, and the stars come out. At half-past eight I ask how much longer we must drive, and am told two hours. At half-past eleven I try to make the man understand he must stop, but he pays no attention. And it is one o'clock when I see the river in front of us, glimmering in the misty moonlight. In a minute we are in the water; two steps more and the swift current is up to the horses' sides, and the tarantass begins to turn over. Ivan, now thoroughly awake, jumps out, the other

Russian helps, and with much pushing and floundering the horses manage to struggle back to shore. This is plainly no ford, and as there is no help in sight we camp on the bank for the rest of the night, no grass for the horses, nothing to make a fire. After a bite of black bread and a tea-cup of the Foreign Office Bordeaux, I curl up in the tarantass, shivering with damp river cold, and Wang, rolled up in his sheepskin, sleeps on the ground underneath. As for the Russians, I commit them cheerfully to all the joys of rheumatism.

For once every one is up at dawn. A passing lama directs us to a ferry down the river, where we cross by means of a flat-bottomed boat worked by an iron cable. On the other side the men start a fire and we get some hot tea. Again I am struck by the familiar way in which the Russians hobnob with the Mongols. Anglo-Saxons of their class would not do it. I wonder if the "hail-fellow-well-met" treatment offsets the injustice and rough handling the natives often get from their northern neighbours, and if on the whole they like it better than the Anglo-Saxon's fairness when coupled with his reserve. A distinguished Indian, not a reformer, once said to me, "My countrymen prefer sympathy to justice." Perhaps that is true of other Asiatics also.

For three or four hours after starting off again we traversed much the same sort of country as the day before, crossing fertile valleys, climbing rough hill-sides to avoid bogs. There were not many signs of cultivation, but along the horizon we could see the dark line of a forest, a welcome change. Just before reaching it we turned off across the plain to the yurts of the helpful lama of the morning. We were expected and given a warm welcome in more senses than one, for the yurt into which I was at once taken was so hot that I thought I should faint. How those people in their woollen clothes could endure the heat was a mystery.

The lama, a well-appearing, elderly man, seemed completely fitted out with wife and children and yurts and herds. He was plainly a person of substance, and the head of quite a settlement. The yurt where I was received was very spacious, and was furnished precisely as Huc described sixty years ago. There was one novelty, a stove-pipe connected with a sort of cement stove, but perhaps this was merely for ornament, as my dinner was cooked in a pot placed upon a tripod over a fire of wood and argols. I was given the seat of honour, a sort of divan, and milk was placed on a small, low table before me. But I at once espied something more interesting than food. Round the walls of the yurt were ranged one or two tables and chests of drawers. On one were some books, detached leaves in leather covers with clasps. These were the lama's sacred books. Very stupidly,

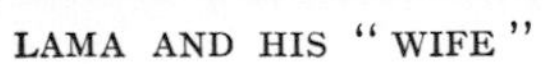

LAMA AND HIS "WIFE"

for I had been told that no secular hand may touch them, I started to pick one up, but the man courteously but very firmly waved me back; hardly would he allow me to look at them from a distance. He assured me he could read them, but that is not true of most lamas. A little altar set out with small images and pictures of Buddha, and among them a cheap photograph of the Gigin of Urga, did not seem half so sacred, for the lama displayed them freely, even allowing me to inspect the dozen or so small metal pots containing oil and other offerings which were ranged in front of the images.

When our food was ready, the lama carried off the Russians to eat in the men's tent; that is the rule, but the neighbours, men and women, who had flocked in, stayed to watch me. Various strange dishes were put before me; best of all, some hard curds decorated with lumps of sugar. Sugar is a great delicacy with the Mongols.

As we were nearing the land of hotels, I emptied my tiffin basket here, making my hosts and their friends happy with tins of jam and marmalade and sardines and beef extract, not to mention enamelled cups and plates and stew-pans. Everything was eagerly taken, even empty jars and bottles, and they seemed as pleased as children with a new toy.

The country changed abruptly after leaving the last Mongol settlement. Houses of Russian colonists occurred frequently, and presently we entered the remnants of a fine pine forest, and from this time on there was no lack of trees. We were now almost at the Russian frontier, and I was becoming uneasy about the fate of my little revolver. It had already undergone various vicissitudes; discovered by the customs officials at Constantinople, they had threatened to fine me for violating the law about bringing in firearms, but finally decided to remit the fine but confiscate the weapon. When remonstrated with on the ground that I was a lady going to Asiatic Turkey and might need it, they made matters straight by returning the revolver, but kept the ammunition. I had paid duty on the thing in Bombay, I had spent hours fitting it with cartridges in Shanghai, many miles it had been carried, kept handy in case of need, although I could not imagine what the need could be, and now I was assured it would be seized and I would be fined if I tried to take it over the Russian frontier. No firearms of any sort may be brought into the empire without a permit procured beforehand. No, the Russians should not have my little revolver. We passed a small pond; one toss and it was gone.

The sun was setting as looking across the valley I caught the white gleam of the great church in Kiakhta, but it was after eleven when we rumbled through Mai-ma-chin, the frontier post of China, and crossing the Russian boundary unchallenged, drove quietly down the long main street of the town. I was too sleepy to notice anything, until I heard the men chuckling softly, and I waked up to find that we were past the custom house. "It would be too bad to disturb the sleepy sentinels, so we took off the bells," they explain. I imagine they had added to their other misdeeds by doing a bit of smuggling.

It seemed to me that we drove for hours through the dark, echoing streets of Kiakhta, but at last we stopped before the white wall of a long, low building, and in a moment I was in another world. Behind me were the wide, open plains of Mongolia and the starlit nights in tent or tarantass. Here was Russia, half Europe, half Asia, and wholly uninteresting. But at least there was a good bed awaiting me, and the most wonderful little supper ever served at midnight on short notice, delicious tea, good bread and butter, and the most toothsome small birds, served hot on toast in a casserole. Where in a Western frontier town could one find the like?

But it was not until I waked the next morning that I realized how very Western Kiakhta is: humble log houses side by side with pretentious stuccoed buildings, rickety wooden sidewalks or none at all, streets ankle-deep in dust one day, a bog the next; but the handful of fine residences, and above all the great white church costing fabulous sums in decorations, tell of Kiakhta's great commercial past, a history that goes back two hundred years, when Gobi was alive with the long lines of camel caravans coming and going between the Great Wall and the Russian border. Those were the days when the great tea merchants of Kiakhta heaped up huge fortunes, to squander them in ways common to the suddenly rich all over the world. But with the building of the railway, trade turned aside, and to-day the town bears the marks of decaying fortunes. The storehouses are half empty, many of the great merchant families have gone away or are ruined, and were it not for the regiments stationed at this frontier post, Kiakhta would be wrapped in the silence of the desert. It remains to be seen what will be the effect of the railway Russia proposes to build between Verchneudinsk and Urga. It may give new life to the town, but of course it is military and political in its purpose rather than commercial. During my four days' trip from Urga there was very little traffic coming or going, and unless Mongolia's resources prove unexpectedly rich, the days of Kiakhta's prosperity are gone beyond recall.

But I did not stop long to investigate either the past or the present interest of Kiakhta, for by the next afternoon I was off again, finally ending my tarantass journey some eighteen miles north of the town, in a great lumberyard on the right bank of the Iro, the starting-point of the steamer to Verchneudinsk. There, together with some scores of people, mostly Russian officers and their families, I kicked my heels among the lumber for ten hours, waiting for the belated boat. It rained most of the time, and the two tiny waiting-rooms were crowded to overflowing with people and luggage; there was no restaurant, and I should have starved had not good Wang made friends with some Chinese workmen and got me some eggs. Finally we were told the boat would not come till morning, so each person tried to find a corner and go to sleep. I had just curled up comfortably, at one end of a great, unfinished shed where the horses had been put out of the rain, when a cry sounded through the dark that the boat was coming. By one o'clock we were off. Everything was in confusion and every one was cross. I had secured a cabin beforehand, and then found I was expected to share it with a young Russian officer going home on leave. I quite regretted my airy, quiet corner in the open shed.

All the next day we were steaming in leisurely fashion down the Iro, making long stops at little hamlets in the forest, where all the inhabitants of the half-dozen log houses clustered round the invariable white church with green domes turned out to meet us, often bringing bottles of delicious milk to sell. They were mostly of the peasant type, large, fair, and stolid-looking. The scenery along the river was dull and monotonous, low, heavily wooded banks, broken now and then by a little clearing. It was a sodden, unkempt, featureless country, and I found myself longing for the journey's end.

On the boat the third-class passengers were mostly Russian peasants and a few Chinese, with a little group of frightened-looking Mongols. I fancy they wished themselves back in the desert; I know I did. In the first and second class there were almost none but military people, the men all in full uniform of bewildering variety. Most of them were tall and large, but rather rough in manner. I imagine one does not find the pick of the Russian army on the frontier.

We reached Verchneudinsk well after dark, and a queer little tumble-down phaeton took us to the inn chosen because of its German-speaking landlord. Here I spent two days waiting for the Moscow Express. After I had started my invaluable Wang off on his journey back to Peking by way of Harbin and Mukden, I had nothing to do but rest and enjoy the charming courtesies of the officials of the Russo-Asiatic Bank. Verchneudinsk has little of interest, however; it is just a big, new town, raw and unfinished, half logs and half stucco, with streets that are mostly bog, and several pretentious public buildings and an ugly triumphal arch marking the visit of the Tsar a few years ago. Civilization has some compensations, but half-civilization is not attractive; and it was a happy moment when I found myself with Jack in my own little compartment on the Moscow Express, westward and homeward bound.

CHAPTER XVI

A FEW FIRST IMPRESSIONS OF CHINA

IT is rather presumptuous for the strolling Westerner who can count only months in China to have any impressions at all of anything so huge, so old, so varied, so complicated as China and its people, and still more inexcusable to put these impressions before the world. And yet it may be possible to find some sort of an excuse if one is bent on doing it.

We live to-day in a time of surprises. Turkey is reforming, China waking up, the self-satisfied complacency of the white race has received a shock, and more are feared. Most of us of the West are anxious to get over the wall, or look around it, — we are told it is there, — and see what that other man is really like. We read books written by those who have spent years in China, in Japan, in India, and we realize that they know thoroughly this or that corner of the whole. We talk with the man who has lived his life among the people of the East, and we feel that he has plumbed them to the core — along one line. He has preached to them, he has healed them, he has traded with them, and he knows them as the doctor or the trader knows his community. The men and women of the West who have spent their lives in the East have usually gone there with definite purpose and compelling duties. They rarely see more than one part of the whole country, their work holds them fast, and they are prone to see it from the point of view of the interest that took them there. Out of these chapters of intimate knowledge can be put together a great exhaustive study of the whole, but no one has done that yet; the time has not come, perhaps.

Now the traveller with no preoccupying purpose, and fresh from a bird's eye view of large sections of the country, is likely to talk a good deal of nonsense, and yet he may tell some things of interest that the old resident has ceased to see from very familiarity. If you mention them, he says, "of course," but to those at home they are not "of course," and sometimes they are worth telling.

My first and my most lasting impression of the Chinese was how very like they are to us. I had been told it was a mistake to approach China from the east: you touched twelve at once. Nowhere would you find another country and people so strange, so different from anything before imagined. Rather you should approach China from the west, then with each stage as you travelled eastward stranger and ever stranger worlds would open before you. That is what

I did; it just happened so. India was already somewhat known to me, and on this trip I stopped there only a few weeks, seeing each day more that was difficult to understand, and then I went on to China, and to my great surprise felt myself almost at home.

Of course at first sight most things were queer, that is to say, different from what they are in the West. The men wore their hair braided down their backs, and the women dressed in trousers, and both mourned in white. The seat of honour was on the left, not on the right, and when people greeted you they shook hands with themselves. All that one is prepared for, but being prepared does not take away from the impression of queerness. But even from the beginning, and the feeling grew stronger as the days lengthened into weeks and the weeks into months, underneath this surface difference the Chinese seemed to me more like ourselves, or maybe our ancestors, more like us at one stage or another, than any other people of the East that I had known.

In India, as every one knows, religion dominates the life of the people. A man is first of all a follower of a certain creed, a Hindu or a Moslem, and the observances of that creed control his daily acts in a way to which there is no parallel in the West — or in China. The principles of Christianity underlie the best of Western civilization, but the majority of men in Europe or America pay little conscious heed to

Christ's teachings as they make the daily round of work and pleasure, and generally they confine their formal religious observances to one day of the week, if as often. The Chinese, to be sure, is one of the most superstitious of men, but there is little more religion in his fears than is implied in the practices of many a Westerner. He never builds a straight entrance into his house, for he believes that evil spirits cannot move in a curved line; and across the world, people who call him names because of this refuse to sit down thirteen at table. The malign influences appeased, the average Chinese goes his way untroubled or unconsoled by any thought concerning that which is to come, or at most he strives to acquire merit, not for a week only, but for the whole year, by some pilgrimage much more strenuous than church-going. Like the Western man of to-day he also is impatient of priestly control, and is apt to say slighting things of his spiritual leaders. His mind is set, not on things above, but on the bread-and-butter, or, more precisely, rice, aspect of life. The scale of rewards is different, but the mainspring of daily living is much the same in the Far East and the Far West.

Or put it in another way: with Chinese and man of the West alike, national standards, national aims, all bear the mark of the industrial world. In America and in Europe the chief concern is industry, — industry in the large sense, agriculture, manufacture, commerce. These are the interests that concern the people, that control their policy. In India religion holds this place, while in Japan the ideals of the old social order were military, and in a measure that is still true of the new. But in China material interests have full possession of the field, and the strong man of the Chinese nation is not the soldier or the priest, but the merchant.

And there is something very Western, very American, as America used to be, in the small part played by the Government in the life of the ordinary Chinese. If he does not misbehave and keeps out of a lawsuit, he rarely comes in contact with his rulers. He is acquainted with the saying of Mencius that "the people are of the highest importance, the gods come second, the sovereign is of lesser weight," and he knows the place of the Government, but he expects little from it, and neither does he fear it.

It is the district officer who represents to the ordinary Chinese the Government, and there are about fifteen hundred of these in the eighteen provinces, about one to every two hundred and fifty thousand of the population. The headman of the village is the only official of whom the Chinese really knows much, and he is one of the village folk, governing by home-made rules of very ancient date, and never interfering if he can help it. Policemen are few, and the various inquisitorial boards and officers that make us clean and sanitary and safe in spite of ourselves are simply non-existent. No one inspects the Chinese garbage pail except the pig, or sniffs about for defective drains, or insists upon a man's keeping the roadway in front of his house in order, or compels him to have his children vaccinated. The tyranny of the majority may exist in China, but it is not exercised through the Government. The Chinese as he is today has been fashioned and shaped by long-inherited custom, and the dead hand rests heavily upon him, but he is not a government product, nor is he likely to be just yet.

And the Chinese is democratic in very much the same way that the American is. If there has been an aristocracy at all, it has been essentially one of race, the conqueror and the conquered, and hereditary distinctions have played a very small part in the past outside Peking and the Manchu circle. An official career is, in theory, and in good measure in practice, open to the man who is fit, no matter what his antecedents; and the poor boy has quite as good a chance to make himself fit for all save the highest posts as in America. Nor is there always much to choose between the American and Chinese standard of fitness. To regard success as commander in a small war as qualifying a man for the civil headship of a great industrial state does not seem much more reasonable than to make skill in writing a literary essay the test for a high military post. And one thing more, the Chinese, in so many things essentially democratic, abases himself before the power of riches as much as the American, and far more than any other Asiatic.

Now, since the Chinese expects little of the government, he has learned to rely upon himself and his fellows. Like the Englishman and the American, and unlike the Frenchman and the German, he takes the initiative. The Government is weak, the individual or group of individuals strong; the Government does little, so the other side does much. All over the East, — in Burma, Indo-China, the Malay States, the Philippines, wherever he can force an entrance, — you find the Chinese merchant and the Chinese coolie, and it is no state-managed enterprise that takes them there. Just as the British workmen emigrate, or the British merchants seek out new markets, so the Chinese make their way without leading or assistance. And they succeed; throughout all that territory that lies between the China Sea and the Bay of Bengal, whether under British or French rule, unless actually barred out, the Chinese is entrenching himself and prospering. Heavy poll-taxes alone keep him from controlling trade and the labour market in Indo-China; in the Malay States he is ousting the native and running the British merchant and banker hard; in Burma he is getting more and more control of trade, and has even succeeded in convincing the

Burmese woman that he makes a better sort of husband than her charming but indolent countryman.

To turn to smaller matters. I am sure I had once known, but I had certainly quite forgotten, that the Chinese, like ourselves and unlike other people of the East, sit on chairs in preference to sitting on their heels. For it gave me a little comfortable shock of surprise when I saw my coolies at dinner sitting on benches around the table, "just like folks," instead of squatting on the ground after the fashion of my Indian servants. It is a small thing, but it marks the Chinese off from all other Asiatics, and brings him a little nearer the West; and I do not wonder at the touch of pride in the answer of the Chinese student at a New England college when some one remarked on seeing her sitting on the ground, college-girl fashion, with a number of her classmates, that it probably came easier to her to do that, as she was used to it, "Oh, no; I think you must be confusing us with the Japanese. We Chinese learned to sit on chairs two thousand years ago."

But not only do the Chinese sit on chairs like ourselves, but they "dine," just as the West does. Not merely are they ready to spend freely on the pleasures of the table, but they make of dinner a social function, longer and more elaborate, and sometimes even more deadly dull than grand dinners at home. The un-Europeanized Indian, rich or poor, is abstemious;

he eats simply to satisfy hunger, and dining is with him no more a social occasion than taking a bath at home, — much less, indeed, than his own bathing, which seems to be often both a religious and a social act. He would not think of entertaining his friends at a dinner party. But my coolies at the wayside inns spent jovial hours over their meals, and the gay Manchu or Chinese diners that I watched at the Peking hotel might have been Americans at the Waldorf-Astoria, barring a few details. And it seemed very Western, only it was quite Chinese, for the chief of the Kalgan Foreign Office to express his regrets that my stay was too short for him to arrange a dinner party for me.

So much has been said of the differences that exist in China, of the wide separation between North and South and West, that I had expected to find repeated there the conditions of India. But externally nothing of the sort was observable. To begin with, almost all Chinese have black hair, almost all wear blue clothes, and almost all eat rice. And the obvious differences between the natives of Chihli and the natives of Kwangtung, for example, are no greater than you would note in passing from Maine to Mississippi; while in Yunnan and Szechuan, just as in the Western States of America, you seem to be among people from "back East," only slightly modified by different conditions of climate and life.

The estimate given me by the Chinese Consul-General at Singapore, a Kwangtung man, as to the proportion of the whole population speaking some form of Mandarin, was about three hundred millions out of a possible three hundred and sixty millions, and this agrees with other statements that I have seen. If this be so, then the enormous majority of the people have the bond of a common tongue. And more than that, all the educated — a small proportion, of course, although many more know a few symbols — have a common written language.

But as Confucius said thousands of years ago, "not all words are in books, nor all thoughts in words," and the traditions of nature worship, Taoism, Buddhism, of Confucius himself, have all put their stamp upon the Chinese, whether of the North or South, and the journeying coolie (and it must be remembered he is a great wanderer), no matter where he goes in China, will find himself among men who recognize the same obligations, cringe under the same superstitious fears, and strive toward the same goal of material well-being as himself. Fundamental differences do certainly exist; North and South China are divided in speech, and the people are unlike, physically and mentally, but I wonder if the separation is really deeper than that between the Northern and the Southern States in America to-day.

We talk of China as in decay, of the Chinese as

aged, and the country as exhausted. It is true the soil has been man-handled for ages, like the soil of India, but over great areas it constantly renews its fertility, and, anyway, most of China's resources are underground, untouched. The Government of last year was rotten to the core; it had outlived its day. But the Government was not the people, and the Chinese are neither worn out nor unsound.

I think it must be because everything seems finished in China that people talk about her decay. The whole thing impresses you as having been made and completed, after a fashion, a long time ago. Nowhere, save where the touch of the West has been felt, do you see things being tried for the first time. Everything has been done in China so many, many times, for so many centuries, and the results have spread abroad all over the empire; everywhere, in the remotest corners, you find the same ingeniously contrived commercial system, the same symmetrical and complicated social order. Being a very clever and resourceful people that has lived a long time, the Chinese have found out a great many things for themselves, and as there was no other clever and resourceful people at hand to incite them to other and better ways of doing some things, they went on as they were, neither spending their strength nor sharpening their wits in trying experiments. Indeed, experimenting stopped centuries ago; each natural difficulty, every social and economic problem had been met and answered in some sort of way, and so the people lived year after year, doing things just as their fathers had done them. And now they impress one as very experienced, though old-fashioned; but not aged, — no, not at all.

On the contrary, face to face with the Chinese at home, one is overwhelmed by an impression of power, — actual power, potential power, power of the individual, power of the group, power well used, power misspent. The impression is almost stunning. You seem to be watching a community of ants, persistent, untiring, organized, only the ant-hill is a town, and the ants are men physically strong, gluttons for work, resourceful, adaptable, cheerful. Then multiply such ant-hills by thousands and you have China. For not merely is the Chinese the best worker in the world, but he also leads in organization. No Chinese stands alone; behind him is the family, the clan, the guild. He does not confront life naked and solitary, he is one of a group; that gives him confidence, and keeps him under control. It makes it both easier and more difficult to deal with him. Treat him unjustly, and you are fighting, not a man but a group. But if he wrongs you, you have a hold upon him, you can call him to account through his group.

And the power of organization smooths greatly the daily machinery of living in China. As I leaned over the side of the steamer in Singapore Harbour, watching the seven hundred coolies come aboard that we were taking home to Kwangtung province, the chief officer remarked to me, "A thousand Chinese make us less trouble than one Indian"; and he went on to explain, "When we enter here, half a dozen Chinese boarding-house keepers come on board and ask how much deck-room we have. They agree on what they want, and then each stakes out his claim, as it were, with bits of red paper emblazoned with Chinese characters. A little later coolies come, bringing the luggage of the home-going Chinese, each thing marked with a piece of red paper with the same black lettering. They ask no questions, but look about until they have found the corresponding marks on the deck, and there they unload. And later the Kwangtung men arrive, each with a red ticket, and they too ask no questions, but just hunt up their things all properly marked, and then proceed to make themselves comfortable. And no one is bothered."

Or to turn to larger things, what was it but this same power of organization that made ready a great revolutionary movement, permeating a population of three hundred odd millions, and spreading over an area of a million and a half square miles, and all so well and secretly done that, though suspected, it could not be discovered? The Turkish Revolution seemed a triumph of secret preparation, but there the task was to convert an organization already made ; here it was necessary both to arouse and to organize.

But then China has ages of experience, both in organizing and in rebelling, back of to-day. Establishing a Republic, however, is something new; the Chinese have never before tried their hand at that, but if they will only bring into play now all their undoubted power of organization, of resource, of moderation, they will certainly make a success of their new experiment in government. Given time, and they will do it. Perhaps my view of China's future is rose-coloured. But the thing seen and felt is of tremendous force, and the impression of power that the Chinese made upon me was rather overwhelming. And, anyway, a friendly opinion may be pardoned in one who, during months of solitary travel in China, never met anything but courtesy and consideration from all, whether coolie on the road, villager or innkeeper, official or priest.

THE END

INDEX

INDEX

The Riverside Press
CAMBRIDGE . MASSACHUSETTS
U . S . A